ABORTION IN THE USA AND THE UK

Abortion ... the USA and the UK

THIS IS A 3 WEEK LOAN
If it is not returned by the date below the charge is
20p PER DAY
THIS ITEM CAN BE RENEWED TWICE

RETURNED
- JAN 2016

ASHGATE

Published by
Ashgate Publishing Limited
Gower House
Croft Road
Aldershot
Hants GU11 3HR
England

Ashgate Publishing Company
Suite 420
101 Cherry Street
Burlington, VT 05401–4405
USA

Ashgate website: http://www.ashgate.com

British Library Cataloguing in Publication Data
Francome, Colin, 1944-
    Abortion in the USA and the UK
    1.Abortion - Great Britain - History 2.Abortion - United
    States - History 3.Abortion - Political aspects - Great
    Britain 4.Abortion - Political aspects - United States
    5.Abortion - Law and legislation - Great Britain 6.Abortion
    - Law and legislation - Great Britain
    I.Title
    363.4'6'0941

Library of Congress Cataloging-in-Publication Data
Francome, Colin.
    Abortion in the USA and the UK / Colin Francome.
        p. cm.
    Includes bibliographical references and index.
    ISBN 0-7546-3015-3
        1. Abortion--United States. 2. Abortion--Great Britain. I. Title.

HQ767.5.U5F71795 2003
363.46'0941--dc22

2003062725

ISBN 0 7546 3015 3

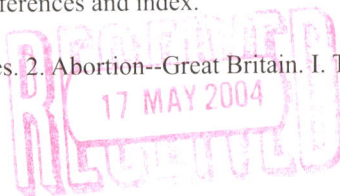

Contents

Foreword

Frances Kissling

The Culture War Continues

It was 1970 and abortion had just become legal in New York State. I was asked to serve as the director of one of the first clinics providing legal abortion services in the state, and accepted. Thus began a career that has spanned almost a generation; involved both the medical and moral aspects of the issue and taken me around the globe as an advocate for legal abortion. During that time abortion has been a hotly contested public policy issue and one that probably has aroused more passion than any other social and cultural issue of our times. Advocates for and against agree on almost nothing, from the complex question of the moral status of the fetus to the simple question of whether or not abortion is medically safe for women.

The public debate has become highly predictable. Whether one is in New York, London, Mexico City, Lagos or the United Nations, the discourse is the same. The television viewer knows exactly what the prochoice spokesperson will say and is fully prepared for the claims of the opponent of legal abortion. As a result, most of us have stopped listening. As we look to the future of legal abortion, listening becomes imperative. In this book, Colin Francome guides us through 50 years of history in the effort to legalize abortion in the United States and the UK. Each country's route to legal abortion has been different and these differences are thoroughly detailed and analysed herein. Understanding these differences may be key to understanding the continued controversy that surrounds current attempts to decriminalize abortion in much of the developing world and to preserve legal abortion in a number of countries where it is challenged by conservatives.

The liberalization of abortion laws did not happen in a vacuum. Francome notes that major reforms to abortion laws began in 1967 and ended in 1982. This should come as no surprise. The 1960s and 1970s in the US and Europe were decades of major social change and economic prosperity. The birth control pill was introduced; civil rights for racial minorities were increasingly recognized; women's rights advanced dramatically and the sexual revolution was in full swing. The backlash began in the 1980s. The economy slowed; Thatcher, Reagan and Khomeini rose in power. Religious fundamentalism in the US and the Middle East came into full bloom. The culture war raged. It is in this context that country by country progress in changing abortion laws and saving women's life came to a near stand still.

The tragedy of this stand still is that those women most in need of legal abortion services are still without them. In the developing world where women's lives are crippled by poverty and patriarchy, it is estimated that more than 60,000 women a year die as a result of botched abortions, most illegal. Countless more suffer physical and psychological complications from botched abortions. These women are the visible proof of the fact that today, as fifty years ago, women who need abortions will risk everything including their lives to end pregnancies they consider unsupportable. They do so not because they are selfish, as the opponents of abortion tell us, but because they understand that bringing new life in to the world is the most important responsibility and right a woman possesses. Throughout history women have proven that they can be trusted to decide when it is appropriate to exercise their right to bring that life into the world. Isn't it time to end the culture wars and recognize that right?

Chapter 1

Introduction

On 4 June 2003 Congress outlawed a form of later abortion often used with handicapped fetuses or where the woman was ill. It was the most significant restriction in the 30 years since abortion was legalized in the case of *Roe v. Wade*. The change led a commentator to state 'Always more conservative about abortion than Britain, America is now in the mood to reverse abortion rights as never before' (Goldenberg 2003). This book considers the differences in the situation on either side of the Atlantic. In the final chapter, it makes a case for the pro choice position. The two chapters on the period when abortion was illegal show that, despite the risks to health and the costliness of illegal operations, they were nevertheless prevalent. This suggests that abortion cannot be legislated out of existence; rather, there are great limits in what legislators can do to prevent it unless they choose the path of education and openness. If this occurs, the better knowledge of contraception is likely to reduce the number of unplanned and unwanted pregnancies. Also in the final chapter, some consideration is given to another aspect of the right to chose. This is that many couples or individual women find that it is very difficult to have the children they want. The percentage of women remaining childless throughout their lives has increased. For some, this will be a conscious choice. However, many are denied maternity by the demands of society; so supporting the right of choice must also include the right of maternity, if this is what is desired.

1.1 The Wider Effects of British Law

As I explained in my previous book *Abortion Freedom*, the British Act of 1967 helped to spark a worldwide trend to relax the laws. In the period until 1982, more than forty countries extended their grounds and only three narrowed them. This change meant that nearly two-thirds of women lived in countries where laws permitted abortion on request or on a wide variety of grounds. Fewer than one in ten lived in countries where abortion was totally prohibited (Francome 1984). The United States was one of the countries to change its laws radically, and the Supreme Court decision of 22 January 1973 led to the individual states having to change their laws. The laws on abortion deal with a variety of issues such as where the operations should be performed, who should perform them, whose consent is required in the case of minors, what time limits should be adhered to and what conscience clauses should be followed. The laws even between countries with liberal legislation vary a great deal on these matters. There are also wide variations as to the method of payment. In some countries abortions are paid for on the National Health Scheme; in Britain the chances of a free abortion depend to some degree on where the woman lives and the attitudes of her doctor, whereas in the United States free abortion is largely conditional on being a Medicaid patient and living in a state which finances the operations.

However, an important distinction for countries with liberal laws is whether they allow abortion on request, or only allow to certain categories of women. This is a fundamental difference between the law in the United Kingdom and that in the United States. In the United States the Supreme Court decided to give women that right on the grounds of privacy. British law does not, and so may be argued to lag behind that of other countries where a woman may obtain an abortion in the early months of pregnancy without restrictions on her reasons. In addition to the USA, this applies to Austria, Belgium, France, Germany, Greece, Italy, the Netherlands, Norway and Sweden.

Although the law in the USA is very liberal, many parts of the country have very conservative attitudes to social matters and here opposition to abortion has been much stronger. One of the crucial differences between the USA and the UK has been the degree of violence against abortion facilities and personnel in the USA. Data show that in the year 2000 more than half (56 per cent) of providers faced harassment against abortion. However, apart from picketing, harassment has declined since 1996 (Henshaw and Finer 2003). In Britain there have been isolated incidents, but by no means such a degree of violence and harassment.

1.2   Supporters and Opponents of Choice

In this chapter the general social forces in the two societies – UK and US – are considered; in later chapters, the more specific groups in each society are examined.

1.2.1   Women's Movements

As far as I have been able to determine it was German feminists at the beginning of the twentieth century who first made the demand for women's rights over their fertility, and in Britain Stella Browne publicly advocated this position from 1915 onwards (Ellis 1928, p. 607). In the USA, the first recorded call for legalization I have noted was that of Hermann Dekker in 1920; however, there were few voices raised in support until the 1960s (Francome 1984, p. 75).

Many people date the start of the Women's movement to the publication of Betty Freidan's book *The Feminine Mystique.* However, what is clear is that there are several strands in the campaign. Some women want to work for equality within the constraints of current society while, in contrast, the socialists/feminists demand freedom of choice in both contraception and abortion as part of a series of steps designed to change the overall values of society. Marie Waters, for example, argued that the restrictions on women's sexual behaviour were designed to support the patriarchal family and to help ensure the safe transfer of property to the next generation. In her view, a revolutionary socialist society would eliminate the economic need for the oppression of women and in this society the state would not be involved in primary relationships. 'Marriage and divorce would become totally personal decisions, subject to no laws, contracts or restrictions: abortion and contraception would be available on demand' (p. 25). Waters went on to argue that women have not always been treated as inferior to men and excluded from many productive roles. On the contrary, she suggested that in earlier societies women were equal, and developed or invented the basic skills that placed humanity on the road to civilization – agriculture, tanning, weaving, pottery, architecture and much else. Women were relegated to an inferior social position only with the rise of a 'class society' – with the division of society into classes: those who owned versus those who did not (Jenness, 1976). In this view, the fight for sex equality is part of an overall struggle for a changed society. It is not isolated from other political changes and Linda Jenness, of the Socialist Workers Party, placed these demands in perspective. She argued that by fighting for day-care facilities, equal opportunities for employment and education, and for the abolition of all laws against abortion, women would not only improve their own position in society but would help to encourage the struggle of other oppressed groups. She went on to say, however, that women could not be fully liberated within the constraints of current American society, but only after a socialist revolution.

The fact that socialists have stressed the priority of the revolution has meant that where fertility control has been regarded as anti-revolutionary they have opposed it. Chapter 8 will show that the linking of contraception to a conservative doctrine in the nineteenth century led to the socialists becoming the major opponents of the spread of contraception in Britain. Although socialists have recently supported sexual rights, left wing theorists have been wary of the spread of certain kinds of commercial sexuality which they do not feel help in the development of personal relationships. For example, Linda Gordon suggested that some developments have been reactionary:

> The marketing of sex cookbooks for the 'connoisseur' is moving, as Commoditization always does, in an antihuman direction, that is, it is carving up the human experience so that sex becomes severed from economic, social, political and emotional life (1977, p. 413).

So the view of socialists/feminists contrasts markedly with those who want liberalization for increased opportunity for profits. However, many within such organizations as the US based National Organization for Women (NOW) work for change without expecting there to be a new society. They are, of course, mindful of the fact that a changed relationship between men and women will have wide repercussions throughout the society. The women's groups have tended to combine their personal development programme with a wider strategy for change – especially on issues directly related to women.

1.2.2   The Professionals

Initially, the major medical bodies such as the British Medical Association (BMA) and the Royal College of Obstetricians and Gynaecologists (RCOG) opposed the passage of the 1967 Abortion Act. One of the reasons suggested for the British law failing to give women the right to choose an abortion was that doctors were concerned that they would be told what to do (Hindell and Simms 1971). However, the inclusion of a conscience clause making it possible for doctors to opt out of abortion addressed this concern to a degree. Surveys of the opinion of doctors in 1970, 1972 and 1973 showed they were in support of the law. In 1973, for example, 52 per cent thought the law should not be changed, 24 per cent thought that it should be liberalized to make abortion easier, and 23 per cent thought it should be tightened to make abortion more difficult to obtain. The medical authorities also changed their position to support a liberal law. For example, when James White introduced a bill to restrict access in 1975, an editorial in the *British Medical Journal* attacked it.

There have been few, if any, other surveys of doctors' opinions until I was invited by Marie Stopes International (MSI) to carry one out. I drew a random sample of 1,000 general practitioners (GPs) and had a creditable 71 per cent response rate. The doctors were asked whether they were broadly 'pro choice' or 'broadly anti abortion'. The results showed that over four out of five (82 per cent) characterized themselves as 'pro choice', while just under one in five (18 per cent) said they were basically opposed to abortion (Francome and Freeman 2000, p. 190). We also asked doctors whether they supported a liberalization of the law along these lines. They were asked whether they agreed or disagreed with the following statement: 'The 1967 Abortion Act should be amended to provide a woman with the right to choose an abortion in the first 14 weeks of pregnancy, after consultation with a doctor.' In response three in five (60 per cent) supported such a liberalization of the law.

The four out of five doctors who considered themselves 'pro choice' is well above the figure of 56 per cent in a study of general practice physicians in Kansas (Westfall et al.). A study of rural Idaho showed that almost four out of five physicians had a religious objection to abortion (Rosenblatt 1995).

1.2.3   *Those Concerned about Overpopulation*

The origins of the contraceptive movement are usually traced back to the Rev. Thomas Malthus. He introduced his conservative doctrine in the wake of the French Revolution. He believed that there was a natural tendency for population size to outstrip food supply and hoped that the poorer groups would engage in self-restraint in order to control their family size. The neo-Malthusian movement revised his doctrine by substituting contraception for restraint and, after the Bradlaugh/Besant trial of 1877, became a major force for change. Its principles were clearly set out in each copy of their journal *The Malthusian*, as follows:

1   That population has a constant tendency to increase beyond the means of subsistence.
2   That the checks which counteract this tendency are resolvable into positive or life destroying, and prudential or birth restricting.
3   That the positive or life-destroying checks comprehend the premature death of children and adults by disease, starvation, war and infanticide.
4   That the prudential or birth-restricting check consists in the limitation of offspring by abstention from sex or by prudence after marriage.
5   That prolonged abstention from marriage as advocated by Malthus should not be followed. Advocacy of abstinence is productive of many diseases and much sexual vice. On the contrary early marriage tends to ensure sexual purity, domestic comfort, social happiness, and individual health. It is a grave social offence for men and women to bring into the world more

children than they can adequately house, feed, clothe and educate.

6   That over population is the most fruitful source of pauperism, ignorance, crime and disease.

7   That the full and open discussion of the Population Question is a matter of vital moment to society, and such discussion should be absolutely unfettered by fear of legal penalties.

Although between the two world wars Malthusianism was at a low ebb as other organizations became much more active and the ideas of Malthus seemed outmoded, after the Second World War there was renewed concern with the size of the world's population. The sheer size of the increase was of course one factor, but the appeal was also due to the stress on population growth in the dominant economic doctrines. A good example is the argument put forward by Walt Rostow (1971). His view was that the poor countries of the world should 'take off' into self-sustained economic growth. However, he saw problems in the expanding population, because if it were growing at around 2 or 3 per cent per annum, the surpluses that could have been used for investment would instead be needed for immediate consumption. The clear implication of this was that poor countries should make extra efforts to control their population size.

There was also support for the spread of fertility control from a section of the business world, and the Rockefeller Foundation helped to finance various projects. It seems that the concern about population size was much greater in the United States than in Britain. Paul Erhlich's book *Population Bomb* (1976) had wide circulation and caused a great deal of interest. It was, for example, distributed to the Hawaii legislators who were subsequently to introduce the first Act to give women the right to choose an abortion in the United States (Steinhoff and Diamond 1977, p. 73). Erhlich later tied his concern with over-population to the ecological movement which gave it wider appeal, and in time the zero population growth movement gained a measure of popular support (Erhlich and Erhlich 1970). So variants of Malthusian ideas have continued to be important. They offer a solution to social problems without any change in the social order. This was their basic appeal in the early nineteenth century, and it is still relevant today. A second reason for their appeal to the dominant members of society is that their recommendations are usually aimed at the poorer sections of the community and so act as an agent of social control. In Britain in the nineteenth century, contraception was regarded as a way of reducing the number of the poor working classes. More recently, others have suggested it as a possible way of reducing the numbers in minority groups.

Where this pressure has been strong, there has often been an element of compulsion in the spread of fertility control. There are documented cases of forced sterilization in the United States (*New York Times*, 4 December 1977), and there were allegations that some men in India were forced to undergo vasectomies. Thus, the advocates of the extension of fertility control on Malthusian grounds do not necessarily support the individual's right to choose, and in fact neo-Malthusians may argue that choice should be curtailed for the good of society. Those who regard population as the crucial problem tend not to challenge the dominant social order, but to regard the problems of the poorer groups as being in large measure of their own making.

1.2.4 Reformists

Those who accept a reformist position on fertility control tend to look for moderate changes. They differ from the socialist/feminists in that they accept the nuclear family and claim that abortion protects it by excluding unwanted children who would otherwise place strains upon the family unit. Historically the reformers have included people with a wide variety of beliefs, depending on the issues involved and the political situation at the time. One of the problems for reformers is that they may be willing to support a degree of social change but become unhappy if more radical developments occur.

A reformer may at any one time be on the side of those working for change, but may at a later stage join with the conservatives in opposition to further liberalization. The clearest example of this was the switch in sides of Aleck Bourne. In the 1930s he had been a member of the Abortion Law Reform Association (ALRA) and worked for a liberalization of the law. In a celebrated case in 1938 he performed an abortion for rape and was cleared in the subsequent trial, so opening the way for operations in similar circumstances in the future (see Chapter 9). However, he opposed the law being extended too far, and in the 1960s he joined the Society for the Protection of Unborn Children (SPUC) and worked against the Bill sponsored by ALRA despite having formerly been its most prominent member.

The British 1967 Abortion Act was debated in reformist terms and the kind of argument advanced was that the legalization of abortion would help women with problems. The reformers asserted that the change they were proposing was not threatening to the social order but would help to improve it. They argued that the Act would not greatly increase the number of abortions because there were already a high number of illegal operations: legalization would simply transfer these to the legal sector. They also stressed that there was no attempt to give women 'abortion on demand' and that doctors would still have the ultimate control. We shall see that this absence of the claim of a 'right to choose' differentiated the British campaign from that in the United States and many other countries.

One of the crucial features of the reformist perspective is a gradualist theory of change, and for this reason its demands tended to be limited to a 'realistic' level. So within a reformist campaign there may be many people holding very radical views who, for political reasons, do not express them publicly. Although the British 1967 Act was argued in reformist terms, there were many in the campaign who would have liked a repeal law (Francome 1984).

1.2.5   Left Wing Groups

It is those of the left who have consistently been the supporters of the right to choose an abortion. In chapter 6 I discuss the voting patterns for 2001 in the US Congress. In April 1978 I published an analysis of the votes of British Members of Parliament (MPs) in the Journal *Political Quarterly*. This showed a similar pattern in the United Kingdom with the Labour politicians being far more in favour of abortion rights than the Conservative ones. More recent votes have confirmed this position.

So these groups are the main sources of support for the rights of fertility control. Let us now consider the main opponents.

i) Right-wing groups   These have generally opposed the extension of contraception and abortion rights. Right-wingers tend to value stability and oppose changes which they see as threatening to their beliefs and social stability. They tend to accept the dominant views of society that act as a method of social control, and to regard problems as being due to deficiencies within individuals rather than structural weaknesses within the system. Poverty was traditionally regarded by conservatives as being largely due to the unwillingness of the poor to work or to their 'wastefulness'. Historically they distinguished the 'deserving poor' from the 'non-deserving poor' and their solution for the latter was to persuade them to change their ideas and to adopt the work ethic.

The traditional conservative view of sexual behaviour is similar. In the United States there have been many campaigns supporting chastity, and in 2002 President Bush proposed chastity as a solution to teenage pregnancy. However, one of the clearest statements on the value of the family and the importance of keeping sexuality within bounds was put forward by N. Dennis. He argued that the greater number of divorces and break-ups of relationships since the Second World War has resulted in an increase in crime. Permissiveness is one factor leading to the breakdown: in earlier times, sex and marriage were more closely related. He commented:

> The intention was to ensure that, as far as possible before a man had sexual intercourse with a woman, he should undertake far-reaching, long-lasting and wide-ranging commitments to his possible child and the mother of his possible child (1993, p. 3).

Thus his view was that, where sex is more freely available outside marriage, men do not have to take on the wider responsibilities of parenthood. He said that, while sex within marriage is perfectly acceptable, pre- and extra-marital sex are threatening. Sexuality is regarded as 'normal' within the confines of the nuclear family, but should be proscribed for single people who would be engaging in it without responsibility and so would not have 'earned' the right to participate.

Conservatives are concerned at any extension of rights to abortion or contraception, even if they take advantage of such facilities themselves. Sometimes they may welcome venereal disease and illegitimacy as 'punishments' for unacceptable behaviour. Indeed at first some people welcomed HIV/AIDS as a punishment for wickedness (Francome and Marks 1996). This finding is not at all surprising in the light of the above reasoning. Those who take an extreme conservative view regard capital punishment as a deterrent to murder, homosexuality as 'deviant' behaviour in need of treatment if not punishment and abortion as a 'prop' to irresponsibility in sexual relationships.

Conservatives tend to regard the social structure as vulnerable. They see threats in social changes and so oppose movements towards greater liberalism. However, once the changes have occurred and may seem to have limited adverse effects, they can then be accepted and even defended. Thus, the hierarchy in the Church of England once opposed contraception but now accepts the right of individuals to use it. The right wing may want a greater adherence to their values. They are concerned that even those rules that do exist are not adequately followed and they may look back to a 'golden age' in the past when 'right was right' and 'wrong was wrong'. A good example of this was when the right wing British Education Minister, Dr Rhodes Boyson, attacked sexual freedom which he said had led to personal isolation and despair. He contrasted the situation to the clear and confident virtues of the

Victorian age (*Guardian*, 20 March 1982). Margaret Thatcher was another British Conservative who wanted a return to Victorian values: in her view, when they were pre-eminent Britain was great.

In the late twentieth century, the right wing forged links with certain Protestant Fundamentalist groups. One of the interesting facts about politicians is that their official position on 'conscience' issues such as abortion, capital punishment and homosexuality tend to correlate. So in both the UK and the USA politicians opposed to abortion rights are also more likely to be opposed to homosexual rights and in favour of capital punishment. Consequently, in the UK it was largely the Conservative MPs who opposed the reduction of the age of consent for homosexual behaviour and who tend to support any anti-abortion bills that are proposed. When I was teaching in the United States, I tested for any similar correlation amongst 700 students: in fact, I found that none existed.

ii) Religious groups The major consistent opposition to both birth control and abortion has come from the Catholic Church. One reason for this, which has distinguished Catholics from many of the Protestant groups, is that sexuality has a crucial place in its beliefs. The Church has placed a high value on virginity, and its doctrines are determined by those who have chosen to forgo sexual intercourse.

Official Catholic teaching traditionally said that the primary purpose of sexual intercourse was the procreation of children. Artificial birth control was regarded as being unnatural and against the will of God. In the 1930s it was often looked upon as murder. However, with changing attitudes and the acceptance of the safe period, the Church's concern with contraception has diminished. Possibly the clearest exposition of the Church's modern theory concerning the problem of sexuality and fertility control was that put forward by Bishop Joseph Bernardin in the *New York Times* (22 January 1978) on the fifth anniversary of the Supreme Court's decision legalizing abortion. He stated that he very much doubted whether 'more and better contraceptive information and services will make major inroads in the number of teenage pregnancies ... [for] ... It will motivate them to precocious sexual activity but by no means to the practice of contraception. In this case the "solution" will merely have made the problem worse'. Bernardin argued that the answer, although not an easy one, was to tell young people that there was no such thing as sex without consequences and, furthermore, to teach them that: 'Sex is not merely for fun or for the expression of transitory affection. It is an enriching and serious business between mature people who are emotionally, socially and even economically able to accept the consequences, of which pregnancy is hardly the only one.' He then called for more education or indoctrination of teenagers in family values, stability of marital relationships and the willingness to accept the consequences of one's actions.

Leading British anti-abortion activists tend to take a similar position. Phyllis Bowman, a Catholic convert and founder of the UK's Society for the Protection of Unborn Children, does not see contraception as the answer. In a personal interview (14 May 1979) she told me: 'When I became involved with abortion I thought contraception was quite definitely the answer to abortion but I don't now.' She went on to say that she felt contraception on demand would lead to an increase in abortion on demand. However, she did not oppose the right of women to use birth control: 'As far as I am concerned a girl can take pills till they come out of her ears. She's then doing what she wants with her own body.' Similar comments were made to me by Ellen McCormack, former Right to Life Candidate for the US Presidency (14 December 1979). In taking this position they were both echoing the dominant Catholic position – which is to concede on the issue of birth control and concentrate on abortion. Madeleine Simms, a well known British activist, suggested to me that one of the reasons Catholicism has stressed abortion is that it is the one social issue on which regular supporters agree. She said it has helped to unite the Church which is hopelessly divided on such matters as contraception. This allegation is hotly disputed by Catholic leaders.

Although in some countries such as Spain, Italy and France, Catholicism is closely identified with the right-wing groups, there is not necessarily such a connection. In Latin America, the Church has taken a very radical stance and some priests have worked with revolutionary groups. Similarly, in both Britain and the United States, the dominant rationale for opposition to abortion has been linked to a radical analysis of society. Particularly in the United States, Republican anti-abortionists have been opposed to giving increased help to deprived groups, yet Catholics have been more likely to see the need to support these. For example John Quinn, President of the United States National Conference of Catholic Bishops, once said, 'If you want to defend the pre-born effectively … see to it that the aged and handicapped are treated decently … support the rights of the hungry and disadvantaged wherever and whoever they are' (NARAL 1976).

In Britain, too, the anti-abortion Catholics have taken a radical position on a number of issues. For example, Phyllis Bowman was an anti-Vietnam war activist and Paul Cavadino was (and is) a prison reformer. Furthermore, both in Britain and the United States the movement leans against capital punishment and for the rights of minority groups. So there are clear differences between the Catholics and the conservatives and in some cases there are strange alliances. For example Paul Cavadino, whose politics are well to the left, often used the arch-Conservative John Biggs Davidson to ask his parliamentary questions.

iii) Moral entrepreneurs All societies try and impose a series of values on its citizens. If it were not so, and if societies developed where, for instance, theft was not proscribed, it would be difficult for them to function. However, there are some issues which are contentious. This applies to the whole area of what Schur called *Crimes without Victims*. These are issues such as drug taking, homosexuality, under-age drinking, under-age sex, under-age gambling, nudity on stage or in the cinema, 'back alley' abortions and contraception. In these areas of crime there is no complainant. In a second book, *Victimless Crimes*, Schur debated the issue of abortion, and whether it should come into this category or whether the fetus should be considered a victim. His definition that there was no complainant indicates that he was right to include it.

In *The Outsiders* Becker argued that in many cases laws were promoted by moral entrepreneurs. Some people believe in wider values to such a degree that they try and impose them on to the wider society and in some cases may make them their life's work. In the nineteenth century we can look back to Anthony Comstock in the USA, and in his autobiography Winston Churchill mentioned the unsuccessful anti-drink campaigner Mrs Chant (1972). Later, in 1979, the USA had the formation of the *Moral Majority* by Jerry Falwell. This group claimed that the backbone of its support came from 'citizens who are pro-family, pro-moral, pro-life and pro-American, who have integrity and believe in hard work' (Francome 1984, p. 188). In Britain, there was Mrs Mary Whitehouse who campaigned to 'clean up' television. On the issue of fertility control, there have been many moral entrepreneurs. In the past they campaigned against contraception, but nowadays their target has increasingly been abortion, as we shall see as the book develops.

These, then, are different perspectives on the issue of fertility control. They are not mutually exclusive, for some socialists have been neo-Malthusians and, possibly more importantly, some conservatives may also have religious beliefs opposing fertility control. In these cases the individuals may well be doubly motivated. There are also, inevitably, some activists who do not clearly fit into any of the groups outlined.

1.3   How Both Sides have their own Facts

Those on either side of a debate on a contentious issue, whether it be legalization of cannabis, abolition of capital punishment, extension of sex education or as in this case abortion, will sometimes agree on the facts of the case but make different value judgements. To give an example from the marijuana debate, both sides may agree that marijuana usage leads to increased sexuality. However, while the opponents may view this as grounds for condemnation, the supporters may cheer the interest in the earthy, the organic, the sensual (Goode 1970, p. 78). On the abortion issue, both socialists and anti-abortionists have argued that abortion will further the breakdown of the nuclear family. However, whereas the anti-abortionists regard the family as the 'cornerstone' of society and see its defence as very important, the socialists have sometimes argued against it. As I have documented elsewhere, they may criticize it on a number of grounds including the fact that it restricts child socialization patterns, that it excludes those who are outside the basic unit and that it supports the capitalist system (Francome 1984, p. 7).

Socialists may agree with anti-abortionists that the increase in availability of contraception will not reduce the number of abortions. They may argue that this does not matter much, for what is important is that women can control their own fertility. However, the anti-abortionists regard this as a crucial point for, if it is true, it supports their view that the high number of abortions cannot be reduced by better sex education and the increased availability of contraception. In these and other ways, socialists and anti-abortionists agree on certain facts but disagree on values. Both sides agree that if a woman becomes pregnant through rape she is going to have a very difficult time in continuing with the pregnancy and may well be without the support of a partner. However, while most people agree with President Bush that she should be able to have an abortion, some anti-choice campaigners oppose it. One commentator stated 'We oppose the killing of an innocent baby for the crime of his father'(Willke 2002, p. 2). To some degree then, both sides on the abortion issue agree on the facts but disagree on the worth or otherwise of these facts.

However, within the abortion debate the most striking feature is not the limited agreement on facts, but rather the extent of disagreement between the groups. Anti-choice groups sometimes argue that fertility control will harm the family. However, NARAL and other pro-choice groups often argue that easier abortion will protect, rather than destroy, the nuclear family. One of its leaflets said 'Legal abortion helps women limit their families to the number of children they want and can afford, both emotionally and financially and reduces the number of children born unwanted. Pro-choice is definitely pro-family'. There are other crucial facts on which both sides of the abortion debate disagree. However, both sides claim that the facts are on their side. Veteran abortion activist Bill Baird said to me 'I always beat the anti-abortionists in debate because I give them the facts. I remember the exact references from the medical journals' (August 2001).

On the other hand, Father Paul Marx commented:

> Pro-abortionists work by propagandistic rhetoric, so their arguments are hard to dismantle. They hide the ugly facts while playing on emotions. It is a technique to use the ignorance of others by keeping the evidence of science and common sense from opening people's minds. Yet it is truth that shall make us free (US-based priest, *Our Sunday Visitor*, 13 February 1977).

Similarly Ellen McCormack, former Right to Life Presidential Candidate, told me in an interview: 'The only way we can get change is for people to have the facts. I am not afraid of people having facts. We are not going to be able to change the hard cases – for example doctors making money out of abortions – but people will be able to see the problems.' Overall, there are five important areas where the facts are disputed between the pro- and anti-choice groups.

1.3.1   The Effects of Abortion on Attitudes to Life

The anti-abortionists believe that legalization leads to an anti-life attitude. They take the view that by legalizing the right to 'kill unborn children' the way is open for euthanasia and the killing of certain handicapped groups (Willke 2002, p. 2). They often draw a comparison with the situation in Hitler's Germany which they say is the only other modern society where the right of the individual to life was systematically abrogated. A highly promoted US anti-abortion book (B. and J. Willke 1975, p. 6) states that the abortion laws:

> Represent a complete about face, a total rejection of one of the core values of Western man (sic), and an acceptance of a new ethic in which life has only relative value. This is a momentous change that strikes at the root of Western civilisation.

In contrast, those in favour of legal abortion dismiss the charge that legal abortion devalues life. They stress the fact that the vast majority of abortions are carried out early in the pregnancy and argue that at this stage a baby cannot be said to exist. They may give the examples that an acorn is not an oak tree nor an egg a chicken. In answer to comparisons with Hitler's Germany, they point out that Hitler was opposed to abortion and argue that in many respects legal abortion can be regarded as pro-life: it saves women from dying from illegal abortions and allows them to look after their chosen children more adequately.

1.3.2   The Effect of Legalization on 'Back-street' Abortions

On the point of legalization, there is disagreement on the effects of legalization on the number of 'back-street' abortions. The supporters of legal abortion usually argue that before legalization there was a division between rich and poor. Rich women were able to pay high fees to a reputable doctor, while poor women were forced to make use of the services of unqualified and possibly unskilled illegal operators. Pro-choice groups argue that the major effect of legalization is to transfer abortions from the illegal to the legal sector, and in support of their case they point to the decline in the number of police prosecutions and deaths from illegal abortions.

In contrast, anti-abortionists argue that the number of abortions before legalization was relatively small but that the change in the law has altered attitudes. They claim that the number of illegal abortions has in fact risen, either because the availability of abortion has given rise to irresponsible attitudes towards contraception, or because of the actual increase in the number of 'promiscuous pregnancies in unmarried women' (Francome 1984). A recent example of the dispute was when, in considering the debate in Portugal, Willke, a former president of US National Right to Life, commented:

> As usual, the pro-abortion side pumped up imagined numbers of illegal abortions and put forward arguments our readers are familiar with. Among other arguments, they claimed that there were 16,000 illegal abortions committed annually – this, without any visible proof of that number (Willke 2002, p. 4).

1.3.3   The Medical Effects of Abortion

A third area of disagreement is on the likely sequelae of abortion. The supporters of legalization point to medical evidence that abortion is much safer than childbirth. For example, the United States pro-choice group NARAL produced a document, 'Abortion Questions and Answers' (1976), which said: 'Approximately 87 per cent of abortions are performed in the first trimester when it is eight times safer than delivering a baby.' Proponents also argue that the psychological effects of abortion are not very great. To quote a NARAL document again:

There is no indication that abortion leads to any detectable increase in the incidence of mental illness. Any depression or guilt feelings associated with legal abortion are described as mild. One study shows an incidence of post abortion psychosis ranging from only 0.2 to 0.4 per 1,000 legal abortions, as compared to a rate for post partum psychosis of 1–2 per 1,000 deliveries (Francome 1984).

Opponents of abortion question these figures. The National Right to Life Committee website (27 July 2002) stated that many people argue that abortion is safer than childbirth and it pointed out that this was the view of the Abortion Surveillance Branch of the Centers for Disease Control. However, it commented that the medical evidence was to the contrary. It was not specific about what medical evidence this was. Earlier, Dr and Mrs Willke, in their *Handbook on Abortion* (1975, p. 82) claimed that the extent of under-reporting was so great that the number of deaths from legal abortion could be ten times as high as those recorded. In place of the official figures for New York of 2–5 deaths per 100,000 abortions, they suggested that the figures 20–50 should be substituted. They also gave some figures for Sweden and Denmark showing that the death rate from abortion is higher than that in childbirth. They criticize Hungarian data showing a low death rate and argue that this is due to under-reporting and censorship by the Communist Bureaux before publication. Phyllis Bowman of SPUC pointed out to me that those women who die of childbirth are older and unfit whereas it is often healthy young girls who die of abortion.

1.3.4   Abortion and Breast Cancer

The dominant medical view is that there is no relationship between abortion and breast cancer. However, the opponents of choice rarely recognize that there is a debate on the issue. For example the Elliot Institute commented: 'The risk of breast cancer almost doubles after one abortion and rises even further with two or more abortions' (Elliot 2002, p. 1).

1.3.5   Public Opinion on Abortion

An important difference between the groups is in their perception of public opinion. The NARAL document 'Twelve Abortion Facts' (undated) reported three surveys all of which showed support for liberal laws. One was a *New York Times*/CBS News poll that found that 67 per cent of Americans agreed that 'the right of a woman to have an abortion should be left entirely up to the woman and her doctor'. Another showed that a majority of Catholics did not support the Church's position that abortion should not be allowed in any circumstances. In contrast, Dr and Mrs Willke criticize these surveys. They say polls are often wrong and draw attention to the two referenda on abortion, in North Dakota and Michigan in 1972, where 78 per cent and 62 per cent respectively voted against abortion rights being extended (B. and J. Willke, 1975, p. 36).

A similar dispute over public opinion occurred in Britain at the time of the Corrie Bill. Overall, the information that opposing sides on the abortion issue receive gives them a totally different perspective on the facts. At one level, the pressure group operators may be criticized for lack of objectivity; but they take the view that their position is similar to that of lawyers. There are so many pieces of evidence that either side can select that which is favourable to their point of view. Dr and Mrs Willke's book *Handbook on Abortion* is a good example. Pro-choice people have also been selective at times. For instance, when I noticed that a Gallup study was missing from a summary of some British opinion polls and I asked the author the reason for the exclusion, she told me she did not see why she should help to 'publicise material helpful to the other side'. The leaders of the pressure groups know the views of the other side only too well because they read each other's literature and meet at debates.

1.4 Social Analysis

This introduction has set out some of the major perspectives, and the rest of the book aims to examine the contribution of various groups to the debate over fertility control. It will concentrate on abortion, but a full analysis cannot be developed if contraception is not also considered. The major interest is in recent events, but they will be set in their historical context. This is particularly important in the case of the United States where the debate on legalization revolved very much around the reasons for making abortion illegal in the nineteenth century. Furthermore, the analysis of the process of social change in sexual norms will facilitate predictions on future developments.

In examining the process of liberalization a number of different factors will be considered. It will be suggested that there is a relationship between the social climate and the development of birth control and abortion rights. Although the prevailing mood in a society strongly influences the possibilities for change, various other factors must be considered. The evidence will show that, in a very real sense, people make history. The presence of well-organized groups can produce important changes, while the opportunity may be lost if the necessary pressure groups or mass parties are absent or ineffective. Certain belief systems may be relevant to society at one time but become much less important when social conditions change. The predictions made by different groups will be considered in the light of subsequent events. The possibility of change also depends on the structure of the social institutions. For example, the role of the Supreme Court in the United States was radical whilst in Germany it was conservative. This book aims to analyse these different effects and their relevance for the future.

Chapter 2

The Experience of Legal Abortion
in the USA

Induced abortion is one of the most frequently performed surgical procedures in the USA. The number of reported abortions in 1973 – the year of the Supreme Court Decision – was 745,000, which meant that one in five pregnancies was aborted. We shall see that even in this first year the abortion rate was higher than that of the UK. Of course by this time several states such as New York and Hawaii had legalized abortion, and in other places what had been illegal operations would start to be performed legally. As would be expected, the number of abortions grew – to 899,000 in 1974, and to just over a million in 1975 and 1.2 million in 1976. Thereafter the numbers grew steadily, and in 1980 they exceeded one and a half million for the first time. Then for ten subsequent years they remained between 1.5 and 1.6 million. In 1990, for the only time in US history, the number rose above 1.6 million before falling for five successive years to below 1.4 million in 1995. Since that time there has been a gradual decline in absolute numbers, and in the year 2,000 there were just over 1.3 million abortions, the lowest number since 1976.

2.1   Abortion in the Year 2000

Apart from the total number, there are two other ways of measuring the incidence of abortion. If the population of fertile women increased then the absolute number would be expected to rise if all else remained equal. It is therefore relevant to identify the abortion rate per 1,000 women aged 15–44 (in the USA, as of July 1 each year). The abortion rate in the year 2000 was 21.3 which was the lowest abortion rate for over a quarter of a century. In 1975 the abortion rate was 21.7, and it rose to a peak of 29.3 in both 1980 and 1981. The other measure is to compare the ratio ending in live births or abortion each year, per 100 pregnancies. In the year 2000, a quarter (24.5 per cent) of pregnancies ended in abortion which, again, was the lowest figure for over 25 years and was below the ratio of over 30 per cent in each of the four years 1980-1983 (Finer and Henshaw 2003).

There could be a number of reasons for this decline. There have been suggestions that teenage sexual activity has declined and that contraceptives have been used more effectively. Finer and Henshaw of the Alan Guttmacher Institute in New York also draw attention to the decline in the number of abortion providers, down from a high of 2,900 in 1982 to around 2,000 in 1996 and 1,800 in 2000. However, on the other hand the approval for use of Mifepristone (formerly know as RU 486) in September 2000 provided women seeking abortion with a non-surgical option.

The number and rate of abortion varies greatly between regions. The figures below relate to where the abortions occurred not where the women generally resided. Six states which accounted for 40 per cent of resident women aged 15–44 accounted for 55 per cent of all abortions. These states were California, Florida, Illinois, New Jersey, New York and Texas. Rates were highest in New York and New Jersey and were above 30 per 1000 women aged 15–44 in California, Delaware, Florida and Nevada. The abortion rates were low in Kentucky, South Dakota, Wyoming, Idaho, Mississippi, Missouri, Utah and West Virginia, at seven or fewer per 1,000. In the period 1996-2000, the abortion rates declined in 35 states and the District of Columbia, while it increased in 15 states. However, the figures should be used with caution because, for example the Wyoming rate of abortion on residents is several times the rate by state of occurrence.

Between 1996 and 2000, the number of providers grew in nine states and fell in 38 and the District of Columbia. The largest increases were in Connecticut, Hawaii and Pennsylvania. In Connecticut, the increase mainly resulted from the identification of several physicians who did a small number of abortions. The two states with the largest number of providers – New York and California – were the two with the largest absolute decreases over the period.

In 2000 there were abortion providers in 404 of the 3,141 US counties, so only 13 per cent of counties had providers. However, as many of these had only small populations, 66 per cent of women of fertile age lived in counties with providers.

2.1.1   Kinds of Provider

Clinics In 2000, these made up 46 per cent of all abortion providers, an increase from 43 per cent in 1996. Slightly over half the clinics, accounting for a quarter of all providers, were specialized abortion clinics where at least half the patient visits were for abortion services. These units carried out seven out of ten (71 per cent) of all abortions in 2000. Caseloads are largest at these abortion clinics and three-quarters of them carried out at least 1,000 abortions in that year, while only 7 per cent of other providers did so. The remaining clinics, where the majority of patients received services other than abortion, made up one in five (21 per cent) of total providers and performed 22 per cent of abortions. Physicians' offices which carried out over 400 abortions were classified as clinics.

Hospitals Although these made up one-third of abortion providers, in 2000 they only carried out 5 per cent of abortions. More than half the hospitals performing abortions carried out fewer than 30 in the year; a quarter (24 per cent) performed five or fewer, and it is likely these were carried out for fetal abnormality or serious risk to the woman's life or health. Overall, 88 per cent of hospital abortions were outpatients procedures, but 8,000 abortions involved actual admission.

Physicians One-fifth (21 per cent) of providers were physicians' offices. Of these, two in five (41 per cent) carried out fewer than 30 abortions in 2000 and only 2 per cent of reported abortions were carried out in a physician's office.

Overall, a majority of providers performed fewer than 400 abortions in 2000. However, four out of five abortions were done in large facilities where 1,000 or more were carried out. The trend since 1996 has been for there to be a decrease in the number of providers except for those very large providers carrying out over 5,000 terminations where there was an increase. Consequently, abortions are becoming increasingly concentrated amongst the small number of very large providers (Finer and Henshaw 2003).

2.1.2 Growth of Medical Abortion

Mifespristone (RU 486) obtained approval from the Food and Drug Administration in September 2000 and distribution to providers began in the November. This was a little behind developments elsewhere. RU 486 was invented in France by Dr Etienne-Emile Baulieu in 1980 and entered clinical trials in Geneva in 1981. Now known as Mifepristone, the drug was developed by the pharmaceutical company Rousel Uclaf. Multi-centre trials began in England and Wales in 1987, and the drug was licensed for use in France in 1988. On 1 July 1991, a licence was granted for its use in the UK in the first nine weeks of pregnancy. Medical abortion is now increasingly approved around the world. Agreement to its use was given in Sweden in 1992, in China in

1998, and in Austria, Belgium, Denmark, Finland, Germany, Greece, Israel, the Netherlands, Russia, Spain and Switzerland in 1999, although not all countries in which it is approved now provide it as a service (BPAS 2002). In its first six months in the USA, one third of all the abortion providers performed at least one early medical abortion using either mifepristone or methotrexate. Half (51 per cent) of the abortion clinics and just under half (45 per cent) of the non-specialized clinics provided early medical abortion, as did just under one in five (19 per cent) of the hospital abortion providers. In the first six months of 2001, an estimated 37,200 early medical abortions were performed which was around 6 per cent of all abortions. Just over seven in ten (72 per cent) were performed with mifespristone and the rest with methotrexate. Amongst the non-hospital facilities not offering medical abortion, three in ten (30 per cent) said they would probably offer it in the future and an additional quarter (23 per cent) said they might offer it. Providers with large caseloads indicated that they were more likely to offer it. By April 2002, seven out of ten (69 per cent) members of the National Abortion Federation offered medical abortion.

In 2001, the Department of Health and Human Services announced that it would pay for medical abortions for Medicaid recipients only in limited situations such as in pregnancy due to rape or incest, or if continuation would endanger the woman's health. This is as in the case of surgical abortions (Goldstein 2001).

2.1.3   Regional Differences in Abortion Rates (USA)

The changes in the abortion rate discussed in this section have been rounded to a single digit. In 1992 the overall (national) abortion rate was 26 per 1,000 women. However regional data showed that it was the west which had the highest abortion rate, at 34 per 1,000 women aged 15–44. In the northeast the rate was 32, in the south it was 22 and in the mid-west it was 19 per 1000 women. Thus, there were wide regional variations. The results for the year 2000 show a reduction in the national abortion rate to 21 while the regional differences were 25 for the west, 28 for the northeast, 19 for the south and 16 for the mid-east; so the sharper fall of the abortion rate in the west meant that it was the northwast which had the highest rate in the year 2000. Within these regions there was, however, a great deal of variation between the 50 states. The urban areas had higher rates than rural ones. The states with the highest rates per 1,000 women were New York 39, New Jersey 36, Florida 32, Nevada 32, California 31, Delaware 31 and Maryland 29. States with rates about the average were Rhode Island 24, Oregon 24, Illinois 23, Michigan 22, Hawaii 22, Connecticut

21, Massachusetts 21, Kansas 21, North Carolina 21, Washington 20, Texas 19 and Virginia 18. States with low rates were Arizona 17, Georgia 17, Ohio 17, Colorado 16, Tennessee 15, New Mexico 15, Alabama 14, Minnesota 14, Montana 14, Pennsylvania 14, Louisiana 13, Vermont 13, Alaska 12, Nebraska 12 and New Hampshire 11. States with very low rates – less than half the national average – were Arkansas 10, Iowa 10, Maine 10, North Dakota 10, Oklahoma 10, Wisconsin 10, Indiana 9, South Carolina 9, Idaho 7, Missouri 7, Utah 7, West Virginia 7, Mississippi 6, South Dakota 6, Kentucky 5 and Wyoming 1. These results show that New York State had the highest rate and that six states had rates above 30 per thousand women of fertile age. A total of 16 states had rates less than half the national average, including Wyoming which had an abortion rate of only one. The trends over time show some wide differences between states. In the eight years 1992–2000, only three states increased their abortion rates these were Florida, New Jersey and Maryland. The rest all reduced their rates, including Hawaii where the rate more than halved, from 46 to 22 over the period. Other states with significant reductions were Vermont down from 22 to 13, Missouri down from 12 to 7, Mississippi which halved from 12 to 6, Kentucky down from 11 to 5, and Wyoming whose rate of one was down from four in 1992. Overall, the area with the highest figure was Washington DC with 68, almost twice that of California. The figure was however, very much down from its rate of 135 in 1992.

Respondents estimated that 8 per cent of women having abortions in non-hospital facilities travel more that 100 miles to the facility and 24 per cent travel over 50 miles. The proportion travelling long distances varies by geographic region: more than two in five (43 per cent) women in the East South Central Region traveled at least 50 miles for abortion, in contrast to just over one in ten (11 per cent) of women in the Middle Atlantic states. The problem of travelling long distances is aggravated if women have to make more than one visit to the facility. In 2001, four states had legislation requiring most or all clients to receive specified in-person counseling at least 24 hours before the procedure was performed. Ten other states required a delay after state-directed counseling, but allowed the consultation to be by telephone or other means not requiring two visits (Henshaw and Finer 2003).

The Alan Guttmacher Institute also provides information about the number of providers in different states. The highest number is in California with 400, followed by New York with 234, Florida with 108 and New Jersey with 86. Every state has at least one provider, but there are only two providers in South Dakota, three in West Virginia and Wyoming and four in Utah and Mississippi. The shortage of facilities may mean that women have to travel great distances for their termination. Providers estimate that one quarter of women receiving abortions in non-hospital facilities travel 50 miles or more for services (Henshaw and Finer 2003).

In their discussion of the reasons for the trends, Finer and Henshaw suggest that the trend towards fewer providers performing more procedures might be due to the increased legal restraints on the circumstances under which abortions may be performed. Specialized clinics may be better able to deal with any new restrictions than physician's offices and non-specialized clinics. This factor may be most relevant in Mississippi and South Carolina, where new licensing laws have created a burden for providers and at least one provider decided to close in response. In addition, the degree of harassment might be a factor. Although it has declined there have still been several high profile incidents which may have left providers unwilling to let their staff face physical threats. This decline in the number of small providers may not have much effect on the total national provision, but may well have a significant effect on accessibility for residents of some rural areas and small towns.

The decrease in abortion may be linked in some states to the recent imposition of restrictive regulations. For example, the imposition in Wisconsin of a two-day delay was probably a factor contributing to a 21 per cent reduction in the abortion rate in this state and possibly to some of its residents going to Illinois, and particularly Chicago, for their terminations. History has shown that women are willing to travel for an abortion; so a reduction in the rates in one state may well be due to the fact that barriers in neighboring states are less onerous (Francome 1984 and 1992).

2.2   International Comparisons

In the past, the abortion rate in the USA was markedly higher than the rate in other industrialized countries. The recent reduction in its rate, to 21.3 per 1000 women, has placed it nearer to the levels of other countries. It is for example below the rate of Australia (22.2) and near to that of Sweden (18.7).

2.2.1   Costs and Travel for Abortion

The average cost of an abortion at ten weeks based on a sample of 637 providers was $468 in 2001. This average cost is raised by a few places charging very high prices. The actual cost of an abortion at this stage varied between $150 and $4,000, so in some ways the median (mid-way) charge is more representative.

This shows that in 2001 the overall median cost was $370, although it varied according to facility. It was $340 in abortion clinics, $375 in other clinics and $500 in physicians' offices. Not surprisingly, the cost also varied according to gestation. So while the median for 10 weeks was $370, at 16 weeks it was $650 and at 20 weeks it was $1,042. The average cost for a mifepristone (RU 486) abortion was $490 which was just above the overall average.

A sample of women in 2001 found that almost three-quarters (74 per cent) paid for their abortions with their own money or with funds they received from their partner, friends and family. However, 12 per cent of these self-payers were treated at a reduced fee. The other abortions were paid for equally by Medicaid (13 per cent) and private insurance (13 per cent). The percentage of abortions paid for under Federal Medicaid is less than 1 per cent. However, in this survey 57 per cent of women lived in states where there was added state Medicaid funding, and in these states over a quarter (27 per cent) received abortions with support from Medicaid (Henshaw and Finer 2003). The effects of this and private insurance led to only just over two in five (43 per cent) paying a full fee for the abortion by themselves, in contrast to nearly four out of five (79 per cent) women in states which were not covered by supplementary Medicaid (Henshaw and Finer 2003).

2.2.2   Gestation Limits

Providers usually set minimum and maximum limits on abortion. More than nine out of ten abortion providers offer abortion at 8–10 weeks since the last menstrual period. Eight weeks after the last menstrual period is typically four weeks after the woman's first missed period. The proportion of clinics offering abortion declines steeply after 12 weeks, and at 20 weeks only 33 per cent of providers offer abortion services. At 21 weeks just under a quarter (24 per cent) do so. Only 2 per cent of abortion facilities provide abortions at 26 weeks, and presumably these are largely carried out for reasons of maternal health or because of fetal problems.

2.3   Reasons for the Decline in the Abortion Rate

One of the reasons for the decline in the abortion rate may well have been the increased use of emergency contraception. In fact, Finer and Henshaw estimate that 51,000 pregnancies were avoided by emergency contraception in 2000 which accounted for 43 per cent of the decrease in abortions since 1994.

The decline in the abortion rate between 1994 and 2000 was greatest amongst teenagers, and it appears that teenagers are using birth control more assiduously. The proportion of females using contraception at first intercourse rose from 67 per cent in 1988 to 77 per cent in 1995, although the proportion using contraception at last intercourse declined (Abma and Sonenstein 2001). Much of the increased protection to women at intercourse was due to a move to condoms. The use of a condom at last intercourse increased from 31 per cent in 1988 to 38 per cent in 1995. There has also been a decline in sexual activity amongst teenagers. An article published in 2001 stated that the proportion of teenagers who had never been married and who reported having intercourse fell for the first time since data collection began in the early 1970s. The overall percentage fell from 56 per cent in 1988 to 52 per cent in 1995. The fall was greatest amongst men – from 60 per cent to 55 per cent, while the figure for women fell only from 51 per cent to 49 per cent. In fact, young women under the age of 16 showed a different trend. The proportion saying they had intercourse before the age of 16 rose from 11 per cent to 19 per cent (Abma and Sonenstein 2001).

The role of poverty on abortion also seems to have become relevant. Finer and Henshaw report that between 1987 and 1994 the trends in abortion rates were similar amongst higher and lower income groups. Since then, however, there has been a divergence, with the reduction in abortion being greater amongst richer women. One suggestion is that poorer women have found it more difficult to gain access to contraceptive services and the reduction in child support has made it more difficult for a poor woman to raise a child.

One factor which may have led to a decline in the abortion rates may be the reduction in prejudice against births outside marriage. This may make it more likely that an unintended pregnancy may continue to term and in 1994 an estimated 46 per cent of unintended pregnancies did so (Henshaw and Finer 2003).

2.4   The Impact of Legal Abortion on Crime

A controversial piece of research was published in 2001. In the 1990s the USA experienced the sharpest drop in its murder rate since the end of prohibition in 1933. In addition, violent and property crime also declined by more than 30 per cent. Several reasons for this have been put forward, including the zero tolerance policing practices of areas such as New York, the increase in the prison population and an increase in expenditure on victim precautions.

However, Donohue and Levitt consider that these explanations have their weaknesses and, rather, point to the Supreme Court decision on abortion. They comment:

> While acknowledging that all these factors may have also served to dampen crime, we consider a novel explanation for the sudden drop of crime in the 1990s: the decision to legalise abortion over a quarter century ago (Donohue and Levitt 2001, p. 380).

They estimate that legalised abortion can account for about half the decline in Crime in the USA between 1991–97. They suggest that legalised abortion might lead to reduced crime either through the reduction in cohort sizes or because of lower offending rates within the cohorts. An increase in the number of abortions would lead, in 16 years, to there being fewer young men reaching their 'high crime' years – that is, their late teens and 20s. However, in addition Donohue and Levitt maintain that children born after legalization may have lower crime rates because the women who seek abortions may be those who would be more likely to produce children inclined to crime. They draw attention to the fact that teenagers, unmarried woman and the economically disadvantaged are all substantially more likely to seek abortions than other groups. As 6 per cent of any birth cohort commit about half the crime, this can be an important effect. Furthermore, some women may have an abortion to space their childrens, so that they would better able to care for their children and nurture them more successfully. Consequently even if the birth rate did not fall it could still be that children were raised in improved conditions. They provide a number of facts to support their case:

- crime started to reduce around 1992. The peak ages for violent crime are around 18–24, and the first cohort born after *Roe v. Wade* reached its criminal peak at about this time;
- five states – Alaska, California, Hawaii, New York and Washington – legalised or quasi-legalised abortion around 1970. They also had higher abortion rates after legalization. These states had greater reductions in crime than the states which legalised later. The cumulative decrease in crime during the period 1982–97 for these states was 16 per cent greater for murder, 30 per cent greater for violent crime and 35 per cent greater for property crime, compared with the other states.

In an analysis of an array of studies, Dagg found that children who were born because their mothers were denied an abortion had poorer life prospects and were more likely to be involved in crime (Donohue and Levitt 2001, p. 388). The decline in fertility amongst black women was three times greater than amongst whites (12 per cent compared to 4 per cent). He argued that, since the homicide rates of black youths were roughly nine times those of white youths, the ethnic differences in fertility rates were likely to lead to a disproportionate decrease in crime.

In an interview, Levitt commented that they were 'not arguing that the relation of crime and abortion was good or bad, just that it exists'. However, Charles Murray commented that the research did not please activists on either side. The 'pro choice lobby does not want to hear that if you stop poor people having children you will help to solve the crime problem' (2001).

The research has been criticized by a number of people. David Murray of the statistical Assessment Unit said that the drop in the crime rate correlates with a number of different social and cultural developments during the same time period – everything from the start of the internet to the demise of popular music. He made the point that it was young males aged 17–25 who committed the majority of crimes. Consequently, if it were true that abortion reduced crime, it would fall first within this group. In fact it fell first amongst older people. He further commented:

> They didn't ask the right questions and as soon as you ask the right questions the effect they think they are seeing disappears and the picture becomes much more obscure, much more cloudy.

Two other authors, Lott of Yale and Whitley of Adelaide, went further and maintained that abortion can lead to an increase in the number of homicides. Their argument was that legal abortion increases the number of births outside wedlock and one parent families. This leads to less likelihood that fathers will be around and that children will be well nurtured by mothers. They went on to argue that abortion increased the murder rate, by between 0.5 and 7 per cent.

However, others have been far more supportive – for example, Andrew Sullivan stated in the *Sunday Times* that 'the methodology is sound, the arguments tight' (15 August 1999).

One problem with the research is that abortion did not start with the limited state legalizations and the Supreme Court decision, but in fact was common before these so the amount of increase in terminations can only be estimated.

2.4.1 Demonstrations and Violence against Abortion Facilities

NARAL reported that, from 1977 to May 1992, there had been 59,000 acts of violence and disruption. These included seven murders, 17 attempted murders, 41 bombings, 165 cases of arson, 370 physical invasions and 343 death threats (www.naral.org).

One article suggested that anti-abortion violence sprang to national attention in 1982 with the bombing of three clinics in the spring, and the kidnapping in August of Dr Zevallos and his wife in Illinois. Two brothers and a third man were convicted of the kidnapping, which they did under the name of the 'Army of God'. In 1983 there were setbacks for the anti-choice groups, both in Congress over the pro-life Constitutional Amendment and in the Supreme Court over the constitutionality of local regulations, and it may have been these which led to radicals taking further militant action. There was a rash of bombings in 1984, by the end of the year, 25 clinics suffered a bomb or arson attack. In 1988 an organization calling itself 'Operation Rescue' organized a mass blockade of abortion clinics across the country. These continued through the late 1980s and early 1990s. Places where things were difficult included Orange County, Los Angeles; Wichita, Kansas; New York City and Buffalo, New York; Houston, Texas; Jackson, Missouri; Philadelphia, Pennsylvania and Cleveland, Ohio. Often, 200–300 people were arrested at one time (Feminist Campus 2003).

In the first seven months of 1993, half of all abortion clinics were under siege, according to the Feminist Majority Foundation's annual survey. Also in 1993, the anti-abortion groups began to intensify their activities by circulating 'Wanted' posters showing much personal information about doctors and other health care professionals. On 10 March 1993 Dr David Gunn was murdered by Michael Griffin. Another anti-abortion activist, Paul Hill who was a former Presbyterian minister, began advocating that the murder was 'justifiable homicide'. Hill was one of those who demonstrated for the acquittal and release of Griffin. In response to these activities, and armed with extensive data on the degree of violence and the lack of local response, pro-choice activists worked for a Federal response.

This resulted in the passage, in May 1994, of the Freedom of Access to Clinic Entrances Act (FACE) which made anti abortion-violence a Federal crime (Feminist Campus 2003). Violence remained high through 1994, with over half (52 per cent) of clinics experiencing violence. In addition, a quarter of clinics said that their staff had experienced death threats (Feminist Campus 2003). In July 1994, Paul Hill killed Dr John Britton and clinic escort James

Barret. Later in the year, on 30 December, two receptionists were killed in the Brookline Clinic in Boston – four murders in a single year. However, by 1995 the FACE Act was increasingly being enforced, and the Madsen Supreme Court decision affirmed the use of Buffer Zones around clinics. In that year, 39 per cent of clinics suffered violence, a reduction. In the following year, 1996, the violence dropped again, being experienced by only 28 per cent of clinics. However, the appointment of a pro-choice president later that year seemed to spark more violence. In December, a doctor was stabbed 15 times and lost four pints of blood. His assailant was arrested while waiting to attack another doctor.

In 1997, three organizations – the Planned Parenthood Federation of America, the National Abortion Federation and the Feminist Majority Foundation – held a press conference entitled 'Violence is still a problem'. During the proceedings, two bombs were ignited at an Atlanta Family Planning Clinic. In that year there were at least 13 arsons and bombings which was nearly twice the level for 1996. Most of the violent groups were small and some even had only one member. The American Life League produced 'A Pro-Life Proclamation Against Violence' which was endorsed by 31 other anti-choice groups by 13 March 1999. However, neither *Operation Rescue* nor *Rescue League* signed it.

The internet seems to have been one way of passing on information leading to violence. One of the creations was the so-called 'Nuremburg Files' which contained details of more than 225 doctors and other people associated with abortion facilities, including their names and addresses. One of the names on the list was that of Dr Sepian, and he was killed on the 23 October 1998 in Amherst. Shortly after the murder, his name was crossed off the web site. Kim Gandy, then the executive-vice president of NOW commented 'Those who call themselves "pro-life" must take responsibility for the climate of hate and fear that they have helped create in the country. This includes lawmakers and law enforcers'.

There have also been web sites promoting violence, often with religious overtones. People have sought out quotations from the Bible and pulled them out of context – for example, Luke 22:36: 'He that hath no sword, let him sell his garment and buy one' and Psalm 58:10: 'The righteous shall rejoice when he seeth the vengeance: he shall wash his feet in the blood of the wicked.'

Pro-life groups in Virginia printed a large picture of Paul Hill with the caption 'Paul Hill, defender of the defenders of life'. They also commented: 'We proclaim that the force used to defend the life of a born child is legitimate to defend the life of an unborn child'. Paul Hill was quoted as saying: 'Much of the joy I felt after shooting the abortionist and still feel today is the joy of having freely obeyed Christ after long being enslaved to fearful obedience of men.'

The NAF has been compiling details of violence since 1977. In 1998, 12 letters were sent out to clinics threatening anthrax; in 1999 there were 35, in 2000 there were 30 and in 2001 there were 550. In one incident, approximately 110 envelopes containing white powder were sent to private abortion clinics and Planned Parenthood facilities, together with a letter stating that the package contained anthrax. In fact, although the letters contained powder it was not anthrax. Vicki Saporta, executive director of NAF, commented 'This is despicable. With the recent confirmation of anthrax in three states it really is unconscionable for anti-choice extremists to be doing this at this time' (NAF 2001). In 2001 there were 9,900 incidents of picketing, the highest level since abortion was legalized (Operation Save America, formerly Operation Rescue). There was one bombing and two cases of arson, however, there were no murders, for the third year in a row (Feminist Campus 2003).

2.5 Conclusion

The fact that one in four US pregnancies ends in abortion indicates that many women are becoming pregnant when they do not wish to do so. Of course, many other women will be wishing for pregnancy and finding it difficult to achieve. Nearly half of pregnancies occur amongst women who have difficulty in using contraception effectively (Finer and Henshaw 2003). The other women used no contraception, and this was likely to be due to the pattern of relationships between the sexes. Even without changing the amount of sexual activity, it would be possible to reduce the abortion rate further by improving accessibility to contraceptive services, especially for vulnerable groups such as the poor and the young.

Chapter 3

The Experience of Legal Abortion
in the UK

The Abortion Act (1967) came into operation on 27 April 1968. The number of abortions increased rapidly at first. In 1969, the first full year of the Act, there were just under 50,000 abortions in England and Wales and by 1972, 108,600 were notified (in the subsequent analysis, figures over a thousand are rounded to the nearest hundred). Some anti-choice writers expressed the view that the country was becoming abortion-minded, and that numbers would continue to rise (Goodhart 1973). However, those from the pro-choice side argued, rather, that a process was occurring whereby abortions were being transferred from the unrecorded illegal sector to the now legitimate hospitals. As the predominant estimate before the Act was that there were 100,000 abortions a year, the expectation would be that the abortion rate would tail off at about that level. In fact, the evidence seemed to support this position. In 1973 there was only a small increase in abortions, to 110,600, and by 1976 the number of abortions on women resident in the UK fell to below 102,000, almost exactly the number predicted before the law came into effect. Evidence of personal stories gives credence to this scenario. In an earlier book I gave a case history of a woman who approached me after I had given a lecture in December 1984:

> When she was young she was 'too embarrassed' to discuss birth control with her boyfriends and in 1971 she became pregnant. She did not know how to get a legal abortion and it did not occur to her to go to her local doctor, so she asked around and was introduced to 'someone who knew someone'. On the designated day, she waited on a corner in Bristol, and was driven to an address where she met a woman who had trained as a nurse who gave her the abortion for five pounds, using a Higginson's syringe. She said this taught her a lesson, so she went to a family planning clinic in Bristol and used the pill for a number of years. However, she became a little casual about regular use and became pregnant again. By this time she knew of the possibility of a legal abortion, so she went to her doctor (Francome 1986, p. 48).

The number of deaths from illegal abortion fell from 47 in 1966 to eight in 1973. Since that date, illegal abortion deaths have been virtually unknown in the UK. One factor that was possibly related to the reduction in the number of abortions between 1973 and 1976 was the introduction of free birth control. From 1 April 1974, contraceptive supplies provided by the NHS were free of charge irrespective of age or marital status. Women were able to go to their local doctor (GP) or to the local Family Planning Association, and receive a method of birth control of their choice. The practice was different from the USA in that a full physical examination was not and is not required; however, there is a requirement for blood pressure to be taken. Men were, and still are, permitted to obtain condoms free from the Family Planning Association, although they cannot obtain them free from their GP.

In 1977 there was a scare about the potential side effects of the pill and this may have been a factor in the rise in the number of abortions in England and Wales from 103,000 in 1977 to 129,000 three years later. In the years 1980–84, the abortion rate fell slightly each year, but for the rest of the decade there was an annual rise, reaching 174,000 in 1990. The number then fell each year until 1995, when there were 154,300 abortions. In 1995 there was yet another scare about the pill, and the number of abortions rose by 13,600 in the next year. The numbers continued to rise slightly, to a peak of 178,000 in 1998. In 1999 there was a 2.2 per cent fall to 174,000, but in the year 2,000 there was another rise, to 175,500. The Office for National Statistics said that the rise in 2000 was believed to be a result of the millennium celebrations. The Royal College of Obstetricians and Gynaecologists (RCOG) stated that at least a third of British women will have an abortion by the time they reach the age of 45 (2000).

In some ways, a better measure of the number of abortions is the rate per 1,000 women aged 15–44. For residents of England and Wales during the period 1971–84, the rate was relatively constant at between 10 and 12 per thousand, but then rose to a peak of 17.1 per thousand in 1998. In the year 2000, the age-standardized abortion rate was 16.9 per thousand women aged 15–44.

3.1   Legal Abortion in Britain 2000

Between the introduction of the Abortion Act on 27 April 1968 and the end of the year 2,000, more than 5.1 million abortions were notified, of which 85 per cent were on resident women. Currently around 95 per cent of abortions in Britain are on resident women, reflecting the fact that other countries have changed their laws. In the year 2000, two improvements were made to the statistics. First, inconsistencies between birth, conception and abortion statistics were removed and, second, in addition to the overall abortion rate, an age-standardized rate was introduced.

The abortion law permits a termination of pregnancy by a registered practitioner within certain conditions. When the Abortion Act was passed, the upper time limit (except to save the woman's life) was left according to the Infant Life Preservation Act 1929, which specified 28 weeks in England and Wales. There was no legal limit in Scotland where the 1929 Act did not apply. However, an upper time limit of 24 weeks in most circumstances was introduced by section 37 of the Human Fertilisation and Embryology Act 1990 which came into effect on 1 April 1991.

3.1.1   Abortion Providers

Abortions in the UK may legally be carried out in certain NHS hospitals, in approved hospitals for the armed services, or in other premises specifically approved by the Secretary of State. At the end of the year 2000, there were 78 such approved places and two services hospitals. Since 1992, there has been a change in that in some cases the independent sector has been carrying out abortions on NHS patients under agency agreements. In the year 2000, 175,500 legal abortions were performed on residents of England and Wales (Scottish and Irish figures are discussed later). Just under half of these (46.2 per cent) were carried out in NHS hospitals. In addition 28.7 per cent were provided by agencies but paid for by the NHS, so three-quarters of women (74.9 per cent) received their abortions free.

The remainder were provided by two major charities, Marie Stopes International or the British Pregnancy Advisory Service, or by private clinics such as the well known Calthorpe clinic in the West Midlands.

If a woman suspects she might have an unwanted pregnancy, she can go either to her local GP or to one of the major abortion providers. If she visits her GP, she will be given a pregnancy test and will then normally be referred to a local hospital, where she will see a consultant or other senior doctor and then be admitted for the operation.

Marie Stopes International (MSI) This organization provides reproductive health services to more than 40,000 women each year. The organization was founded in 1921 when Dr Marie Stopes, the family planning pioneer, opened the UK's first family planning clinic. Since then MSI has expanded to work in more than 30 countries across Europe, Africa, Asia and Latin America, annually providing services for over a million and a half couples. The organization is known to challenge the medical establishment to take a more progressive approach. In 1960 Lady Brook started an evening birth control session for unmarried women at the MSI clinic in Whitfield Street London and in 1963 the MSI board agreed to sponsor a young people's advisory session in their clinic.

In 1982, MSI joined other members of the UK's Pro-Choice Alliance to launch *Voice for Choice*, a national campaign seeking what it felt were long overdue reforms of current abortion legislation which, it argues, is failing women, who are faced with discrimination and inequality. MSI has carried out some important research including a report on doctors' attitudes and another dealing with the experiences of Irish women coming to Britain for their abortions entitled *The Irish Journey* (2000).

British Pregnancy Advisory Service (BPAS) This organization was formed originally in 1968 as the Birmingham Pregnancy Advisory Service. Doctors in the West Midlands Region were disproportionately opposed to performing abortions, so activists set out to overcome that situation. BPAS is the country's biggest single provider of abortion services with, by 2002, a national network of twelve clinics and day care units supported by 35 consultation centres covering England, Scotland and Wales.

It is a specialist provider of services to the NHS on an agency basis. From 1 April 2000 to 31 March 2001, it carried out 42,500 abortions on women from England and Wales and a further 240 on women from Scotland. Between 1 April 2001 and 31 March 2002, the figure rose to a total of 43,300 abortions on women from England and Wales and a further 250 from Scotland. More than two-thirds (68.5 per cent) of the abortions in this latter period were paid for by the NHS but provided free to the women. This percentage shows an increase from 59.5 per cent in 1989 and 63.8 per cent from April 2000 to March 2001. BPAS now sees itself firmly positioned as a specialist NHS provider, while also remaining committed to those women who are unable to access free treatment or who prefer to pay for their care (Nicholls 2002, p. 2).

BPAS was represented on the working party which developed the RCOG evidence-based guidelines *The Care of Women Requesting Induced Abortion*; it complies with the guidelines' recommended quality standards, including those on waiting times.

3.1.2   Marital Status, Age, Previous Children and Abortion

In the year 2000 the abortion rate amongst married women was 7.3 per thousand which is less than half the overall average. There are several reasons for expecting a lower rate of abortions amongst married women. Whenever I have conducted a survey into the reasons for an unwanted pregnancy, the one stated most often is: 'had intercourse unexpectedly' (Francome 1986, 1992, 1996). This situation will obviously not exist within a regular marital relationship. Furthermore, being in a stable relationship makes birth control easier to plan and consequently leads to lower rates of unwanted pregnancy. In addition, married women might expect the support of their husband and consequently an unexpected pregnancy might more easily be accepted. For those who have completed their family size, female sterilization or vasectomy is an option. On the other hand, sex surveys reveal that married people tend to have sexual intercourse more often than single people, so married people might face more unexpected pregnancies through contraceptive failure. The 2000 figures revealed that just over 90 per cent of conceptions within marriage led to maternity, compared to two-thirds of the conceptions outside marriage (Office of National Statistics 2002).

However, the lowest abortion rate in 2000 overall was not for the married but for the divorced, at 4.4 per thousand. This is attributable to a number of reasons including the fact that divorced women tend to have less sexual intercourse; they may also be in an older age range, and so less fertile. Women who were widowed had an abortion rate of 14.7 which is just below average. In fact, younger widows in the age range 24–34 had high rates of abortion – about twice the average rate for all women. One in 20 of the few widows in the age group 20–24 had an abortion (Office of National Statistics 2001, p. 3). Just over seven out of ten (70.8 per cent) of all the abortions were carried out on single women and their overall rate was 24.0 per thousand, well above the average for all women. Many of these women will be in long-term relationships and be able more easily to plan their contraception, however, a large percentage will not be having sexual relations on a regular basis. Many of these women will, of course, be hoping to have children at a later stage in their lives, when the social conditions are more appropriate for them.

The age group with the highest abortion rate is that of 20–24 years with a rate of 30.9 per thousand, followed by the 16–19 age group with a rate of 26.7. As the age groups rise, the risk of an abortion recedes. Thus, amongst the 25–29 year olds it is 20.7 per thousand, amongst the 30–34 year old group it is 13.8, amongst the 35–39 year group it is 9.1 and in the 40–44 year group it is 3.3. Single women had a higher abortion rate than married women for every age group except those aged 16–19 years. A total of 404 married women in their teens had abortions in 2000, giving an abortion rate of 50.0 per thousand – that is to say, one in 20 of this sub-group of married teenagers had terminations. The reasons for such a high rate are not clear (Office of National Statistics 2001, p. 3).

In the year 2000, the majority of women (52.7 per cent) undergoing an abortion had no previous children, just under one in five (19.0 per cent) had one child, 17.3 per cent had two children, 7.3 per cent had three children, and the other 3.7 per cent had four children or more. These latest official figures do not give a breakdown comparing the number of children with marital status. However, in earlier years it was largely young single women who had no previous children. As far as married women were concerned, they were more likely to have an abortion either to space out their child-bearing or when they had reached the final number of children they desired. Some evidence of this can be adduced by considering the 24,800 women aged over 35 at the time of their abortion. Only 15.6 per cent had no children, 17.3 per cent had one child, over a third (36.1 per cent) had two children and almost a third (31.0 per cent) had three children or more. So this older group would appear to contain a high percentage of women who felt they had completed their child-bearing.

Gestation at abortion The gestation at time of abortion for all residents of England and Wales was as follows: just over two in five (43 per cent) were under nine weeks, fewer than half (45 per cent) were 9–12 weeks and fewer than one in ten (8 per cent) were 13–16 weeks. Later abortions were rare: under 3 per cent were at 17–20 weeks and 0.1 per cent over 21 weeks.

Gestation varied according to the abortion provider. Just over one-third of NHS abortions (35.6 per cent) were at under nine weeks, compared to slightly more (37.6 per cent) agency ones and almost two-thirds (63.7 per cent) of non-NHS abortions (Office of National Statistics 2001, p. 6). NHS abortions occur later, in part due to delays within the system, but also because the NHS dealt with the more difficult cases. Thus, all the 99 abortions occurring after 24 weeks took place within the NHS.

Examination of the relevant statistics shows that the number of abortions occurring under nine weeks has increased. In 1971, only one abortion in six (16.6 per cent) occurred this early, while in 2000 it was at an all-time high of more than two in five (43.2 per cent). This is in part due to the change in abortion methods discussed below. Perhaps surprisingly, in 2000 there was also the highest percentage ever of women having their abortions after 20 weeks. This was 1.5 per cent, a rise from 1.4 per cent in 1999 and 1.3 per cent in 1998 (Office of National Statistics 2001, p. 68).

Regional variations in NHS abortions The percentage of abortions provided free on the NHS for resident women rose from 50 per cent in 1991 to nearly 71 per cent in 1995. This increase seems to have been an unplanned result of government health care changes and the introduction of a division between the providers of care and the purchasers. However, the percentage was still below the recommendation of the 1979 Royal Commission on the NHS that local authorities should aim to provide for 75 per cent of abortions over the subsequent few years (ALRA 1997, p. 4). The RCOG report of 2000 stated that there were wide variations in the provision of free abortions on the NHS. In 1997, for example, only 19 of 105 local authorities in England and Wales funded more than 90 per cent of abortion procedures and 48 of the authorities funded less than 75 per cent. In the Greater London region of Thames, only two of 26 authorities funded more than 76 per cent of all abortions. The RCOG Guidelines Development Group took the view that abortion is a healthcare need and reiterated the policy, proposed by the RCOG working party on unplanned pregnancy, that 'health authorities should accept responsibility for abortions needed by women resident in their districts' (RCOG 2000, p. 11).

In a piece of research begun at the end of 1999 but published after the RCOG report, the Abortion Law Reform Association (ALRA) wrote to all the 119 Health Authorities in England, Scotland and Wales. A total of 109 responded providing a creditable 92 per cent response rate. The overall percentage of abortions carried out on the NHS was 74 per cent in England, 88 per cent in Wales and 99 per cent in Scotland. The survey found that at least nine of the Health Authorities set their own restrictive criteria for the provision of free abortions on the NHS. Some of these were intended to be punitive – for instance, the woman would not be given an abortion if she had not used contraception. Others gave abortions to women on income support or a low income, or to the young or old who are presumably deemed too young or old for childbirth. One health authority delayed abortions until at least ten weeks gestation, in the declared hope that women would either change their minds or opt for immediate private treatment. The survey also found that few authorities had any information on which of their local doctors had a conscientious objection to abortion (ALRA 2000, pp. 8, 9).

Sequelae During the triennium 1994–96, there was one death as a direct cause of a legal abortion (RCOG 2000, p. 34). The absolute risk of complications from abortion is low. A study of 83,500 procedures reported 571 immediate complications, which is 0.7 per cent. These included haemorrhage, cervical laceration, uterine perforation, retained products, infection and maternal death. In the year 2000, the complication rate was lower, at 0.25 per cent, which is just over a third of the total reported in the RCOG study. More than half the problems were due to haemorrhage, which occurred in 1.3 cases per 1,000. Perforation occurred in 0.5 cases per 1,000, sepsis in 0.4 cases and other problems in 0.4 cases, so overall, the complication rate was low. It did, however, vary according to gestation. For women having an abortion before 13 weeks there were 2.2 complications per 1,000; for women at 13-19 weeks it rose to 4.6 and for women over 20 weeks it was 9.8 per thousand. However, in the case of late abortions there may have been other problems which resulted in medical indications for a termination (Office of National Statistics 2001, p. 14).

3.2   Legal Abortion in Scotland

The Scottish abortion rate has always been lower than that of England and Wales. In 1971, for example, the crude non-age standardized rate, including abortions on Scottish women going to England, was 7.3 per thousand. The comparative rate for England and Wales was 10.1. In the early years after legalization, many women travelled to England for their abortions. This was in large part due to the lack of private clinics north of the border. In 1973, for example, 7,500 women had abortions in Scotland and a further 1,100 Scottish women had abortions in England and Wales. This number stayed remarkably constant for a number of years. For instance, in 1980, 7,900 Scottish women had abortions in Scotland and a further 1,200 had them in England and Wales (Macfarlane and Mugford 1984, p. 101).

In the year 2000, a total of 12,000 abortions were performed in Scotland, and an additional 345 women normally resident in Scotland had abortions in England. Scotland has comprehensive NHS abortion services and only 1.5 per cent of these operations were performed privately.

3.3   Legal Abortion in England and Wales for Women from Other Countries

Women have often had to travel to other countries to obtain abortions. We have seen that British women went to France in the early part of the twentieth century, and this was followed by French women coming to the UK in great numbers in the 1970s. In the 1960s Swedish women went to Poland while, following the implementation of the 1967 British law on 27 April 1968, women from the USA came to London. New Zealand women went to Australia and German women to Holland. After 1970, Canadian women went in great numbers to New York State. When the USA imposed financial restrictions on poor women obtaining abortions, many travelled instead to Mexico for cheap operations (Francome 1984, p. 222). The British experience in providing abortions for non-resident women had far-reaching effects.

In 1969, the first full year of the Act, there were 5,000 abortions on non-resident women. This number more than doubled in 1970 to 10,600 and then almost tripled to 32,200 in 1971. In 1972 there were 51,300 abortions on non-resident women, and in 1973 there was an all-time peak of 56,600. At this time, non-resident women made up just over one-third (33.8 per cent) of the total number of abortions for residents of England and Wales. The number of non-resident women having an abortion in England and Wales declined to 33,500 in 1975 and 27,800 in 1976. The numbers then rose slightly again, as women from other countries began to come in increasing numbers, and in 1983 the number of non-resident women had risen to 34,800. By 1988 the number had halved to 15,500 and it then continued to decline marginally over the next few years. In every one of the six years 1995–2000, there were between 9,300 and 9,900 abortions on non-resident women (Office of National Statistics 2001, p. 1).

British law has helped to change the law in other countries. There was a pattern where women have increasingly made use of the British 1967 Act and simultaneously argued the case for change at home so that they did not have to travel. For over two years, from the implementation of the British Act and the legalization of abortion in New York in June 1970, it could be argued that women from the USA were being discriminated against by being made to travel for their operations. In 1970, 1,100 women from the USA had their abortions in the UK, but in the following year it was only 187. In 1973, the year of the Supreme Court decision, the number had fallen to 104 and in 1974 it was down to 63 (Macfarlane and Mugford 1984, p. 102). 297 Canadian women came to the UK in 1970, but in the following year it was only 67. This was probably in large measure because they found it easier to travel to New York than to cross the Atlantic.

In 1970, it was women from the Federal Republic of Germany who came to the UK in the greatest numbers – 3,600 did so in that year. The number rose to 13,600 in 1971 and to 17,500 in 1972. However, thereafter the numbers from Germany began to fall to 11,300 in 1973, 6,000 in 1974 and 3,400 in 1975. This was largely due to the fact that they began to go in increasing numbers to the Netherlands which was more easily accessible. In 1970, 816 Dutch women travelled to the UK for abortions, but by 1973 the number had dwindled to 101 as availability improved (Francome 1984, p. 136). However it was French women who were perhaps best placed to take advantage of legal abortion in the UK. In 1970, 2,267 French women had their terminations in the UK and two years later there were more than ten times as many – 25,200. The total rose to a peak of 36,500 French women having their terminations in the UK in 1974, at a time when there were only three times as many indigenous women having abortions. French law legalized abortion on request in the first ten weeks of pregnancy on 17 January 1975, replacing the 1920 abortion law. In that year, the number of French women travelling to Britain declined to 14,100 and in 1976 to 4,600. It then stayed at about this level with, for example, 4,100 travelling in 1980. French women continued to travel to England mainly because of the early time limit in France; however, the numbers declined in subsequent years.

The experience of Italy was in some ways similar to that of France, although the numbers were smaller. The first record of Italian women having abortions in the UK was in 1972, when 480 came. By 1974 the number had more than doubled to 1,300, and there was a rapid rise to 7,900 two years later. In that year (1976), an Italian Supreme Court decision slightly liberalized the law and soon afterwards, on 28 May 1978, women were given abortion on request in the early months of pregnancy. The number of Italian women coming to Britain fell to 4,200 in 1978, and to fewer than 1,000 in 1979 and subsequent years (Francome 1984, p. 143; 1986, p. 57). One of the factors behind the legalization of abortion in Italy may have been the earlier legalization in France. As *The Times* of London stated:

> France's decision to legalise abortion has left many Italians with a feeling of bitter isolation … all Italy's northern neighbours have now given their women the right to terminate pregnancies under decent and controlled conditions (6 December 1974).

It was Spanish women who were the next to start travelling to Britain in great numbers. The first record of Spanish terminations in the UK was in 1972, when 730 were completed. The number rose to 2,900 in 1974, and it had reached 14,100 by 1978 and 22,000 by 1983. Spanish law was changed in 1985 and by the year 2000 only 32 residents of Spain had their abortions in Britain.

In the year 2000, more than four out of five (80.5 per cent) of the 9,800 non-resident women having abortions in Great Britain came from Ireland. In 1971, 578 women came from the Irish Republic, with the number trebling to 1,800 by 1976. Five years later, in 1981, the number had doubled again to 3,600. There followed a steadier increase to 4,200 in 1991 and to 4,900 in 1996; then, in 1999, there were 6,200, rising to an all-time high of just below 6,400 in the year 2000. The Irish Family Planning Association is aiming to make a challenge to the European Court in the hope of liberalizing the law.

As far as Northern Ireland is concerned, the rise has been more moderate. In 1971, 648 women came to Britain from Northern Ireland, a higher number than came from the Republic. This rose to 1,800 in 1991, but for the rest of the 1990s it levelled down to around 1500 a year. In the year 2000, there were just over 1,500 abortions on women normally resident in Northern Ireland. MSI surveyed women from Northern Ireland attending its clinics and found that 91 per cent would have preferred to have had their abortions at home. Of the clients surveyed, 41 per cent were Catholic and 51 per cent were Protestant (Furedi 1995, p. 10).

In 1992 I carried out a survey of Northern Ireland's 43 consultant gynaecologists and had a 93 per cent response rate. The survey revealed that only two would not carry out an abortion in any circumstances, while two more said they would carry one out only if the fetus would not survive. It found that there was inconsistency in abortion practice. For example, one consultant indicated that he would give an abortion for rape but not for fetal abnormality while, in contrast, another would not provide one for rape but would do so for fetal handicap (Francome 1994). In 1994/95, I carried out a survey of 123 GPs in Northern Ireland randomly selected by a medical organization. The survey showed that, on average, the doctors had each received one request for an abortion during the previous six months (Francome 1997).

Individual case histories show the problems some women face. This one was told to Family Planning Association counsellors. A woman we shall call Patricia was 20 when she had a second unplanned pregnancy; her first was when she was 17 and her boyfriend at the time had said he would stand by her if she kept the baby, but he did not. She did not have sex for a while, but one night at a party she did. The following morning she went to her GP for emergency contraception, but he said he disapproved, for moral reasons and refused to prescribe it. She was very embarrassed and could not wait to get out of the surgery. She tried to forget about it but when her period was late she knew she was pregnant again. Patricia commented:

I love my son Tom but he's very demanding and I know there's no way I could have another baby. I would end up hurting the baby or myself. I'm on income support, so where am I going to find £450? And how can I explain to my family why I need them to look after Tom for three days? I have never been away from home even for one night. Besides, they would disown me if they knew what I was planning.

So the absence of the 1967 Abortion Act caused great financial and personal hardship for women in Northern Ireland, and we shall see in chapter seven that it has led to much discussion.

Apart from Irish women coming to Britain for abortions, a number of abortions also occur in Ireland as we have seen. It seems that most of these are for fetal handicap. Women are offered amniocentesis, and abortions are carried out when the fetus has Downs Syndrome (Lee 1995a, p. 40). This practice has doubtful legality, although it seems unlikely to be challenged in the courts. Lee pointed out that one result of the uncertainty over abortion is that there is uncertainty over what the laws are as they pertain to the infertile who wish for treatment (Lee 1995a, p. 44).

3.4 Non-surgical Abortions

RU 486 was invented in France by Dr Etienne-Emile Baulieu in 1980 and entered clinical trials in Geneva in 1981. Now known as Mifepristone, the drug was developed by the pharmaceutical company Rousel Uclaf. Multi-centre trials began in England and Wales in 1987, and the drug was licensed for use in France in 1988. On 1 July 1991, a licence was granted for its use in the UK in the first nine weeks of pregnancy. Medical abortion is now increasingly approved around the world. Agreement to its use was given in Sweden in 1992, in China in 1998, and in Austria, Belgium, Denmark, Finland, Germany, Greece, Israel, the Netherlands, Russia, Spain and Switzerland in 1999 – although not all countries in which it is approved now provide it as a service (BPAS 2002). In the year 2000, the number of abortions for residents of England and Wales using drugs rather than operative procedures was 19,500, which was a 40 per cent increase compared to 1999 and accounted for 11.1 per cent of all abortions. Its use is increasing, in part because the licence was extended in 1995 to cover abortion between 13 and 20 weeks gestation (RCOG 2000). Currently, a medical abortion entails four appointments. The first takes place at a consultation centre. The pregnancy is confirmed and discussed and the woman referred to a clinic. The second takes place at the clinic where the woman's suitability for an early medical abortion is assessed by a nurse. At this meeting, possible side effects such as cramping and bleeding are discussed. If the decision is positive, the woman takes 200 mg of mifepristone and, if all is well, goes home having been provided with a 24-hour helpline. The third visit is again to the clinic where there will first be a discussion about any cramping or other symptoms that have occurred within the previous 24 hours. The woman will then have 800 mcg of misopristol (a prostoglandin) administered vaginally, and told about what she might expect to experience. She will then be allowed to leave, if all is well and she is accompanied. At the fourth visit, again at the clinic, the woman will be checked to ensure that the abortion has been completed (BPAS 2002a, pp. 3,4). In June 2003 BPAS proposed that women could administer the drug at home.

3.5   Teenage Pregnancy

The legal age of consent to sexual intercourse for all the countries in the UK is 16 years (RCOG 1999, p. 18). However, sometimes doctors or Family Planning Clinics may be faced with women under the age of 16 who request contraception. Under English law, the ability of those under the age of 16 to consent to their own treatment is controlled by common law. The leading case in this area is that of *Gillick v. West Norfolk and Wisbech Health Authority* (1985). Mrs Gillick, a mother of ten children, instigated a court case aiming to prevent children under the age of 16 from being allowed to have birth control without parental consent. She won her case, but on appeal to the House of Lords, it was held that 'the law did not recognise any rule of absolute parental authority until a fixed age, and such rights yielded to children's rights to make their own decisions when they reached a sufficient understanding and intelligence to be capable of making up their own minds' (RCOG 2000, p. 19).

Following this landmark ruling the Department of Health issued further guidance. It said that doctors have an obligation to encourage a young person to involve her parents, but that should not override the patient's views except in exceptional circumstances such as incest, child abuse or exploitation. The doctor should also be satisfied that the young woman understood the moral, social and emotional implications, and that it was in her best interest to have contraceptive advice without parental consent, since she appeared to be having, or was likely to have, unprotected sex whether she received advice or not (RCOG 2000, p. 19).

The question of teenage pregnancy, or of the 'gymslip mums' as some of the tabloid newspapers call them, raises different issues according to the relationship status, and the age, of the woman concerned. Let us take the data for all women under the age of 20. In 2000, 98,000 conceived, a slight reduction on the previous year. The rate of conception was 62 per thousand, a reduction from 65 in 1998. Earlier years had shown fluctuations. In 1970, before birth control became widely available, the rate was much higher at 82 per 1,000. There was a substantial fall to 59 in 1980, followed by a rise to 68 in 1990. So the figures for 2000, while not the lowest ever, do tend to be on the low side. Just over three in five of these conceptions led to maternity, the rest ending in abortion. Among single women who became pregnant in 2000, 40 per cent went on to a maternity outside marriage registered by both parents, and a further 16 per cent to a maternity outside marriage registered by the mother alone. Only two per cent led to a maternity within marriage. The remaining 42 per cent progressed to an abortion (Office of National Statistics 2002, p. 91).

The overall figure of 62 conceptions per 1,000 teenagers masks some regional variations. The London region had the highest rate at 77 per 1,000, and the southwest, including Somerset, Devon and Cornwall, the lowest at 51 per 1000. The variations recorded in the smaller Health Authorities are even greater. The two Health Authorities with the highest rates are both in London: the rate for Lambeth, Southwark and Lewisham was 114, and that for East London and the City 107 per 1,000. In contrast, the lowest rates are in Surrey at 37, and north and mid-Hampshire and Oxfordshire each at 40 (Office of National Statistics 2002, pp. 94–5).

As far as the under 16s are concerned, conception rates are much lower with just under one in 100 women aged 13–15 becoming pregnant in any one year. However, unlike the figures for all teenagers, they have shown a rise from 1970. In that year there were 7,700 conceptions, while in 1980 there were 8.600, and in both 1990 and 2000 there were 8,100. In terms of the rate per 1,000 in the age group, in 1970 there were 7.9 per thousand, which rose to 9.4 in 1985. However, in 2000 the confirmed figure is likely to be 8.1 per 1,000. In the year 2000 just over half (54 per cent) of the pregnancies amongst the under 16s ended in abortion (Office of National Statistics 2002, p. 91).

Figures for Scotland show that the conception rate per 1,000 for the 16–19s fell in 2000 to 69, from 72 in 1998. However, at this rate it was still above the rate for England and Wales. These conceptions led to maternity in 40 per cent of cases. The conception rate amongst the under-16s was the lowest for many years at 7.8 per 1,000 and below that of England and Wales. Just over half (53 per cent) of these conceptions led to an abortion (National Statistics Scotland 2002).

3.6   Good Abortion Practice

The Royal College of Obstetricians and Gynaecologists produced evidence-based guidelines in April 2000, with the aim of developing better standards of abortion to improve women's health. It took the view that unwanted pregnancies occur because women are unable to control their fertility with contraception alone. It stated that the complexities of managing sexual behaviour, together with contraceptive failure, meant that some unwanted pregnancies were inevitable. It then commented:

> The aim of these guidelines is to ensure that all women considering induced abortion have access to a service of uniformly high quality. It is hoped that they will be implemented across all relevant healthcare sectors, and promote a consistent standard, regardless of the sectors in which an individual woman is managed (RCOG 2000, p. 11).

3.6.1   Conscience Clause

The report drew attention to the conscientious objection clause which allows doctors (and nurses) to refuse to participate in terminations, and to the fact that the British Medical Association (BMA) had completed a comprehensive review of the relevant legal papers. Several points emerged:

- although doctors can refuse to help with terminations, if the woman's life is at risk then they have an obligation to help her;
- doctors who have a conscientious objection to abortion may not impose their views on others but may, if invited, explain their position;
- refusal to handle paperwork surrounding abortion lies outside the terms of the conscientious objection clause;
- the conscientious objection clause was only intended to apply to participation in treatment. However, hospital managers have been asked to use their discretion in applying the principle to ancillary staff who may be involved in handling fetal tissue;
- conscientious objection can be used by medical students to opt out of witnessing abortions;

• practitioners cannot claim exemption from giving advice or performing the preparatory steps to help in the arrangement of an abortion, where the request meets the legal requirements. Where appropriate, this may include referral to another doctor.

3.6.2   *Service Arrangements*

The RCOG recommended that, ideally, all women requesting an abortion should be offered an assessment appointment within five days of referral; however, the longest a woman should have to wait was two weeks. Ideally, all women should be able to undergo the abortion within seven days of the decision to proceed being made; however, as a minimum standard all women should be operated on within two weeks (RCOG 2000, p. 24). Another development was the increased use of day care, which the RCOG stated was cost-effective and also reduced the disruption to the lives of women and their families. One study of women undergoing mid-trimester abortions found that two-thirds were treated on a day care basis, while a study in Aberdeen showed that 96 per cent of women undergoing early medical abortion did so as day patients (RCOG 2000, p. 25).

The RCOG report stressed that women should be provided with good information. The professionals providing abortion services should possess accurate knowledge of the possible complications and sequalae of abortion. This would enable women to have the information they needed to be able to exercise informed consent. The information should also emphasize the duty of confidentiality by which all concerned with the benefits of health care are bound (2000, p. 26).

The report also pointed out that evidence from a number of surveys indicated that women value being offered a choice of methods appropriate to the gestation of their pregnancy (2000, p. 36). With regard to abortions under seven weeks, the evidence reveals that suction terminations performed at this time are three times more likely to fail to remove the gestation sac than those carried out between 7–12 weeks. It went on to say that if an abortion provider can only provide a suction termination, it would be better to defer it until the pregnancy exceeded seven weeks. One appropriate method earlier than seven weeks is to provide a medical abortion using mifepristone plus prostaglandin. The evidence, in fact, shows that, unlike the suction technique, this method is most effective at the earliest stages of pregnancy. A second technique for under seven weeks is early surgical abortion using a rigorous published protocol such as that developed at Planned Parenthood of Houston and southeast Texas. The schedule includes urinary pregnancy testing, ultrasound assessment and, later, tests to ensure that the abortion was successful. A survey showed that a complete abortion rate of over 99 per cent was obtained in 2,400 procedures performed at under six weeks gestation (RCOG 2000, p. 37). Both the major UK abortion charities have introduced early surgical abortion to their UK clinics. BPAS has introduced a protocol conforming to the one described using local anaesthesia, MSI has developed manual vacuum aspiration without anaesthesia, and both agencies report low failure rates and high patient acceptability.

The drugs used for an early medical abortion are also used for abortion later in pregnancy, from about 12 weeks. The abortion takes longer than a natural miscarriage and more than one dose of prostaglandin may be needed. This kind of abortion is like having a natural late miscarriage. After 15 weeks of pregnancy, an abortion may be carried out by surgical dilation and evacuation (BPAS 2002a, p. 3)

In the year 2000, more than four out of five (81 per cent) abortions were carried out by vacuum aspiration only, and a further one in 25 (4 per cent) were carried out by vacuum aspiration with D and E. Just one in nine (11 per cent) were carried out by antiprogesterone with or without prostaglandin. The other methods used were D and E 3.0 per cent, prostaglandins 0.4 per cent, prostaglandins with other agents 0.4 per cent, and other methods 0.2 per cent. (Office of National Statistics 2001, p. 68).

In addition, the RCOG report stressed the importance of after care. Women should be provided with a written statement of the symptoms they may experience, with a list of those which would make an urgent medical consultation necessary. They should be given a 24-hour emergency helpline telephone number, and urgent assessment and gynaecological admission must be available. A follow-up appointment should be offered within two weeks of the procedure and referral for further counselling should also be on hand for the minority who might need it. Future contraception should be discussed with the woman, and supplies offered. The chosen contraceptive method should be initiated immediately following the abortion, for ovulation occurs within a month of a first trimester abortion in over 90 per cent of women (RCOG 2000, p. 60). Evidence indicated that it was safe to introduce an interuterine contraceptive device immediately following an induced abortion, and there was no significant increase in post-abortion infection (RCOG 2000, p. 61).

3.7   A Woman's Right to Choose

This rallying call of the major feminist groups in both the UK and the USA is not always heard, for a variety of reasons. One of these is that the law in the UK does not give women this 'Right to Choose', and we will be discussing this in chapter five. However it does have some practical implications. In 1999 at the request of MSI, I helped to carry out a study of doctors' views, which was published in *Family Planning Perspectives*. The finding was that four out of five doctors considered themselves broadly pro-choice, and three-quarters felt that abortions should be provided free on the NHS. However, the study also found that there was a minority of doctors (18 per cent) who were basically opposed to abortion, and that just over a quarter of these (27 per cent) felt that it was not necessary to declare this to a women requesting an abortion (Francome and Freeman 2000). Sometimes, this could lead to problems. In 2002 one woman went to her doctor, and was told that she had grounds for an abortion. On a subsequent visit, she decided on a termination but was told her usual doctor was on holiday. She saw another member of the practice, who said that she did not have grounds, so she had to wait two weeks until the first one returned from holiday (private communication).

Another issue is whether men should have the right to a say in the abortion decision. The 1967 Abortion Act provided no rights in relation to men. There have been two high-profile cases on this issue. In 1978, in *Paton v. BPAS*, a woman consulted her doctor who certified that she needed an abortion on health grounds. She did not consult Paton, her estranged husband, a steelworker from Liverpool, who sought an injunction to prevent the abortion. The judge ruled that the injunction 'was completely misconceived and must be dismissed' (Lee 1998). In the second case, Richard Carver, an Oxford university student and a member of the Society for the Protection of Unborn Children (SPUC), tried to prevent his 21-year-old ex-girlfriend from having an abortion. This case was different from Paton in that the pregnancy had reached 21 weeks. The case made was that the abortion was unlawful under the 1929 Infant Life (Preservation) Act in that the fetus was 'capable of being born alive'. The lawyer Gerard Wright QC, a founding member of the Association of Lawyers for the Defence of the Unborn, argued that the fetus, if born, would be born alive, even though it would die shortly afterwards. However, the case was made that under the terms of the act it was 'capable of being born alive'. The case, known as *C v. S*, was one of the quickest in British legal history, going from the High Court to appeal in 36 hours. Although the case was dismissed, the controversy affected the woman, and she continued the pregnancy and gave the baby to its father to look after (Lee 1998, p. 223). Nolan reports that the great majority of abortions are carried out on the criterion that continuing the pregnancy would be detrimental to the health of the women. He suggested that, ipso facto, any attempt to incorporate the rights of men into the law would run counter to the authority of doctors, and would have far-reaching implications for the provision of all health care (Lee 1998, p. 223).

Nolan also reported that, in 1994, a 2,000 strong UK Men's Movement was formed to promote men's rights. One of their arguments was that a woman can decide to have a child against the wishes of a man, and then claim maintenance through the Child Support Agency. In their view, therefore, fairness dictates that men should have a say in encouraging a woman to continue the pregnancy, or not. This theme is also taken up in the literature of LIFE:

> Men are told it's none of their business to have a view about whether or not their child should be born. They are deliberately excluded from the decision about abortion. But when the baby is born, the law requires the mother to name the father as the person to be pursued for child maintenance (Forgotten Fathers n.d.).

The LIFE literature went on to suggest that this situation is the worst of all worlds for men, and results in there being more pressure on men to exert pressure on women to have an abortion. This factor is one that has not often been discussed in the available literature, and is an area which would clearly be difficult to research. However, three separate women have each approached me with their story. The first was a mother of two girls who had her abortion before the 1967 Act. She did not relate very well to her husband and they had separate bedrooms. She began an affair which led to pregnancy; her husband told her that she should seek an abortion and promised that, if she did so, he would return to her and give her another baby. She obtained a legal abortion after seeing a psychiatrist, and was very upset that her husband did not keep his side of the bargain and refused to make her pregnant again. When I spoke to her, she told me that she regretted the abortion and that she lost respect for her husband after his insistence. A second woman already had a small baby, when she became pregnant again. Her husband threatened to leave her if she did not have an abortion. Much against her own wishes, she acceded to his demand, but as soon as she could arrange her financial independence she left him and sought a divorce. She never did manage to have another child, however, which is a source of regret to her.

The third woman told her story for me:

We were together for three years and had a son. He was nearly three when we got married and my new husband adopted my other two children from my first marriage. I conceived my second daughter on honeymoon. When I was carrying her, I found out about one of his affairs. The baby was planned, and then three months after she was born I became pregnant again, which was really weird because I was still breast feeding. My husband went ballistic and said if I went ahead with the pregnancy he would end the marriage and leave as he did not want more children. In addition we were about to move. He said: 'You have a choice: either you get rid of it and we start a new life in Surrey, or you stay here on your own as a single mother with five children.' Because he was in BUPA he took me to a clinic which was full of foreigners. They did a sterilization at the same time, which I was hysterical about. I had a friend who a very similar thing happened to, but it is not the kind of thing you talk about with other people.

These examples question the role of men in abortion and the situation can clearly become complicated. In some cases men may agree with their partners' decision but in other circumstances there may be major disagreements.

3.8   Conclusion

The evidence outlined in this chapter shows that the British 1967 Act has had wide effects, not only for women in this country but also for women of many other countries. Although a few other countries such as Sweden had liberalized their laws ahead of Britain they were not so much at the forefront of international opinion. So in many respects the British Act could be seen as a watershed. I called my first book *Abortion Freedom* because it monitored the fact that in the period from the passing of the 1967 up until 1982, over 40 countries extended their abortion laws and only three narrowed them. The change meant that in that year over two-thirds of women then lived in countries where the laws permitted abortion on request or on extended grounds.

There are, however, acknowledged weaknesses in the British Act. The fact that women do not have the right to choose an abortion in the early part of pregnancy means the British law is behind that of other countries. Furthermore, the fact that in some areas there are a lack of facilities clearly leads to problems of access especially for a poorer women who could do without added stress at this critical stage in their lives. The fact that the law is a British and not a UK law means that the women in Northern Ireland have to travel for their operations and cannot benefit from NHS provision available to others.

Chapter 4

Legalization of Abortion in Britain

Legalization in the two countries followed totally different paths. In Britain the law was liberalized after a fierce political campaign, but women were not given the right to choose an abortion. In contrast, in the US legalization was the result of a legal pronouncement of the Supreme Court on the 22 January 1973. This led to its law being arguably the most liberal in the world. In British law, such issues as capital punishment, abortion, fox hunting with dogs and homosexual reform are considered issues of conscience and not issues which the government of the day will introduce into Parliament. Those MPs who are not part of the government are called Private Members and there is a ballot to see which of them can introduce a bill. The first six MPs in the ballot have the potential to see their Bill become law. However, the path is difficult and bills regularly run out of time. There are three readings in the House of Commons. The First Reading is a formality. If the Bill passes the Second Reading it goes into committee to be considered more fully and the composition of the committee is reflected in the vote. It then moves to the House of Lords where a further committee considers the Bill, after which it returns to the House of Commons for the Third Reading. At this point, the vote will be based on any amendments, and the Bill will then go to the House of Lords for consideration, possible amendment, and final vote. After all these stages the Bill receives the Royal Assent and becomes an Act. Parliament is itself considered to be a court, and the highest court in the land is the House of Lords.

The constitutional position in the US is different. There is a doctrine of the separation of powers between the Presidency, Congress – which consists of the House of Representatives and the Senate – and the Supreme Court. The nine members of the Supreme Court are appointed for life by the president, so they do not have to seek re-election or respond to public opinion.

4.1   Legalization of Abortion in Britain

Along the way towards legalization, four groups of factors have been particularly relevant: concern for women's health, the general climate of opinion, the relative strength of the pressure groups, and the composition of the House of Commons.

4.1.1   Concerns for Women's Health

A crucial factor was the drug Thalidomide which was first marketed for morning sickness in 1957 and was, by 1962, known to be responsible for the birth of deformed children. The drug was not cleared for use in the USA, so it is perhaps surprising that it was an American, Sherri Finkbine, who focused attention on the drug when she was refused termination in the US and had to fly to Sweden for an abortion (Guttmacher 1967). In July 1962, questions were raised in the British House of Commons and the House of Lords as to whether women who had taken Thalidomide could obtain a legal abortion. The minister replied that abortion was legal on the grounds of physical or mental health of the woman, but not on the grounds of possible deformity of the fetus (Hindell and Simms 1971, p. 110). The *Daily Telegraph* attacked Lady Summerskill for daring to ask the question, but the opinion polls at the time revealed that there was public support for abortion for fetal deformity (Hindell and Simms 1971, p. 110). Thalidomide was thus a reason for many people becoming concerned with the abortion law. Diane Munday, arguably the most effective activist to take up the cause of abortion reform, told me that this was the reason she began campaigning:

> I joined at the time of Thalidomide. I was offered it when I was carrying my third son. I was sleeping badly and I had two babies at the time to look after. I was nearly going mad and my doctor actually gave me a prescription for it. It sat on the mantle-piece of the living room downstairs. Sometimes I was very tempted to take it after a sleepless night and then I realised what could have happened (personal communication).

She learned that if she had taken the drug she could have been carrying a badly deformed fetus with no access to a legal abortion; so she decided to join ALRA to work for a change in the law. Others were similarly influenced, and Thalidomide was a key factor both in showing the inadequacies of the law and in galvanizing public opinion.

4.1.2   Climate of Opinion

In the later chapters on illegal abortion, the changes in attitudes towards sexual behaviour have been observed – in particular, the liberalization of attitudes after the First World War. However, after the Second World War such changes do not seem to have occurred, and with some exceptions the period of the late 1940s and 1950s was not one of tremendous upheaval in terms of sexual morality. The war produced deep-seated social changes in UK and US society, and did much to reduce social class differences (Titmuss 1963, pp. 75–87); the position of women in society also improved (Myrdal and Klein 1968). But in the case of sexual morality, it appears that the closing of the social distance between the classes meant that chastity which, as has been shown, is mainly associated with the middle class, became normative amongst the working classes, too (Pierce 1963). In the early 1950s, even some social commentators were likely to accept chastity as an ideal, and to assert that the problem of morality was being able to persuade young people to accept it. In fact Rowntree and Lavers (1951) put the causes of promiscuity down to the poor conditions of the working class and suggested that, if these were improved, a campaign in favour of chastity might lead to a great improvement in the nation's moral fibre. This argument would seem very old fashioned within 15 years, but it reflected the dominant middle-class view at the time. The problem was seen to be to persuade the working classes to accept the middle-class value of deferred gratification. There were obviously some opponents of this view amongst the radical members of the middle classes, but in the major countries of Europe chastity was accepted as the ideal pattern of behaviour. Even in Sweden, the sex education programme introduced in 1955 was designed to teach chastity. Attitudes in Britain, the United States and most of Western Europe changed in the 1960s, with the growth of what was popularly called the 'permissive ideology'. There were several factors behind this development. One was the decline in religion: attendance at the Church of England declined and, whereas at the turn of the century 70 per cent of people were married in an Anglican church, by 1962 the percentage was less than half (Martin 1967). There was also a change in doctrine and a movement within the Church against the idea that life should be governed by strict rules. Bishop John Robinson's book *Honest to God* (1963, p. 118) challenged many of the religious assumptions in place at that time, saying that it could not be argued that sex relations before marriage are wrong, for the only intrinsic evil is the lack of love. This decline in the practice of religion and the change in emphasis meant that the conservative influence of the Church of England declined a great deal during the 1960s.

Other religious groups also began to challenge contemporary standards. The report *Towards a Quaker View of Sex* (Heron 1963) stated unequivocally: 'We reject almost completely the traditional approach of the organized church to morality, with its supposition that it knows what is right and wrong.' The report went on to propose that the new morality should be based upon tolerance and understanding of the issues of homosexuality, and of premarital and extramarital sex. These challenges to the traditional position were opposed in September 1963 by the Archbishop of Canterbury and the Convocation at York, but their opposition just served to suggest that the Church was divided on the issue (Eppel and Eppel 1966).

The nature of the education system also changed. The expansion of higher education meant that many young people were ending their education in a more radical way. This, too, served to diminish the conservative influence of both the Church and the education system. One factor leading to the 'new morality' was thus the changed nature of the traditional conservative forces, but even more important was the growth in strength of new radical groups within the middle class. The mass media managed to break free from some of the constraints it had faced in earlier periods. In terms of literature, a key factor was undoubtedly the trial of Penguin Books for obscenity, for publishing D.H. Lawrence's *Lady Chatterley's Lover*; the trial ended with their acquittal, in 1960. This well-publicized case led to a re-evaluation of ideas about what it was permissible to publish, and a liberalization of standards in other media. In 1967, the musical *Hair* introduced nudity to the London stage, and this and other changes were largely the result of the middle-class media feeling free to challenge former restraints.

There was, too, a growth in the size and strength of radical middle-class youth. Young people in the 1960s had been brought up with little knowledge of the post-war privations. When people talked in the 1950s about the problems of youth and the generation gap, they were often referring to the fact that 'teddy' boys and girls were not following the middle-class patterns of deferred gratification. However, in the 1960s the 'generation gap' referred to the differences in values between the younger middle class and their parents' age group. A significant minority of these young people had the confidence to challenge many of the assumptions of the dominant ideology, and with the development of the 'pill' and the opening of birth control clinics for single people in 1964, they were able to engage in pre-marital intercourse with fewer worries. In a featured address on the BBC, George Carstairs welcomed the change (1962, p. 51):

> It seems to me that our young people are rapidly turning our own society into one in which sexual experience with precautions against conception is becoming accepted as a sensible preliminary to marriage, a preliminary which

> makes it more likely that marriage, when it comes, will be a mutually satisfying
> partnership (1962, p. 51).

This statement was given a great deal of publicity. When previous writers
had challenged the belief in chastity, their views had not gained widespread
acceptance, but by the 1960s, the climate of opinion had changed sufficiently
for it to be socially acceptable to challenge tradition.

4.1.3   Strength of the Pressure Groups

In the period up to the passage of the 1967 Act, ALRA dominated the campaign.
This was the only pressure group solely concerned with abortion, and in some
senses the 1967 Act shows what it is possible to achieve in the right social
conditions with good organizational skills, even without mass mobilization.
During the early 1960s younger members of the organization began to become
increasingly involved in it, and during the few months up to March 1964, the
leading positions on the ALRA executive committee changed hands. The chair
was taken by Vera Houghton, wife of a prominent Labour politician, who
had been actively involved with International Planned Parenthood (IPPF) for
many years; and Madeleine Simms and Diane Munday also joined (Hindell
and Simms 1971). The new composition of the committee led to a much more
energetic approach. These three women worked closely together, with Dilys
Cossey, also, who was an effective secretary to the organization. Madeleine
Simms was an active Fabian socialist and, in terms of her personal behaviour
and outlook, the most conservative of the women. She recalls how she was
taken aback when Diane Munday told her that she had had an abortion: 'No one
had ever told me that they had had an abortion because people in that period
did not generally talk about this experience. It was really taboo' (personal
communication, 2 February 2003). Madeleine drafted the newsletter and did
the major part of the writing for the Association. Diane Munday combined a
flair for public speaking with enormous tenacity, so she did the larger part of
the broadcasting. Vera Houghton helped mould the executive committee by
giving each member an area of responsibility. Hindell and Simms (p. 118) say
of her: 'Cool, detached, objective, and tolerant, within a short space of time
she had acquired an unquestioned authority over all the disparate elements
on the committee.'

   The committee also contained a number of men who made an important
contribution to its work – Alastair Service, for example, was the main political
lobbyist, while Malcolm Potts and Peter Diggory were medical advisers. This

involvement of men is an important part of ALRA's tradition. Madeleine Simms told me that one of the benefits they had at the time of liberalizing the Act, compared to the feminists who later became responsible for defending it, was that they were supported by their husbands. They were therefore relatively free to work for their cause. In later years, the increase in female employment meant that there were fewer supported women to take an active role, and full-time workers had to be paid.

The Opposition to abortion was at first sporadic and unorganized. It faced the problem that the law was on its side, which made it difficult to generate enthusiasm. Diane Munday set out their problem: 'If you are a fighter, you fight against something. There is no glory or satisfaction in fighting for something that exists' (personal interview, 22 June 1979). So the opponents of the Act had to attempt to overcome the feelings of apathy of their potential supporters, especially in the early part of the campaign. Norman St John Stevas (Lord Fawsley), Britain's leading Catholic layperson, noted the lack of opposition from Catholics at the time of the second reading of the Abortion Bill:

> Last Friday was a bad day for public morality in Britain … The response of Catholic MP's was all the more disappointing because of the very considerable effort made by the Catholic Union to rally opposition to the Bill. An excellent brief was provided, and meetings were held in the House to inform members on the issues involved (*Catholic Herald*, 29 July 1966).

Only 14 out of the 32 Catholic MPs turned up to vote at the Second Reading and it seems that the Catholic Church was caught off guard. Lord Craigmyle, leader of the Catholic Union, said that the vote 'was a shock to us' and talked of 'the appalling weight of the abortion lobby'.

The major organization opposing abortion was the Society for the Protection of Unborn Children (SPUC). It was formed after correspondence in the Church Times and for tactical reasons initially excluded Catholics from its executive. This changed when Phyllis Bowman, its mainstay, converted to Catholicism.

4.1.4 Composition of the House of Commons

There were several early attempts to introduce legislation. Joseph Reeves drew a place in the ballot in 1952, and decided to introduce a Bill. He was, however, not high enough in the order and had only a minute and a half in which to speak. Soon after this, Lord Amulree, a liberal peer, attempted to introduce a

Bill into the Lords but subsequently withdrew it. In 1961, the Second Reading of a liberalizing Bill in the Commons, introduced by Kenneth Robinson, was talked out without a vote. In 1965 Renee Short attempted to introduce a Bill under the ten-minute rule – a device for airing a subject with a view to future change. A Bill introduced by the Conservative MP, Simon Wingfield Digby, was talked out. Lord Silkin introduced two Bills into the House of Lords, one of which fell at the end of the session; but it was not until Liberal MP David Steel drew third place in the ballot that a change in the law looked likely.

There were several factors that had changed in terms of the parliamentary situation. First, after the 1966 election Labour had a large majority, and its MPs were more sympathetic to abortion reform than the Conservatives. Next, there were people in key positions who could be relied upon to help its passage. Roy Jenkins, the Home Secretary, was known to be a supporter of change, and the Minister of Health was Kenneth Robinson who, as has been shown, had previously introduced his own Bill. Douglas Houghton was in the Cabinet and ALRA had in him an impeccable contact in the government. There was also the advantage of a long parliamentary session due to the timing of the election; this would make it easier for the Bill to pass through all its stages. There was no attempt from the opposition to talk out the Bill and it passed its Second Reading on 22 July 1966 by 223 votes to 29. The vote showed clearly the left-wing nature of the support. Fifty-one Conservatives voted for the Bill, which was about a fifth of their total strength, whereas 161 Labour members were in support, which was more than two-fifths of their total. The Liberals supported the Bill by ten to one. Steel's Bill thus had the overwhelming support of the House, and the problem of its passage was largely a technical one, although there was also the danger that the medical profession might become alienated.

4.1.5   Reform or Repeal

The proponents of change had to make a crucial decision as to whether to aim for the total repeal of the abortion law up to a specified time in the pregnancy, or simply to reform the law by increasing the categories of women eligible for abortion. This question was brought to a head by the suggestion of Professor Glanville Williams, at the ALRA Annual General Meeting in October 1963, that abortion be legalized on request until the thirteenth week of pregnancy. This proposal was not as radical as some would have liked since they wished for it to be legalized until later in the pregnancy – but that would have been a very great change (Jenkins 1964). In support, Williams claimed that limited changes related to the 'hard cases' would leave untouched the mass of illegal abortions in the country, and he had some support for this assertion: Lord Gardiner agreed with him, as did Dorothea Kerslake, ALRA's most prominent female gynaecologist. The full executive had to decide whether or not to back this proposal. On 14 February 1964, Vera Houghton made a proposal as to the future aim of the organization, for consideration at the next meeting:

> The Association's aim is to secure such changes in the law as will provide that a registered medical practitioner may lawfully terminate or advise termination of pregnancy up to the 13th week, if he considers it to be in the best interests of the patient. Terminations after the 13th week would only be undertaken to preserve the life of the mother ... To the question: 'Does the Association advocate complete freedom for women to decide whether or not they will bear a child?', the answer is 'Yes', provided that there is a clear indication that this is what the public wants.

However, four days later the executive reversed the last sentence and its reply became 'No, it depends on the medical opinion of the doctor, not the personal opinion of the patient'. With this decision ALRA turned its back on a *woman's right to choose*, and it seems that it was a tea party at the House of Lords (12 February 1964) which caused ALRA to turn back from taking such a step. In a letter (23 March) Vera Houghton said of the event: 'It was pretty clear from the discussion which followed that the Association would not stand a chance of getting a bill introduced, in the present climate of opinion, along the lines recommended by Dr Williams.' Thus, the main aim became to introduce a 'reform' rather than a 'repeal' bill.

4.1.6   Tactics of the Pressure Groups

ALRA used various tactics to garner support for change, one being to gain as much institutional backing as possible. The Magistrates' Association had passed a resolution in favour of reform as early as 31 October 1955 (Hindell and Simms 1971, p. 83), and by 1963 an ALRA leaflet claimed backing from the National Council of Women, the Family Planning Association, the British Social Biology Council, the Eugenics Society and the Women's Cooperative Guild.

However, more were needed. In August 1964 a special leaflet was prepared by ALRA which asked voluntary organizations, particularly women's groups, to support change by passing a resolution at their annual conference, circulating leaflets and helping financially. During the next three years support was gained from many organizations, whose resolutions fell into two main categories. A few were calls for the repeal of the law up to a certain stage in the pregnancy – for example, in 1964, the University Humanist Group Federation Annual Conference supported a resolution which called for it to be lawful to perform an abortion 'on any grounds, provided that the termination of pregnancy is performed before thirteen weeks of pregnancy are completed'. The following year, the Socialist Medical Association passed a similar motion. These two organizations specified that the abortion should be carried out early, but this was not the case with the resolution of the Progressive League at its AGM in 1964. This simply called for a change so that it should be lawful for a doctor to terminate a pregnancy 'if the expectant mother so requests'.

These kinds of resolution, however, were in the minority, and far more common were the ones calling for limited extension. Typical of these was that of the National Union of Townswomen's Guilds which, in 1965, urged Her Majesty's Government to introduce legislation to legalize abortion, when personally desired by the woman concerned and when advised by a medical panel and performed by a suitably qualified member of the medical profession in the following circumstances:

- where it is necessary to preserve her physical or mental health;
- where there is serious risk of a defective child being born;
- where the pregnancy results from a sexual offence such as rape or incest.

These conditions were the same as those contained in ALRA's aims. In the period 1965–67, 17 other organizations passed resolutions similar to this, including the Conservative Political Centre, the Methodist Conference, the Law Society, the British Council of Churches and the United Free Church of Scotland General Assembly (Francome 1984, p. 87).

A second task of the organization was to build its individual membership. In the early 1960s it had had fewer than 200 members, but with the impetus of the new leadership and a more active approach it grew steadily, and by 1966 had passed the 1,000 mark. The membership was of course atypical in comparison with the general population. Nearly two-thirds were women, two-thirds had a higher education and one-fifth had medical qualifications. A third of the women had undergone an abortion at some time, and politically there was a higher than average number who were left wing. Overall 51 per cent were Labour supporters, 21 per cent Conservatives and 13 per cent Liberal. A fifth were members of the Fabian Society (Hindell and Simms

1971, p. 120). But although the membership was to the left, there was also important support from the right wing. For example, David Steel's medical adviser, Peter Diggory, was a member of the Conservative party. This kind of all party support was valued by the ALRA executive as giving a broader base upon which to campaign.

Although there was not mass membership, ALRA tried to show the support of the public through opinion polls. One, in 1962, found that 72 per cent of the poll agreed with abortion for fetal deformity. Three years later, NOP found that 70 per cent agreed with abortions if the woman's health would be seriously affected, and only 24 per cent said it should be illegal in all cases. In the following year, three-quarters felt that abortion should be easier to obtain. ALRA also tried to show support from the clergy and the medical profession. In 1966 the South East London ALRA group distributed a questionnaire to non-Catholic clergy. The 450 replies showed that a huge majority favoured a change. Only 6 per cent said they were satisfied with the law, while 89 per cent said they were not happy with it. A medical survey carried out by NOP in 1967 wrote out the first and major clause of the Bill, and asked doctors if they agreed with it. A total of 1,180 interviews were reported, and the results showed that 65 per cent thought the new grounds were satisfactory or too restricted, 21 per cent felt the proposals were too liberal and 10 per cent disagreed with all abortions. 4 per cent were undecided. With these results, therefore, ALRA was able to claim widespread support for change.

ALRA used a variety of techniques to keep abortion in the news. Sometimes it would simply exploit an event, as with Thalidomide, but on other occasions it actually set out to make newsworthy discoveries. A good example of this was a study of the abortifacient drugs racket in 1965, under the direction of Dr Martin Cole. Three investigators, two women and a man, visited forty shops in London and Birmingham asking for products to bring on a delayed period, and a twelve-page report was produced. This said: 'The impression was gained that this sort of request was so common as to occasion no distinctive reaction' and that, while the preparations were never labelled 'abortifacients', they made claims such as 'bring swift and blessed relief'. The findings showed that the use of abortifacient pills was still being tried by women unable to obtain a legal abortion (Hindell and Simms 1971, p. 34). ALRA was able to make political capital out of this fact, and Madeleine Simms wrote in her press release:

> Our present antique abortion laws have the effect of encouraging women to resort to drugs when they wish to end unwanted pregnancies, instead of consulting their doctors to discuss the problem. It is suspected that these drugs

rarely produce the desired results but may sometimes poison the mother or damage the foetus if taken in large doses (undated).

ALRA could therefore argue that a change in the law would lead to a great improvement in the health of women who would no longer need to resort to such remedies.

Those in favour of a new abortion law stressed the fact that they were not particularly radical on other issues. When speaking, they dressed conservatively in order not to alienate the support of the majority. The personal problems associated with the lack of availability of abortions were particularly emotive, and an effective leaflet entitled *In Desperation* contained 'a small selection from many such letters received by the Abortion Law Reform Association each week'. One of these read:

> I went to the hospital to terminate my pregnancy. I was only a few weeks and I had to wait to see one doctor and then another and so on till I got into such a state I thought it would be done, but they said 'No'. I begged them, as this was my tenth child. My husband has a bad heart and is off work a lot. My children's ages run from 16 years to my youngest who is 13 months and it's just too much for me. I go mad with worry, also I get so upset I sit and cry for hours. If I could have had £15 I could have got it done from a woman, but who would have that amount of money with all my children? I can tell you sometimes I wish I had the nerve to end it all. That is how I get, so I think if a woman wants it done she is entitled to it.

Using cases such as this, ALRA was able to show the suffering of women faced with poor social conditions or the illegal abortionist. Overall, ALRA was thus a highly effective pressure group.

At first the Catholic Church was not ready for this particular battle, and the fact that it was opposed to artificial birth control diminished its credibility. It was easy to understand Lord Craigmyle's complaint: 'If a Catholic makes a speech on abortion, his views are dismissed, he is not heard with respect … we are, as it were, being persecuted, for Christ's sake' (*New Society*, 9 March 1967). Prominent Church of England clergymen were willing to attack the stance of the Catholic Church. For example, an article in the *Evening News* (15 November 1966) by Nicholas Stacey, the Rector of Woolwich, entitled 'Why Rome is Wrong', blamed the Catholic Church for being responsible for a large number of illegal abortions because of its attitude to birth control. This kind of attack raised questions about the Catholic Church's position, and its leadership was not particularly astute in putting forward its views.

One particularly clumsy attempt was made at the Annual Conference of the Institute of Directors on 10 November 1966, when Cardinal Heenan attacked the Abortion Bill and then astonished his audience by saying: 'You directors, if you stand men off, may be responsible for the death of countless unborn children' (*New Society*, 9 March 1967). The supporters of the Bill were quick to point out that unemployment was not a criterion for abortion and the attack was counterproductive. The feelings against Catholic intervention therefore grew, and possibly led to the SPUC decision to exclude Catholics from its committee. However, although the Catholic hierarchy was not involved in the organization of the major pressure group, it was Catholics who became one of the main sources of opposition. By December 1966, Peter McDonald, a wealthy Manchester lawyer, had distributed over 300,000 copies of a pamphlet entitled *To Be or Not to Be* – possibly the first of the emotional leaflets from the anti-abortionists. It drew comparisons with Dachau and Belsen, saying 'If the Abortion Bill goes through, Herod will laugh in Hell. There will be perpetuated in our name a massacre of the Innocents more dreadful than any Herod could have imagined'. It also opposed abortion for rape, thereby implying a need to tighten the British law. Eventually there was a growth in the Catholic grassroots movement. One group based in Manchester duplicated 1,500 copies of a petition against the Bill. The Union of Catholic Mothers urged its 30,000 members to write to their MPs opposing change, and several leagues representing 6,000 Catholic doctors announced that their members would perform no abortions. But though pressure was being brought to bear against the Bill, it was already too late. Perhaps the biggest coup of SPUC was gaining the support of Aleck Bourne, the doctor who was responsible for the legalization of abortion for rape. The credit for his involvement is taken by Phyllis Bowman, its press secretary at the time. In a speech, she heard Bourne say that if he could have saved both the raped girl from suffering and also the fetus he would have done so. He was against any extension of the grounds feeling that his case had made the law sufficiently liberal, and so became a willing supporter who was able to provide a great deal of credibility to the SPUC campaign. His presence also prevented SPUC from making the absolutist position the official policy of the organization. SPUC used the usual techniques to attempt to sway Parliament. A petition calling upon the government to set up a Royal Commission to consider all the relevant facts was distributed in April 1967 to all the 10,000 Anglican vicars, who were asked to collect signatures. However, it seems that most were not sympathetic, one pointing out in a circular letter that the petition was launched by two Roman Catholic MPs, Norman St John Stevas and James Dunn. Furthermore, the

British Council of Churches met and concluded that Christian compassion in the face of human suffering did require a measure of reform (Hindell and Simms 1971, p. 100). The aim of a million signatures on the petition was not reached but, on 1 July, 530,000 names were taken to 10 Downing Street, in the company of sympathetic MPs, and various medical personnel including six uniformed nurses.

As well as organizing various activities such as lobbies and letter writing campaigns, SPUC commissioned a Gallup Poll. The questions were directly related to the Bill and phrased in such a way as to show support for the SPUC campaign. One seemed to show public support for a Royal Commission which would have postponed a change in the law indefinitely. In fact SPUC became quite skilled in a short time.

Those who disagree with an issue on ethical or moral grounds need to formulate their argument in a way that is acceptable to the rest of the population. A major argument of the advocates of reform was that there were many illegal abortions each year, often performed in dangerous circumstances and with great risk to the woman. The main effect of legalization would be to transfer these from the illegal to the legal sector. Furthermore, the reformers stated that rich women have always been able to gain access to doctors willing to perform abortions for the right fee, so reform would give poor women what rich women had always been able to afford. This was a powerful argument for legalization, for it suggested that there would be little change in the overall number of abortions. The opponents of the Bill had, therefore, to try to promote an alternative scenario. They argued that the number of illegal abortions was relatively low and that the advocates of reform were inflating the number for political reasons. Furthermore, they suggested that a change in the law would not lead to a reduction in illegal abortions but would just make people more 'abortion minded', and both legal and illegal abortions would increase. They also argued that it would fundamentally alter the moral values of society and lead to a lack of respect for life in general.

In the light of these comments it is interesting to contrast the statements of two Conservative MPs in the Committee on David Steel's Bill (Hansard, 8 and 22 March 1967):

Pro-Choice Sir George Sinclair (Dorking):

The object of this Bill, as I see it, is not to encourage abortion on demand, but to help women in cases which it defines, as clearly as is practicable, to obtain abortions legally and not to be driven, as many of them are today, to seek illegal operations. As it now stands, the Bill seeks to transfer as many of these defined cases as possible from the illegal to the legal list. If it is successful it will considerably increase the number of legal operations and reduce the number of illegal ones.

Anti-choice Norman St John Stevas (Chelmsford):

It is essential, therefore, that we should have the maximum amount of information available so that action will be taken if necessary. My belief is that action will be necessary, because not only will it be found that the illegal rate of abortions will rise but that the legal rate will bound up as well, and there will be a general increase in demand for abortion throughout the country.

This argument that the number of illegal abortions would increase was used by virtually all those opposed to liberalization. The findings of the academics also reflected their side of the debate. Glass's suggestion (1940) that there were 100,000 illegal abortions a year was given widespread publicity. However, SPUC academics were putting forward a much lower figure. For example, C.B. Goodhart (1973) claimed that 100,000 was much too high and that 'the true figure could not have exceeded 20,000, and was probably nearer 15,000 criminal abortions a year in Britain before 1967'. He also raised the spectre of the abortion rate continuing to rise to enormous levels rather than tapering off as the abortions in the illegal sector were transferred. Thus, even at the academic level there was serious dispute. It is interesting to note that, in a report, the Royal College of Gynaecologists suggested a figure of 14,600 criminal abortions each year rather than 100,000, and repeated the assertion that liberalization might not eliminate illegal abortion but rather make the population 'abortion minded' as it claimed had happened in Japan, Hungary and Czechoslovakia (*BMJ*, 2 April 1966). The anti-abortionists also emphasized the dangers of abortion, saying, in particular, that it was more dangerous than childbirth. SPUC claimed this in its literature calling for signatures for a Royal Commission, and we shall see that this claim was an important factor in the final shaping of the law.

Some support for the SPUC campaign came from two of the major medical bodies. A short time before the Second Reading, the Royal College of Gynaecologists produced a report which suggested that major change was not necessary since no gynaecologist would hesitate to induce an abortion under the existing law whenever 'the continuation of the pregnancy would be detrimental to the physical or mental welfare of the woman'. It set out its misgivings as to the dangers of the operation and stated categorically: 'the

majority of gynaecologists in this country can see no urgent need for reform
of the law governing abortion' (Hindell and Simms 1971 p. 168). However,
since it recognized that some change was inevitable, it took the view that the
grounds should be strictly limited and that abortions should be authorized by a
consultant gynaecologist. The *BMJ* published in July 1966 was also opposed to
much change but disagreed with the restriction of authorization to a consultant
gynaecologist. A survey of doctors conducted in 1967–68 found that only 22
per cent thought that a woman with several children should be able to have
an abortion on demand (Cartwright, 1970).

4.1.7   Action in Parliament

In November 1966, after pressure from the British Medical Association, the
Royal College of Gynaecologists and the Church of England, David Steel
issued a statement that he intended to withdraw the social clause which had
provided for abortion where the woman's capacity as a mother might be
overstrained. This action was regarded as a betrayal by ALRA who had to
face the fact that they did not have control over the Bill. This point was made
to me by Vera Houghton: 'There comes a time when your Bill becomes their
Bill. Members of Parliament are not the puppets of the pressure groups.' It was
not until 18 January 1967 that the Bill went into Committee, where 22 people
voted for it, three opposed it and five abstained. The opponents did what they
could to slow its progress by introducing as many amendments as possible,
and the Bill's supporters did their best to oil its passage. The unofficial whip
of the supporters was Peter Jackson and he told me (private communication,
1977) that, for the most part, the policy of those on his side was to keep quiet.
The Catholic and other opponents of the Bill kept the Committee Stage going
for 12 sessions in the hope of killing it; bills usually only have two or three
sessions. After the Committee Stage, the Bill returned to the House for the
Report Stage, where attempts were again made to prevent its progress. But
after an all-night sitting, the Bill passed its Third Reading on 13 July 1967 by
167 votes to 83. This was a much smaller victory than the Second Reading,
but reflected the fact that some, like Leo Abse, had voted for the Bill at an
earlier stage even though they were basically anti-abortion.

 The Bill then moved to the Lords. Lord Silkin, who seemed the obvious
person to pilot it through because of his previous interest in the subject, was
at first doubtful, feeling that the Bill was too weak now the social clause had
been 'given away by the sponsor to pacify the opposition'. He felt it might be
better to introduce a stronger Bill at a later time, but eventually changed his

mind. In the Lords some amendments were introduced. A clause specifying that only consultants should carry out abortions was introduced at one stage, but then voted out again; and various other changes were suggested. But by far the most important alteration came at the end of the debate. One of the problems was to define the degree of risk to the pregnant woman necessary for a legal abortion. Lord Parker, the Lord Chief Justice, who was generally opposed to the Bill, noted that all the suggestions such as 'grave risk' or 'serious risk' would cause problems of definition in the courts. He therefore proposed a much simpler criterion: that abortion should be legal if the risk to life or the risk of injury to health was greater by continuing the pregnancy than by terminating it. This amendment seems to have been accepted with little thought – even the Home Office said that it was not a profound change. However, Norman St John Stevas pointed out that if abortion were really as safe as Renee Short and the other reformers claimed, then abortion would always be legal. The anti-abortionists were in a difficult position on this matter for, as we have seen, they had been claiming that abortion was more dangerous than childbirth. Now they were caught out by their own arguments and the amendment was included as the Act received the Royal Assent on 27 October 1967.

Chapter 5

Legalization of Abortion in the USA

The abortion laws in the USA were overthrown in a campaign that lasted only 12 years. During this relatively short time the laws of all states changed from being restrictive to being amongst the most liberal in the world. This change was much more marked than the more gradual liberalization in Britain, and was due to a combination of social, medical, political and legal factors.

The discussion on the background to the British 1967 Act has shown that one of the important influences was the liberalization of sexual attitudes. This occurred also in the USA, and for largely the same reasons. There was a similar growth in the power of the radical middle classes with the expansion of education and decline in the conservative forces. The number of young people had increased as it had in Britain. In fact Coleman (1966) pointed out that the baby boom beginning in 1946 caused a 50 per cent increase in the age group 14–24 by the end of the decade 1960–70. With an increasing proportion of students in higher education, as in Britain, the increase in this highly visible group was much greater (Francome 1976a).

There was also growth in the availability of contraception. The Supreme Court decision of 1965 overthrew restrictions on married people using birth control on the grounds of the right to privacy, and other decisions in the courts were important in a move towards liberalization. The legalization of *Lady Chatterley's Lover* was discussed earlier, and these kinds of changes paralleled those in Britain. However, there were also some social differences, of which three are particularly important. First of all, due to the greater heterogeneity of the society and the greater number of religious conservatives, the acceptance of 'permissiveness' was much less universal than in Britain. Secondly, the sexual divisions in the USA were stronger. Betty Friedan (1963) put this kind of difference down to what she called *The Feminine Mystique*, the belief that women should have a totally different role in society from that of men. This concept seems to have been much more prevalent in the USA, and to have frustrated women's attempts to gain equality. In terms of sexual behaviour, the double standard is stronger in the USA, and although liberalization of attitudes occurred, it was more because sexuality began at an earlier period of the relationship rather than that the sexist nature of the relationship ended (Francome 1980a).

Thirdly, the change in attitude towards radicalism was much stronger in the USA. Radicalism amongst students developed from issues which deeply affected their lifestyle. The civil rights movement grew from activists involved in the summer project of 1962, and concerned itself with manifest and institutionalized racism at home. The war in Vietnam was not just an ideological issue but affected those who were threatened with the draft. The direct relevance of these issues led to a much more fundamental re-evaluation of the basic values of society than occurred in Britain (Francome 1976a).

These important differences in radicalism between the two societies, with other factors, led to the US abortion campaign ending in a very different way from that of the British liberalization. In the USA, in fact, there was not really one campaign but two separate ones – first a campaign for liberalization, and then a demand for repeal.

5.1   Revival of the Reform Movement

In the USA during the 1930s, the demand for legal abortion had faded away; and after the Second World War, there was at first no pressure to get it restarted. Planned Parenthood (1945) took the view that it should push for contraception as an alternative. A pamphlet entitled 'Planned Parenthood's Campaign for 1945' argued that one reason for birth control was the high number of abortions which were 'the second largest cause of maternal mortality, and for every woman who dies, three are made sterile or invalid'.

This argument that abortion was dangerous and that the numbers could be reduced by contraception meant that Planned Parenthood continued to take an anti-abortion stance until the 1960s. In fact, as late as 1963, a pamphlet stated: 'Abortion requires an operation. It kills the life of the baby that has begun, it is dangerous to your life and health' (Planned Parenthood 1963). Notwithstanding this comment, Planned Parenthood was the source of the first major event to consider abortion in 1957. The participants proposed the establishment of consultation centres for women seeking termination along the lines of those in Scandinavia (Lader 1967, p. 2). It also called for a study of the various abortion laws to be carried out by authoritative bodies such as the Council of State Governments and the American Law Institute (ALI), in order to frame a model law that could be presented to the states to replace existing statutes. ALI responded to the call in December 1959 when its model Bill was revealed (Lader 1967, p. 145). It recommended that a doctor be permitted to terminate a pregnancy:

- if continuation of pregnancy 'would gravely impair the physical or mental health of the mother';
- if the doctor believes 'that the child would be born with grave physical or mental defects'; or
- if the pregnancy resulted from rape or incest.

This proposed Bill was revealed to the public in 1962 as part of the Model Legal Code approved by ALI. Its presentation aroused a great deal of interest and Alan Guttmacher, President of Planned Parenthood, commented: 'Its mere promulgation opened the medical profession's eyes to the preservation of health as being a justification for abortion' (Walbert and Butler 1973, p. 68). In the following year, the American Medical Association (AMA) 'took note' of the ALI Bill. However, until 1967 there was little interest from the states. From 1962 to 1966 only five legislatures considered an ALI-type Bill, and in no case was the law changed. The biggest pressure during this period was in California. An attempt at reform failed in 1961. Two years later Assemblyman Alan Beilenson believed he had a better opportunity for success. He had a clear majority in committee for a 'do pass' recommendation (Lader 1967, p. 146). However, pressure against the bill grew, and in this, as in subsequent years until 1967, it was unsuccessful. Furthermore, there was organized opposition to the Beilenson Bill within the pro-choice movement. The first organization to concentrate solely on abortion was set up in California by Patricia Maginnis and was called the Society for Humane Abortion (Lader 1967). Maginnis called for outright repeal of the law; she felt that the Beilenson Bill was inadequate since it would not cover all women in need. The second abortion organization to be set up was the Association for the Study of Abortion, founded in 1964. One of its aims was to educate the public by providing speakers for civic gatherings, radio and television shows (Lader 1967, p. 148). However, it would not carry out any political activities because its tax exempt status limited its sphere of influence. Thus in the mid-1960s there was no national organization pressing for abortion reform, and the early changes in the law in 1967 were the result of local activity.

5.2   Reform v. Repeal

In 1967 the situation in the USA seemed to be moving in the same direction as in Britain, with a limited liberation of the laws and an extension of rights only to some categories of women. One of the most important campaigners during this period was Alan Guttmacher, and he consistently argued the case for reform rather than repeal. In 1959 he said, 'I do not want blanket permission to abort any women who is unhappily pregnant; I do not think our civilization is ready for this or that it ever should be' (p. 237).

Eight years later, he reiterated his view that the path of reform was preferable. He pointed to the ALI Bill and the British law and commented:

> I believe with stubborn conviction that our archaic abortion laws should be overhauled. They should be made more lenient so as at least to grant legal sanctions for all women to be legally aborted for those indications which many doctors now recognize for their individual private patients. In addition certain social, humanitarian indications should be added which even today's more liberal doctors deem untouchable. What would such a revision accomplish? It would not eradicate the legal, social and medical blight of illegal abortion. This can only be done by legalising abortion on demand, as has been done in Japan and Eastern Europe. I am opposed to this for the US in 1967. I believe that social progress is better made by evolution than revolution. Today, complete abortion license would do great violence to the beliefs and sentiments of most Americans. Therefore I doubt that the US is as yet ready to legalise abortion on demand, and I am therefore reluctant to advocate it in the face of all the bitter dissension such a proposal would create (Guttmacher 1967, p. 12).

So Guttmacher at this stage still placed himself fully within the reformist camp, and it seems that the medical groups were of the same opinion. At its meeting in Atlantic City in June 1967, the AMA House of Delegates considered a policy recommendation on abortion. It suggested that the AMA should adopt a policy which was a modification of the Model Penal Code of the American Law Institute. This proposed that abortion should be allowed for threats to the life or health of the woman, where the infant might be born with incapacitating physical or mental deformity, and where there was evidence of rape or incest. The policy also recommended that three doctors should examine the patient. and that the operation should be performed in a hospital. The statement, with minor changes, was accepted as AMA policy. So there were reform Bills with institutional support, and a number of states passed them. Colorado was the first in 1967, California and North Carolina followed shortly afterwards. In 1968,

Georgia and Maryland liberalized their laws, followed in 1969 by Arkansas, Kansas, Delaware, Oregon and New Mexico. It seemed at first that New York was also going to have a reform Bill. In 1968 Governor Rockefeller set up an 11-member commission to examine the law and to make recommendations for change. The Commission proposed a Bill on the ALI model, with an additional clause allowing abortion on request for any mother of four children. The Bill was, however, rejected by the New York State legislature in 1969, and it must have seemed to many at that time that a repeal Bill would have no chance of success. Yet in July 1970 the New York legislature passed a law giving abortion on request in the first 24 weeks of pregnancy – an unlikely sequence of events in the context of theories of gradualism in the process of social change. However, the overall victory of the repeal forces was due to a number of factors specific to the situation in the USA (Lader 1973). First of all, there was the lack of a recognized national reform organization that had the allegiance of most of the activists. The Association for the Study of Abortion, the nearest group to this, was not political; so when the National Association for the Repeal of Abortion Laws was formed, it did not compete with anyone. Lader (1973, p. 88) tells how he, Lonny Myers and Ruth Smith met in his apartment in late 1968 to discuss a national conference on abortion laws at which the aim would be to set up an organization for repeal. That this was a possibility reflected the fact that there was a substantial body of support amongst the radical groups. The involvement of the feminists around the right to choose was one important factor and, furthermore, they were supported by those who had been organizing the referral services. Parts of the New York clergy had set up a consultation service and they noted that the reforms being proposed would leave many women without access to legal operations:

> Our day-to-day work taught us how few women wanted abortions for the reasons most liberals conceded were justifiable. When we started, most of us favoured some liberalisation of the law, but within a six month period every member of the clergy believed passionately not in liberalisation but in repeal of the law (Carmen and Moody 1973, p. 102).

Other radicals argued a similar case, and by the time of the NARAL conference in February 1969 there was a solid base in the formation of New Yorkers for Abortion Law Repeal. There was also a change of mind amongst some of the older advocates of reform. Alan Guttmacher described his conversion:

The more I studied early results from the five states which had been the first to liberalize their laws, the more I began to espouse the opinion that abortion statutes should be entirely removed from the criminal code. The number of legal abortions being undertaken under the new liberalized laws, when contrasted with the figures for the previously undertaken illegal abortions, were far too low (Walbert and Butler 1973, p. 60).

Guttmacher went on to discuss the fact that in 1968 California had only 5,000 abortions under its new law, and told of a visit to Colorado where there were many bureaucratic obstacles. He concluded:

Abortion on request – necessitating the removal of 'abortion' from the penal codes – was the only way to democratic legal abortion and to sufficiently increase the numbers performed so as to decrease the incidence of illegal abortions. I came to this conclusion in 1969, forty-seven years after abortion first came to my medical attention when I was a third year medical student (Walbert and Butler 1973, p. 60).

Thus with the additional support of the older generation of radicals, repeal won out over the reform position. However, the question remains as to what were the social and political conditions that allowed it to succeed.

5.3   Role of the Constitution

If the legislators in the USA pass a law, it can be challenged on the grounds that it infringes guaranteed rights. The courts have a great amount of formal power and can decide that a law is completely invalid. In Britain, courts do have some power of interpretation, as witnessed in the Bourne judgement, but the courts' role is within narrow limits. They are not allowed to declare a law passed by parliament unconstitutional. In contrast, it is possible within the US system to try to have a law totally annulled by a declaration of unconstitutionality. This is illustrated by two important court decisions in 1969 which changed the nature of the abortion debate.

On 5 September 1969, the California Supreme Court declared the state law unconstitutional after the trial of Dr Leon Belous. In its decision, the Court defined the rights of a woman over her own procreation for the first time. The ruling was also the first State Supreme Court decision in US history to declare an abortion statute unconstitutional (Lader 1973, p. 110), and it set a precedent for other pending cases. Belous had been tried under the pre-1967 law, not the one that was in operation by the time the case came to court. However, a similar decision was taken two months later in the trial of Dr Milan Vuitch who had been accused of breaking the abortion law of Washington DC. On 10 November 1969, the law was declared unconstitutional, and Washington became the first area of the country where abortion was completely legalized (Francome 1980b, p. 615). According to the decision, there was no necessity for hospital treatment and any licensed physician could perform an abortion if his equipment met the required standards. Thus, it was in the courts that the advocates of repeal had their first success.

5.4   The Medical Profession

A second factor, and one that was again different from Britain, was the attitude of the medical profession. In the USA it seems that there was much greater support for change. A survey by the journal *Modern Medicine* in 1969 showed that 51 per cent of US physicians wanted abortion to be available to any woman upon her request to a competent physician (Lader 1973). This reflects both a more liberal view and the different roles played by doctors in the two societies. In Britain there is quite strict control of medical practice, especially in hospitals where a consultant is in charge of the medical care and other doctors are regarded as being in training. In the USA, professional independence is much more guarded and individual doctors act more freely. They are allowed to enter hospitals and carry out operations based on their professional judgement, and the general practitioner has much greater freedom than a British doctor (Bunker 1970). Thus the belief in non-intervention of the law could in part be due to a general belief in the right to freedom from interference. Furthermore, doctors in the USA stood to gain financially by legalization, whereas the British surgeons were concerned that a large increase in the number of abortion patients would draw resources from other services.

5.5   The Women's Movement

A third difference between the societies was the role of the women's movement, which was much more active in the USA. Paradoxically it was a man, Lawrence Lader, who was the catalyst in this direction. He told me (personal interview, 1978) that he first came to the conclusion that abortion should be a woman's right after discussions with Margaret Sanger; and in his book *Abortion* (1966) he called the complete legalization of abortion 'the one just and inevitable answer to the quest for feminine freedom' (p. 169). Lader had known Betty Friedan for a number of years, and when she became the first president of the National Organization for Women (NOW) he persuaded her that abortion should be one of its main aims. This became NOW policy at its convention in 1967, and from that time on the abortion movement in the USA had the backing of a strong and articulate women's movement.

It is possible that if the British movement had adopted a more militant position it might have received more support from women. Lucinda Cisler, talking of the USA commented:

> Part of the reason that the reform movement was very small was that it appealed mostly to altruism and very little to people's self interest: the circumstances covered by 'reform' are tragic but they affect very few women's lives, whereas repeal is compelling because most women know the fear of unwanted pregnancy and in fact get abortions for that reason (Cisler 1970).

This statement was echoed by Assemblywoman Constance Cook, the sponsor of the New York repeal Bill: 'I knew that women did not want reform, at least not enough to go out and work for it, whereas I suspected they would work for repeal, and they did' (Lader 1973, p. 125). In Britain, the women's movement did not become involved with the abortion campaign until after the Act had been passed.

5.6 Confrontation Tactics

A fourth difference between the two societies was the much greater appeal of confrontation tactics in the USA. I have already shown how the movement towards radicalism was more relevant to the immediate position of those involved. They were also much more likely to engage in direct action, as could be seen from the invasion of the segregated Woolworth's shop in 1960. Black students waited in vain for a white waitress to serve them, and later returned with many of their colleagues (Lauter and Howe 1970, p. 27). This kind of approach to political activism had direct relevance to the abortion campaign. Members of the movement not only worked for changes in the law but also set out to provide abortions. One of the earliest exponents of this tactic was Pat Maginnis, and in 1966 the *New York Times* (4 December) carried the headline 'Abortion Classes Offered on Coast'. The article reported that Maginnis was touring California, giving advice on abortion methods and information on countries where they could be obtained. At the time Maginnis was 38 years old and had had three pregnancies and three abortions, two of these self-induced. Her organization, the Society for Humane Abortion, had a mailing list of 2,000 and her lectures on abortion techniques were usually attended by 30–60 people. She was arrested in the summer of 1966 by the San Francisco police, and charged with violating the city's anti-abortion ordinance by distributing handbills calling for a change in the law; but the court dismissed the charges as a violation of her rights of free speech. It seems clear that her lectures were in breach of the wording of the Californian law, but the police refused to prosecute her a second time. A spokesperson for the San Francisco Police Department said: 'All we'd do is give her publicity. We believe the courts would turn her loose' (*New York Times*, 4 December 1966). The District Attorney made a similar point, and said he believed she had a constitutional right to state her position. So Maginnis continued her lectures, and her actions suggested that the laws were unenforceable. On the East Coast there were similar challenges to the legal system, one of the most important being the formation of the Clergy Consultation Service. Lader proposed that the clergy should take action, and the fact that 21 Protestant and Jewish clergymen were going to refer women for abortion was revealed in a front-page article in the *New York Times* on the 27 May 1967. Women who rang up were counselled and referred to sympathetic doctors. The leader of the movement was the Reverend Howard Moody of New York's Judson Memorial Church, and a women's committee, headed by Arlene Carmen, set out to evaluate potential doctors' medical training, professional experience, and the quality of their offices.

The clergy kept accurate records and so were able to provide the women with increased protection. Their actions were illegal within the letter of the law, but they decided to be open about their referral system in the belief that it would be better to let everyone know what they were doing:

> At all times we were to behave as though we were acting within the laws of New York State and that, as clergy, we were bound to follow a higher moral law (Carmen and Moody 1973, p. 25).

The fact that the clergy was able to set up such a service is very surprising, and it is difficult to imagine a British group performing such a role. In part, it reflects the fact that they had much greater freedom of action than their British counterparts. However, it seems that another crucial factor was the radicalizing effect of other social movements. It was the clergy who had been involved in both the school integration battle in New York and in other areas of civil liberties, who were willing to be most active in the abortion campaign (Carmen and Moody 1973, p. 21). The counselling service was in demand right from the start, and in 1968 6,500 women were passed through the referral system of New York City. Moody wanted to prevent women from having to travel far, so he encouraged the setting up of consultation services in other major cities. These clergy services decreased much of the mystique surrounding abortion and led to its increased acceptance. Their agency lasted until the New York law came into operation in 1970.

Another referral service on the East Coast, and the only one with its own clinic, was that of Bill Baird in Hempstead, which also opened for abortions in 1967. Baird took a much more aggressive approach in his campaign for contraception and abortion. In August 1974, the *Boston Globe* reported that a church had refused to allow a mother to have her daughter baptised because she had publicly supported Baird. Lader points out that although many in Planned Parenthood were outraged by his inflammatory tactics:

> Still, after each Baird hurricane, the movement made considerable progress. Each of his arrests affected the law in questions. Each innovation – the mobile van, for instance, with which he brought contraceptive and abortion information directly into ghetto areas – set a pattern that was finally followed elsewhere (Lader 1973, p. 51).

In the struggle for legalization, Baird scored some important victories. Possibly the most notable was the Supreme Court decision of 1972 which overthrew the laws against contraception for single people. People like Pat Maginnis and Bill Baird, who were willing to risk prison for their beliefs, helped to bring the campaign into the open.

5.7 The Nature of the Opposition

A fifth and final difference between the two societies was the nature of the opposition. In Britain, the dominant opposition was not publicly opposed to abortion in all circumstances, and in its early days it remained separate from the Catholic Church. However, in the USA the 'Right of Life' movement was more overtly linked to Catholicism and less willing to compromise. This meant that some of the right wing who might have been opposed to abortion on extended grounds were alienated from the movement. The uncompromising nature of the opposition was due to the same cultural factors that led to the dominance of the repeal groups, and also to the much greater involvement of the Catholic Church. As was mentioned in the British context, there is a tendency for pressure groups to take an extreme position, since the activists are always those who are most strongly committed. However, while in Britain both sides managed as far as possible to contain this tendency, in the USA this did not happen. In fact, the whole nature of the debate was far more acrimonious. When the first reform Bill was being considered in New York, the opposition forces became so rowdy that two members of the Catholic Lawyers Guild left the hearing to draft a formal apology (Lader 1973, p. 64). With both sides entrenched in stances so widely divergent, further confrontations were inevitable and have continued at a high level of intensity.

Two of the key anti-abortion activists, Dr and Mrs Willke, used their *Handbook on Abortion*, first published in 1971, as a basis for their campaign, and also used pictures of aborted fetuses. They had some successes in changing public attitudes, possibly the most notable from their point of view being a referendum campaign in Michigan. A referendum on the abortion law was due to take place in November 1972, and on 15 October it looked as if the reform, which would allow abortion on request up to 20 weeks of pregnancy, was going to be passed. An opinion poll in the Detroit News showed support from 59 per cent of the electorate, with only 37 per cent in opposition. However, in the later stages Dr and Mrs Willke visited Michigan and ran an aggressive campaign. They appeared on television, radio and in debates and helped to organize the distribution of their 'fetus brochure' to nearly all the 2 million homes in Michigan. There was also a massive amount of television advertising, with one advertisement being repeated as often as 13 times a day in the two weeks before the election. This intense activity resulted in the referendum being defeated by 62 per cent to 38 per cent, an extraordinary turn-around. A referendum on abortion in North Dakota was also defeated, and by a larger margin (Willke and Willke 1975, p. 36). If the anti-abortion forces could have mounted this kind of campaign all over the USA, the law might never have been overthrown in the Supreme Court. However, they did not have the resources to do so. Furthermore, the opponents of abortion were not even guaranteed the support of all Catholics. In this respect, a key role was played by Robert Drinan, a Catholic priest who was Dean at the Boston Law College. At first Drinan was opposed to the abortion law changes. In 1965 he argued:

> Any change of a substantial kind in America's abortion laws would be a notable departure from that body of Anglo-American law which regulates conduct deemed to constitute a crime against society … However convenient, convincing or compelling the arguments in favour of abortion may be, the fact remains that the taking of a life, even though it is unborn, cuts at the very heart of the principle that no one's life, however unwanted and useless it may be, may be terminated in order to promote the health or happiness of another human being (Drinan 1967, p. 122).

At first, Drinan was one of the major debating opponents of those in the Clergy Consultation Service. However, once the argument moved away from abortion on specific grounds towards removal of all the laws, Drinan found it much easier to give his support. In a paper at the International Conference on Abortion in Washington DC in September 1967 entitled *The Right of the Fetus to be Born*, he criticized the fact that certain states were considering passing reform laws:

> The right of the fetus to be born, now protected in Anglo-American law, may be seriously compromised within the near future by changes in the laws of England, Canada and several states in America. In eliminating the right of some fetuses to be born, the law enters an area which it has never entered before – an area where it will be required to decide by what norms and by whose judgements what persons are to be born and what persons are to 'die' before their birth (Buck 1968, p. 57).

Although Drinan opposed reform, paradoxically he continued to accept the case for total repeal:

> One way to avoid the necessity of making these choices would be for the law to withdraw its protection from all fetuses during the first 26 weeks of their existence. Under this arrangement the law would not be required to approve or disapprove the choices of parents and physicians as to who may be born or not born (Buck 1968, p. 57).

This argument, put at a conference sponsored by the Joseph P. Kennedy Foundation where there was a general anti-abortion feeling, led to some urgent rethinking amongst many who had opposed any changes. Drinan's views effectively split the Catholic opposition and gave respectability to the argument that, while abortion was wrong, the law should not be imposed on those who did not accept this view.

These, then, were some of the social and political forces that led to the possibility of repeal laws, and in 1970 the states of Hawaii and New York both gave a woman the right to choose an abortion during the early part of her pregnancy. I have described the process in the two states more fully elsewhere (Francome 1984, pp. 114–22). However, the crucial difference between the states was that New York did not have a residential requirement; this meant that women from all over the USA could go there for a legal abortion.

5.8   Supreme Court Decision

In theory the judges should just interpret validity of laws in terms of the constitution. In practice, of course, they are influenced by the climate of opinion. Views on abortion continued to liberalize after the passage of the New York Act, and in August 1972 a Gallup Poll showed that 64 per cent of the public, including a majority (56 per cent) of Catholics, believed that the decision to have an abortion should be left solely to the woman and her doctor. An article discussing the results in the *New York Times* (25 August 1972) suggested that there had been a strong movement towards liberalization. It stated that in 1968 fewer than 15 per cent wanted liberal laws, but this percentage had risen to 40 per cent in 1969 and 50 per cent in 1971. By 1972 medical opinion had similarly moved towards a repeal position. In March 1971, a survey of specialists in obstetrics and gynaecology in New York found that two-thirds favoured the new abortion law. A couple of months later liberal laws were endorsed nationally, when the American College of Obstetrics and Gynecology urged that the decision on abortion should be left to doctors and their patients. It seems that the working of the New York Act was one factor which led to the liberalization of views. In October 1972, the New York City Health Services Administrator stated that the experience of two years' legal abortion on a mass scale had cut the maternal death rate, reduced infant mortality and had reduced illegitimate births for the first time since the keeping of statistics had started in 1954 (*New York Times*, 7 October).

A further reason for the change in the climate of opinion was the general movement to the left in response to the war in Vietnam. It is probable that the liberalization of attitudes amongst students and anti-war protesters was concentrated on the coasts rather than the mid-west or the south. However, in terms of political importance the liberal areas carried more weight. Thus effective public opinion was to the left of overall opinion in the country. These changes all worked together. The challenge to the law came from two cases.

One woman was assigned the pseudonym Jane Roe to protect her privacy. She instigated an action against Henry Wade, the district attorney of Dallas County, Texas, where she lived. She claimed the Texas anti-abortion statute violated the United States Constitution (Mohr 1978, p. 247). Sarah Waddington, the lawyer who argued the Texas case before the Supreme Court, told me in an interview in 1978 that the decision they finally took would not have occurred in the climate of opinion even two years earlier. She also said that the Court's prior decisions were important, as was the fact that the advocates of legal abortion had largely won the academic debate about the genesis and maintenance of the abortion laws. There were two major issues involved: the first was the question of privacy, and the second was the background to the laws and the question of the origin of life.

The right to privacy had already been decided in particular reference to the question of contraception. In 1965, in *Griswold v. Connecticut*, the Supreme Court had recognized the existence of a constitutional right of privacy within marriage: in this case, it was decided that the states could not prohibit a couple from using contraceptives within their marital relationship. This decision for married people was extended to single persons: in *Eisenstadt v. Baird*, 1972, it was argued that the marital couple was not an entity, but two individuals who both had the right to ensure that the government did not interfere in such fundamental matters as the decision as to whether or not to have children. This right of privacy was a key factor in the Supreme Court decision striking down the Texas law, in *Roe v. Wade*. A second factor was related to the concept of the fetus as an unborn child, and the academic work of NARAL's legal adviser Cyril Means was particularly important on this point. Means (1968) wrote on the background of the abortion laws, and his work was widely quoted in the Supreme Court decision. He pointed out that under English common law abortion had been legal until movement could be detected in the womb – 'quickening' – which normally occurs around 15–17 weeks. He stated that from the moment of conception until quickening, there was no protection under common law (Means, 1968). Explaining the reasons for the abortion laws, Means stated that it had been an unsafe operation in the nineteenth century (p. 211), and he argued that the main purpose of the laws was to protect the life and health of women with unwanted pregnancies. He went on to quote the evidence of Christopher Tietze that at some time in the early twentieth century abortion became a safe operation and, indeed, safer than childbirth. It followed that the previous reasons for abortion restrictions were no longer valid (Means 1968, p. 512). He drew attention to the fact that the British 1967 Abortion Act had reasoned in terms of safety, and commented:

> As a matter of meaning, it uncannily recaptures the intentions of all the British
> and American legislators on this subject in the nineteenth century … The
> new British clause would not have looked 'radical' at all to the nineteenth
> century parliamentarians and legislators. It looks radical now only because
> it has so widely been forgotten what the real purpose of the abortion statutes
> was (Means 1968, p. 514).

Means went on to question whether the legislators had the right to insist
that a woman must risk the hazards of childbirth rather than being allowed a
relatively safe legal abortion.

A second paper went further, arguing that under common law women had
the right to abortion throughout pregnancy 1971 (Means 1971, p. 359). This
finding obviously had important constitutional implications:

> Were the American Medical Profession now suddenly to remember the reason
> for the passage of these laws, they would grant an abortion to every woman in the
> first or second trimester who requested one; for, today, abortion is always safer
> than childbirth, as the New York figures now show, not only through the first
> trimester but during the first 24 weeks of pregnancy (Means 1971 p. 396).

Mr Justice Blackman recognized the importance of Means' research in
delivering the opinion of the court. The Judge noted Means' point that even
post-quickening abortion was not established as a crime, and agreed that the
major reason for the introduction of the laws was to protect the health of the
woman. In his ruling, Mr Justice Blackman outlined three major areas of
interest. First, the right of privacy, next, the interest of the state in protecting the
health of the woman involved, and finally, the interest of the state in protecting
potential life. He noted that some were arguing that the woman's right of
privacy was absolute throughout pregnancy, but he rejected this contention.
He took the view that it applied during the first three months of pregnancy and
that within this period the decision on abortion should be left to the woman
and her attending physician. After this time, however, the interests of the state
in promoting the health of the woman became of increased importance, and
so the state could regulate abortion procedures in ways that were reasonably
related to maternal health. Once viability had been reached, the states could
proscribe abortion in pursuit of its interest in the potential human life except
when it was necessary to preserve the life or health of the woman (Osofsky
and Osofsky 1973). This decision was won with a 7–2 vote, and the only
Catholic Judge was included in the majority. With it, all the state laws were
overthrown, and even the New York law was unconstitutional because it did

not allow abortion for 'health' after viability. At the time of the decision, four states had abortion on request – Alaska, Washington, Hawaii and New York; fifteen states had relatively new laws based on ALI-type conditions – Alabama, Arkansas, California, Colorado, Delaware, Florida, Georgia, Kansas, Maryland, Mississippi, New Mexico, North Carolina, Oregon, South Carolina and Virginia. Some other states, such as Wisconsin and New Jersey, had liberalized their laws by means of court decisions, but many still had their traditional nineteenth-century laws.

5.9   Conclusion

Not all advocates of legal abortion were entirely happy with the Supreme Court's decision. For example, Congresswoman Bella Abzug said she would introduce a Bill that would go further and eliminate state laws of any nature concerning the regulation of abortion (*New York Times*, 23 January 1973). However, realistically the major problem was that the law was seen as being imposed from outside. Although the polls showed that most people were in support, there were various areas of the country which were very conservative and strongly opposed to abortion. In Utah for example, the State legislature opposed the Supreme Court decision by 66 votes to one (Francome 1984, p. 184). This meant that the ruling was necessarily going to introduce a great deal of conflict.

Chapter 6

The Politics of Abortion in the USA

There are a number of reasons for the strength of the opposition to abortion in the USA. After the 1973 Supreme Court decision, even states most opposed to liberal laws were prevented from retaining such legislation. Further, much of the general population is very conservative. Opinion poll results indicated a sizeable minority totally opposed to the activities of the abortion clinics. Furthermore, the right-wing pressure groups have had increasing success. Three issues – capital punishment, homosexuality and women's rights – show this clearly. It seemed in the early 1970s that there were going to be liberal laws in all these areas. The Supreme Court struck down all death penalty laws in 1972, and some thought that that would be the end of capital punishment. However, in 1976 it ruled that the death sentence could be constitutional if certain conditions were met, including the fact that the law concerned gave the jury or judge discretion in imposing the penalty. Consequently, the USA stands alone as a major Western industrialized nation that allows capital punishment. By 1999, 38 of the 50 states had restored the death penalty, and 24 states carried out at least one execution in that year (Wright 2002, p. 316). On the matter of homosexual rights, there has also been a great deal of controversy. Logically, the right of privacy established during the birth control cases should make laws against sodomy unconstitutional (Barnett 1973). However, in May 1978 the Supreme Court allowed the North Carolina law to stand and it took until 2003 to extend privacy laws to homosexuals. The right wing has been effective in its opposition to the Equal Rights Amendment (ERA). In order for ratification to occur, 38 states needed to support it, and by January 1977 35 had done so. However, in the next 18 months, in the face of skillfully organized opposition, no further states gave their assent and, furthermore, four states voted to rescind their earlier approval. In the late seventies, therefore, the USA moved away from the liberal developments which occurred in other countries, and it is generally to the right of other major countries. There are still concerns about the ERA amongst anti-abortion groups. For example, on 10 December 2002 Missouri Right to Life commented that if the ERA were to be passed it would provide further grounds for the right to abortion and wipe out the gains that the movement had made in the past quarter of a century; it commented 'the ERA thus represents a dire threat to the pro-life movement'.

Let us consider some of the major groups involved in the issue of abortion.

6.1   Major Groups Opposing Abortion Rights

The modern anti-abortion movement seems to have begun in 1970, and its origin was closely linked to the Catholic Church in New York State. In a candid description Arlene Doyle, has explained its beginnings: 'For publicity purposes, the Catholic Church in New York State had put together the names of some people and placed them on a New York State Right to Life letterhead. In fact, however, the people involved never held a meeting and most of them never even met each other' (Doyle 1977). However, over time the opponents of abortion grew in organizational ability and formed a number of different organizations. Some of the major ones are discussed below.

6.1.1   *National Right to Life Committee (NRLC)*

This now has branches in each of the 50 states and, in 2003, more than three thousand local groups. It is absolutist in that it wants all abortions banned. In the meantime, it works to support more piecemeal changes and we saw in the introduction how the organization encouraged senators to vote for minor restrictions.

Some of the literature is a little gory; it said, for example, that in a partial birth abortion 'the abortionist jams scissors in to the back of the baby's skull … the baby's brains are sucked out'. It is basically a Catholic organization and one possible point of conflict is that Church members do not share the official Church view on the subject. Various polls have shown a wide disparity between official doctrine and the beliefs of the laity. For example, as far back as 1978, Fr Andrew Greeley reported in the *Long Island Catholic* (26 January) that 66 per cent of Catholics said they would have an abortion or encourage their wife to have one if there was a chance of a defective child, and 76 per cent said they would favour one if there were a serious health threat.

6.1.2   *Americans United for Life*

This Chicago-based group has a vision of the future in which abortion and euthanasia are neither desired nor legal. It conducts the major part of the legal work for the movement. Its website argues that abortion is dangerous because of 'unsanitary and unsafe conditions at abortion clinics, with the accompanying deaths and injury of an untold number of women'.

6.1.3   March for Life

This organization prides itself on not compromising over this issue. For example, in opposing the use of abortion where a woman has been raped, it placed this comment on its website:

> Abortionists are now trying to use the loathing we have for rape in order to justify their own dastardly crimes of torturing and killing an innocent pre-born child conceived by rape … Women's-libbers wrinkle their noses and ask if a pro-lifer would force a woman to carry a rapist's child for nine months and be reminded all the time and at the birth of the child of the tragedy of the rape. The pro-lifer says 'put down the killing knives and drugs and offer real help to the victimized woman.'

6.1.4   Feminists for Life

This group began in 1972 as a 'non-sectarian' grass roots organization. It said it opposes all violence including abortion, rape, capital punishment and euthanasia and its website comments 'Every 36 seconds in America a woman lays her body down, forced to choose abortion out of a lack of practical resources and emotional support'. In 2000, the president, Serrin M. Foster, challenged the incoming President Bush to hold a national enquiry into pregnancy and abortion. She went on to say 'We can create a plan to systematically eliminate the root causes that drive women to abortion – the lack of financial resources and emotional support'.

6.1.5   Moral Majority

This was formed by Jerry Falwell in 1979. It was against 'sin, abortion and communism' and for Reagan and South Africa. 'We are fighting a holy war', said Falwell, 'and this time we are going to win' (Goreau 1981). One of the claims was: 'There are an estimated 85 million Americans; 50 million born again Protestants, 30 million morally conservative Catholics, 3 million Mormons and 2 million Orthodox and Conservative Jews, with whom to build a pro-family, bible believing coalition.' One of the weaknesses of this assessment, of course, is that even at this number, it is still a minority of the population in the USA. However, on some issues the new right does have public support. For example, an opinion poll conducted for *Time* magazine (May 1981) found that 71 per cent agreed that 'The Supreme Court and Congress had gone too far in keeping religious morals and values, like prayer, out of our laws, our schools and our lives'.

Especially in its early years, some of the claims were extravagant. One of the most prominent political supporters, Senator Jesse Helms, wrote in a fund-raising letter: 'Right now your tax dollars are being used to pay for grade school courses that teach our children that cannibalism, wife swapping and murder of infants and the elderly are acceptable behavior' (Francome 1984).

The fact that this kind of rhetoric can find favour amongst a segment of the population shows the appeal of the simple solution to parts of the US society. Hunter (1981) noted that right wing politicians put forward the idea that the vast majority of people were 'hard-working, sober, tradition-minded patriots fed up with welfare handouts, "peace-creeps", hippies, black militants and street violence'. They also stressed law and order, and posed the image of an eastern establishment out of touch with the people. It was this feeling that the new right aimed to galvanize, and single-issue topics such as abortion were useful to add dynamism to the movement. 'Our success is built on four elements – single-issue groups, multi-issue conservative groups, coalition politics and direct mail', wrote Richard Viguerie in *The New Right* (1981).

The National Conservative Political Action Committee (NCPAC – pronounced Nik Pak), founded in 1975, funnels money to conservative candidates and targets liberals for defeat. Its program, apart from the abolition of abortion, calls for support for prayer in state schools and other 'pro-family' issues. It is controversial, even amongst the right, because it claims to be an 'independent' political organization and is able to finance campaigns without breaking election laws limiting contributions – it says it does not support candidates but opposes them. As we might expect from our knowledge of the difference in perspective of anti-abortion Catholics and the right, liberal Catholics have doubts about the developments in the new right.

6.1.6   The Catholic Church

A study I carried out amongst students on Long Island suggests reasons for Church pressure to be able to succeed. Only a quarter of my sample of nearly 600 Catholic students were opposed to abortion on request in the early months of pregnancy (Francome 1978). However, those who were regular church attenders were much more likely to support the official teaching. Amongst those who had been in church in the previous week, 41 per cent disagreed with the right to legal abortion in the early months of pregnancy compared to 17 per cent of those who had been to church in the previous month, and 16 per cent of those who had not been to church in the previous month, showing wide differences between the regular worshipers and the rest. Regular churchgoing, then, is one factor which allows the Catholic Church to keep up its pressure. A second is its hierarchical structure. The power to make decisions is concentrated in the higher levels of the bureaucracy, and the lay members are expected to follow this lead. Furthermore, the support of the Church's position is a question of numbers. Only 20 per cent of Catholics may believe fully in its position, but with 50 million Catholics this amounts to around 10 million people. Once a proportion of these have become organized, they are bound to make an impact.

This direct involvement of the bishops was a very important factor in organizing the political power of the Church behind the anti-abortion movement.

6.2   Sources of Support for Abortion Rights

After the 1973 Supreme Court decision, many of those who had been active for abortion rights moved off into other areas of political concern. There were a few who predicted a great deal of further opposition, but these were in the minority, and in a sense this is understandable.

6.2.1   National Abortion Rights Action League (NARAL)

This is the largest of the pro-choice organizations. In 2003, its website stated that it was 'The leading political force dedicated to preserving the right to choose' (http://www.naral.org). Its earlier newsletters set out political plans: it should identify pro choice incumbents who will need help to be re-elected; it should identify anti-choice incumbents who have a strong challenge from a pro-choice candidate and it should identify pro-choice candidates with a good chance of winning open seats (1978, Vol. 10, No. 1).

It is divided into three sections – NARAL incorporated, NARAL Political Action Committee and the NARAL Foundation. This last was founded in 1977 as a charity to carry out indepth research, and it has nearly 300,000 members and supporters. Its president, Kate Michelson, said in 2002:

> The freedom to choose is at a critical crossroads. Down one road lies an America where women have no access to legal abortion and no right to choose. Down the other road lies an America where women have the right to make their own reproductive health decisions.

NARAL also collates statistics on important issues. One such was its information on clinic violence, which said that there had been over 59,000 acts of violence between 1977 and 22 May 2002. These included seven murders, 17 attempted murders, 41 bombings, 165 arsons, 370 physical invasions and 343 death threats.

There is no real political organization in Britain on abortion that approaches NARAL in size or degree of activity.

6.2.2 Planned Parenthood Federation of America

This is the largest voluntary reproductive health care organization (http://www.plannedparenthood.org). It provides reproductive and complementary health care services, and is an advocate for reproductive rights and health. In addition, it provides technical and training assistance to its affiliates.

It produces a great deal of literature arguing the case for abortion rights. One paper printed in November 2002 was entitled 'The Medical and Health Benefits since Abortion was made Legal'. This asserted, for example, that before legalization many women suffered the adverse effects of illegal operations, that 193 women died of illegal abortion in the USA in 1965, and that in 1969 almost a quarter (23 per cent) of pregnancy-related admissions to New York hospitals resulted from illegal abortion.

6.2.3 National Abortion Federation

This is the professional organization for abortion providers in the USA and Canada (http://www.prochoice.org). It includes 400 non-profit clinics, women's health centers, Planned Parenthood facilities and private physicians as well as researchers, clinicians and educators. Together, each year, they care for more than half the women who have abortions in the USA. Since 1979, NAF has had an abortion hotline which provides free information about services.

6.2.4   Catholics for a Free Choice

This organization is actively chaired by Frances Kissling and provides information about abortion. Not surprisingly, it provides information about Catholics in particular. Its website (2003) points to research showing that in the USA Catholics are 29 per cent more likely to have abortions than Protestants, that 64 per cent of Catholics disagree that abortion is immoral in every case, and that 69 per cent of Catholics believe a woman who has an abortion for a reason other than to save her life can still be a good Catholic.

6.2.5   Other Groups

There are various other organizations which have been reported in literature from the National Abortion Federation (URLs shown in brackets). These are the Abortion Access Project (http://www.abortionaccess.org), the American College of Nurse Midwives (http://www.midwife.org), the American College of Obstetricians and Gynecologists (http://www.acog.org), the American Medical Woman's Association (http://www.amwa-doc.org), Association of Reproductive Health Professionals (http://www.arhp.org), Center for Reproductive Law and Politics (http://www.crlp.org), Clinicians for Choice (http://www.cliniciansforchoice), National Women's Health Network (http://www.womenshealthnetwork.org), National Women's Law Centre (http://www.nwlc.org), Physicians for Reproductive Choice and Health (http://www.prch.org), Population Council (http://www.popcouncil.org), Pro-Choice Resource Center (http://www.prochoiceresource.org) and Reproductive Health Technologies Project (http://www.rhtp.org).

Another organization which is helpful to the pro-choice groups is Republicans for Choice, and this assists in widening the political spectrum of supporters. In addition several groups, while not primarily concerned with abortion, nevertheless have an important effect. Primary amongst these is the National Organization for Women (NOW). This has abortion rights as one of its prime targets. Various religious groups also support the right of women to have abortions. The Unitarians have probably been the most outspoken in this direction, but their numbers have been relatively small. Some groups have worked together under the Religious Coalition for Abortion Rights which has helped to organize their campaign against restrictions. Amongst the more prominent members are the American Baptist Church, the Disciples of Christ, the Lutheran Church of America, the Presbyterian Church, the United Church of Christ, Reform Judaism, Conservative Judaism, the Unitarian Universalistic

Association, the United Methodist Church, the United Presbyterian Church and the YMCA.

These, then, are the major pressure groups involved in abortion rights and, as discussed, they get majority support from the liberal politicians and from those in the population who take a liberal point of view.

6.3   Nature of Political Action

Although the sources of strength of the anti-abortion movement are clear, there is a question of tactics. At one time the major aim was a constitutional amendment. A problem here was that there were several kinds that could be chosen, and various methods of trying to get one accepted. The amendment could, for example, be relatively moderate. One suggestion put forward by Coffey (1976) in a journal orientated towards Catholic doctors was for a restriction based on the length of gestation: 'Perhaps in the United States today, the best that pro-lifers can realistically expect is the establishment of an amendment giving the unborn protection against unjust homicides from the end of the first trimester onwards.' However, calls for moderate change did not hold much sway in the anti-abortion movement, for the membership wanted a very tough law. There are some advantages to a group in taking an extreme position. In examining pro-choice groups during the battle for legalization, we saw that organizers of the activists thought women would be much more willing to work for a change that would provide them with all or almost all their demands.

The pro-and anti-choice groups have been working at a number of different levels. These include the Presidency, the Supreme Court, Congress and in the States.

6.3.1   The Presidency and Legal Abortion

In recent years US presidents have largely taken two positions on abortion. The Democratic position as taken by Jimmy Carter or Bill Clinton is that, while they may personally be opposed to abortion, they believe that women should have the legal right. The Republican position is one of opposition to abortion in all or nearly all circumstances: the law should be changed to make it largely or totally illegal. However, within these overall positions there are differences in emphasis. Jimmy Carter, for example, disappointed pro-choice groups in the late 1970s by not standing up for the provision of abortion funds for poor women. Bill Clinton proved a more reliable ally to the pro-choice movement.

The anti-choice groups have sometimes had their doubts about the commitment of Republican presidents to their cause. At the 1976 election, the Republican platform supported 'the efforts of those who seek enactment of a constitutional amendment to restore protection of the right of life for unborn children' (*New York Times*, 18 August). In 1980, Ronald Reagan was quoted as saying: 'I strongly believe that the rights of unborn children must be protected in a civilized and humane society; therefore, as President, I will ask Congress to pass a constitutional amendment to protect the rights of all innocent human life' (*Catholic Herald*, 14 November 1980). However, Reagan, as governor of California, had approved a measure liberalizing abortion, and although he assured anti-choice groups he had changed his mind and now opposed abortion, when he kept his promise to appoint a woman to the Supreme Court he chose Sandra Day O'Connor, a past supporter of abortion rights. Paul A. Brown described the anti-abortion forces as 'devastated', and she had to pass anti-abortion pickets to get to the Confirmation Hearings (*New York Times*, 10 September 1981). However, the Senate supported her appointment by a vote of 99 to 0. This action distanced Reagan from the Right to Life groups, and many of the anti-abortion leaders were concerned that he was not proving a reliable ally.

When the elder George Bush followed Reagan into office in 1988, he urged the Supreme Court to overturn *Roe v. Wade*, vetoed ten bills that would have provided easier access to abortion, barred abortion from military installations and prohibited 4,000 federally-funded family planning clinics from counseling and referring for abortion. In addition, he prohibited the abortion pill (then called RU 486), vetoed US funding to UN Family Planning programs citing the organization's supposed support for forced abortion in China and enforced the 'Mexico City Policy' which prohibited US-funded aid organizations from performing abortions or supporting pro-choice laws in the Third World.

When Bill Clinton was elected, he reversed these decisions. He gave support to *Roe v. Wade*, urged Congress to make abortion part of mandatory health insurance benefits packages, allowed abortions in the military, allowed federally-financed family planning associations to counsel and refer for abortion, allowed research into fetal tissue and restored funding to pro choice-organizations (Rochester 1996). During his term of office, there were several attempts to ban late abortions or what, in the USA, were called 'partial birth abortions'. In 1996, the Associated Press reported that a Bill to ban partial birth abortions was the first measure to ban a specific abortion procedure since the 1973 Supreme Court decision. Clinton vetoed the bill 'in an emotional ceremony where five women who had undergone such abortions spoke tearfully about the experience and the fetal disorders that led to their decisions'. Clinton commented that the 'procedure is a "potentially lifesaving, certainly health saving" measure for a small but extremely vulnerable group of women and families in this country, just a few hundred a year'. He released a letter to Archbishop Bernardin of Chicago in which he commented 'This is a difficult and disturbing issue which I have prayed about for many months'. He went on to say that at first he thought he would support the bill, but then realized that the procedure was rarely used and then only to save the woman's health or life. Kate Michelson of NARAL commented that the president had chosen compassion (Associated Press 1996).

Before the election on 1 Feb 2000, George Bush told Associated Press:

> I support the goal of a Human Life Amendment with exceptions for rape and incest and to save the life of the mother. Recognizing that there is currently insufficient support for that amendment in Congress and the states, I will provide leadership to take positive, practical steps to reduce the number of abortions: ending partial birth abortions, helping women in crisis through maternity group homes, encouraging adoptions, promoting abstinence education, and passing laws requiring parental notification and waiting periods (Associated Press 2000).

When Bush was controversially elected in 2000, one of his first actions on the anniversary of *Roe v. Wade* was to re-establish the ban on abortion funding being provided for Family Planning groups. This restriction was originally instituted by Ronald Reagan in 1984 and reversed by Bill Clinton in 1993. Bush commented 'It is my conviction that taxpayer's funds should not be used to pay for abortions or to advocate or actively promote abortion, either here or abroad'.

Another issue which affected the presidency was the question of research which could help the victims of Alzheimer's disease. His decision in 2001 to oppose stem cell research led to him receiving plaudits from the US anti-choice lobby. The technique, which is also known as therapeutic cloning, involves using human embryos. However, this decision led to opposition from scientists who believed that the research could lead to a cure for Alzheimer's, Parkinson's disease and diabetes, and might let the severely paralyzed move again. Bush was even opposed from within his own party. One article talked of him being opposed by 'one of the most revered icons of the Republican Party' – the former president's wife, Nancy Reagan (Burkeman 2002). Alzheimer's has destroyed the memory of her husband and 81-year-old Mrs Reagan has been campaigning and complaining that 'a lot of time is being wasted'.

Another controversial decision was the announcement by the Bush administration, at the end of January 2002, of a proposal to expand the definition of a child to include a fetus, so that women on a low income could receive taxpayer-funded health care. The announcement was made by the Health and Social Services (HHS) Secretary, and a spokesperson, Bill Pierce, was quoted as saying 'It is about better health for pregnant women, particularly poor women, and the children that are born'. However, in response Kim Gandy, the president of NOW commented 'If a fetus is defined as a person, which is a legal term, then even first trimester abortions would be murder'. Opponents of abortion hailed the statement. But Douglas Johnson legislative director of Nationwide Right to Life said the proposal was one to which 'only the most extreme pro-abortion ideologues will object'. Abortion rights activists supported the provision of pre-natal care for poor women, but prefer it to be achieved by the granting to states of waivers to children's programs (Enda 2002).

In 2002, the actions of President Bush led to Jessica Reaves writing a letter to him, pointing out that during his race for the presidency he had avoided the issue of abortion. However, after the election the Conservative activists 'cashed in their chips and you are back on the case'. She then asked if it meant he would appoint anti-abortion Supreme Court judges who would vote against *Roe v. Wade* and would campaign for Republicans who were opposed to choice. She said that if that was the case the president should note that:

- the majority of Americans support abortion rights;
- inciting enemies makes them more powerful. For example, the introduction of the 'gag rule' led to Planned Parenthood taking an extra $600,000 a month;
- before legalization women had illegal abortions, and WHO estimated that 78,000 women died of an illegal abortion each year;
- the president should listen to the women in his life. His mother Barbara Bush – a former first lady – supports abortion rights in the first trimester; his wife Laura Bush states that she supports *Roe v. Wade*.

She argued that these are major points that should restrain the extent to which the President supports anti-choice groups.

Professor Arkes, of Amherst, proposed a bill which resulted in the 'Born Alive Infants Protection Act'. Bush signed into law, on 16 August 2002, this unusual law which protected the civil rights of new-born infants who survived an abortion.

6.3.2   Legal Abortion in the Supreme Court

Although the court decision of 1973 had legalized abortion in a wide variety of circumstances, it left a number of issues open for opponents of abortion to use to try to restrict rights. Some of the areas not ruled on in the decision were:

- to what extent could states regulate abortion in the second trimester?
- what regulation could be forced upon abortion clinics?
- what restrictions could be placed upon the distribution of information and advertisements?
- how far could a woman be forced to seek the consent of other parties such as her husband or parents?
- could states prohibit abortions by non-physicians?
- may public hospitals refuse to perform abortions?
- must Medicaid payments be made to women who want abortions?
- may states require records to be kept?
- could a woman be forced to take note of certain information before making her decision?
- should a doctor try to save the life of a viable fetus?

With all these areas of doubt there was obviously wide scope for court cases. From 1973–2000, there were 31 Supreme Court decisions on abortion, of which the following were particularly important:

1976 On the consent of the husband, the court ruled by six to three (*Danforth v. Planned Parenthood*) that, since the government has no authority to veto an abortion, it cannot delegate such authority to the woman's husband. The decision stated: 'It is difficult to believe that the goal of fostering mutuality and trust in marriage ... will be achieved by giving the husband a veto power exercisable for any reason whatsoever or for no reason at all' (*New York Times*, 2 July). In this year, too, the Supreme Court overthrew attempts to restrict the rights of under 18s to an abortion.

1977 The Supreme Court held by six votes to three that states were not required to pay for elective abortions, and effectively returned to Congress and the States the decision as to whether or not to pay for abortions.

1978 The Court agreed to review the Pennsylvania law, struck down by a lower court, that required physicians to try to protect the life of a fetus in an abortion if they thought it could survive (*Twin Circle*, 25 June 1978). However, on 9 January 1979 the Court voided the law by a six to three margin.

1979 In the case of *Baird v. Bellotti*, it struck down the Massachusetts law. However, it set out guidelines for a law controlling minors' rights. It must, for example, make available to minors an alternative authorization to their parents. A judge might decide that a minor could demonstrate the mature and informed consent required to make her own decision.

1980 In *Harris v. McRae*, the Supreme Court upheld by five to four the Hyde Amendment which ruled that the federal government was not obliged to fund abortions for poor women, even when such abortions were medically necessary.

1981 In *H.L. v. Matheson*, the Supreme Court upheld a Utah statute requiring a doctor to seek parental permission before performing an abortion. If her parents refused, the young woman had the right to go to a judge in the hope of gaining approval.

1992 The Supreme Court in *Planned Parenthood of Southeastern Pennsylvania v. Casey* allowed to stand a Pennsylvania Statute mandating that women wait at least 24 hours after receiving state-provided information on abortion before having a termination. By the year 2000, 19 states had passed 'waiting period' legislation (Joyce and Kaestner 2000). In this case, the Court supported restrictions wanted by the anti-choice groups. For this, it was strongly attacked by pro-choice supporters, who said that the attack on the rights of poor women represented 'a hazardous retreat from the philosophy of pluralism on which this democracy is based' (Jaffe, Lindheim and Lee 1981, p. 196).

1992 In *Penn v. Casey*, although the court upheld the essentials of *Roe v. Wade*, it also upheld a provision of a Pennsylvania statute that required a physician to provide a patient with information on the medical risks of abortion and to show her pictures of a fetus at different stages of development, and that also introduced a 24-hour waiting period, and the reporting of abortions for statistical analysis.

1994 In *Madsen v. Woman's Health Center*, a Florida injunction was upheld which created a 36-foot buffer zone outside the entrance to abortion clinics, and prohibited excessive noise from being heard in abortion clinics. However, it struck down a ban on pro-life signs, and also a provision for a 300-foot buffer zone.

1997 In *Schenck et al. v. Pro Choice Network of Western New York*, the Supreme Court upheld a New York injunction banning demonstrations within 15 feet of doorway or parking lot entrances; these were regarded as fixed buffer zones. However, the Court struck down the part of the law which restricted people from approaching within 15 feet of any vehicle or person; these were regarded as floating buffer zones.

2000 The Supreme Court upheld a Colorado statute making it illegal for any person within 100 feet of the entrance of any health care facility to 'knowingly approach' within eight feet of another person, without consent, to engage in oral protest, pass on leaflets or handbills; or to display signs to, or attempt to counsel, such a person.

2000 In *Stenberg v. Cahart*, the Court upheld, by five votes to four, a lower court's ruling which declared unconstitutional Nebraska's 1997 law banning 'partial birth abortion'. It took the view that such a law prevents doctors from giving patients appropriate and necessary medical care. In the Court's view, doctors must be allowed to give the most appropriate method of care for their patients.

6.3.3   Congress

In the USA, Democratic politicians tend to support abortion rights to a much greater degree than Republicans. This is similar to the situation in the UK, where Labour politicians are for more supportive than Conservative ones. In the 107th Congress in 2001, there were three votes on abortion in the Senate. One of these was on the question of abortion amongst service personnel. The 50 Democratic senators therefore had a potential 150 votes, and they did in fact vote 148 times. The Nationwide Right to Life group reported that Democrats voted only seven times, to support its anti-abortion stance; so in fewer than one in 20 cases the Democrats supported restrictions on abortion in agreement with the Nationwide Right to Life Committee. At the start of the session, there were 50 Republican senators; however, on 5 June 2001, Senator James Jeffords from Vermont became independent. This left 49 senators and a possible 147 votes in the three divisions. Of these, the Republicans voted 141 times. Their voting pattern was totally different from that of the Democrats: on 114 occasions they supported the Right to life position, while they opposed it on only 27 occasions. Overall, Democrats supported the Nationwide Right to Life in only 5 per cent of cases while for Republicans it was in 81 per cent of cases. So there is a strong correlation between the position on the political spectrum and the vote on this issue. However, the Republicans' support for

National Right to Life was not quite as solid as the Democrats' opposition. In fact, both the Republican senators for Maine and one each from Rhode Island and Pennsylvania opposed the Right to Life position in all the votes.

In the months immediately following the 1973 Supreme Court decision, two senators and a congressman introduced Constitutional amendments to oppose abortions, this still being a main, if distant, aim of the anti-abortionists. By May 1980 19 states had called for a Constitutional Convention. By 1982, two alternative strategies were being put forward. The first was the Human Life Statute, which aimed to take advantage of a section of the Supreme Court which had made the decision that it was unable 'to resolve the difficult question of when life begins' (Isaacson 1981). The Bill would simply state that 'For the purpose of enforcing the 14th Amendment not to deprive persons of life without due process of law, human life shall be deemed to exist from conception'. This Bill would only need simple majorities in both Houses, but there were doubts about its constitutionality. An alternative strategy was therefore put forward by Senator Hatch. He proposed a 'Human Life Federation Amendment', which would authorize Congress and the states to regulate or prohibit abortion in order to 'restore to the representative branches of government the authority to legislate with respect to the practice of abortion' (Donovan 1981). The proposed wording was:

> The right to abortion is not secured by this constitution. The Congress and the several States shall have the concurrent power to restrict and prohibit abortions, provided that a law of a State more restrictive than a law of Congress shall govern.

The idea was that this constitutional amendment would have an easier chance of passage and ratification by three-quarters of the states. Thereafter, restrictions could be imposed constitutionally.

In order to support their case in Congress, both sides on the abortion issue tried to oust members who did not share their views. Anti-choice groups, however, seem to have had the greater success in influencing members of Congress.

Anti-abortionists have also targeted certain members. As Senator Bob Packwood stated: 'If the Right to Life groups can defeat 8 or 10 House members, and maybe one or two senators, others will get the message' (Eccles, 1978). One person they were particularly keen to unseat was Fr Robert Drinan of Boston, as can be seen from this advertisement (*Wanderer*, 7 September 1978).

URGENT!!

Please Help Retire Father Drinan
America is seeing the tragic spectacle of a Jesuit priest in Congress for eight years, who has been voting for public funding of the destruction of innocent pre-born children.

BUT AT LAST WE CAN HAVE A PRO-LIFE CANDIDATE WHO CAN RETIRE FATHER DRINAN!

NORM WALKER IS A STAUNCH PRO-LIFER AND OUTSTANDING MORAL LEADER!

There is no Republican candidate. The September 19th Democratic primary is our only opportunity. We need the help of everyone who is concerned. Time is running out.

In this campaign the anti-abortionists were unsuccessful, but Fr Drinan was 'retired' under instructions from Rome. Furthermore, several well known pro-choice Senators targeted by anti-abortionists have lost their seats.

6.3.4 States

The separation of powers between the presidency, Congress and the courts which occurs at the national level is mirrored in each of the states, with the state governors being the nearest equivalent of the president. The Supreme Court now allows states to regulate abortion in the following ways:

* they can ban elective abortions after viability;
* they can allow parental control or notification for those under 18 years;
* they can introduce waiting periods;
* they can introduce informed consent or counseling;
* they can enforce record keeping.

These areas mean that many state legislatures will have abortion bills before them. For example, four out of five states ban non-therapeutic abortions in the last three months of pregnancy (Kaiser 2001). We have discussed the fact that many of the states are very conservative. An interesting article from a disgruntled opponent of abortion was entitled 'Catholic States are pro-abortion'. In this, he drew attention to the fact that there are four states with an over 40 per cent Catholic population, namely Rhode Island, Massachusetts, New Jersey and Connecticut. However, their Senators are all pro-choice. He pointed out that, in contrast, the five states most opposed to abortion – Utah, Oklahoma, Wyoming, Idaho and Kansas – have only an 8.2 per cent Catholic population (Kendra 2002).

Anti-abortion groups have tried to persuade the states to pass laws restricting funding for abortion, and also to reduce rights in areas where the Supreme Court was not specific. After the Hyde amendment became law, states were forced to discontinue the funding of abortion using state monies without matching federal funds. They could stop funding altogether, or only allow abortion in restrictive categories such as rape or incest. However, they could decide to pay the full cost of abortions for poor women unless barred from doing so by the state's legislature. These possibilities meant that the conflicts that occurred at the federal level were often replayed in the states.

By September 1981, only nine states, including New York, voluntarily funded Medicaid abortions. In addition, Massachusetts and California paid for them because their state constitutions provided for equal treatment, and Pennsylvania and New Jersey funded abortions during court proceedings. Overall, the Government's Centre for Disease Control reported that 85 per cent of needy women who might get Medicaid abortions lived in states that continued paying (*Newsday*, 5 September 1981). The most recent information for 2000 showed that over three in five women seeking abortions lived in states where there was state coverage towards the cost for the poor (Henshaw and Finer 2003).

We have seen that, since the anti-abortion lobby persuaded the Supreme Court to allow it to restrict the rights of minors, many states have passed laws doing just that.

Another area where many states have been active is on the question of 'partial birth abortions'. Laws have been passed against these in 30 states including Alabama, Alaska, Arkansas, Louisiana, all in 1997; Kentucky, Oklahoma, Virginia, and West Virginia in 1998 and Montana in 1999. More than 20 states have had their laws challenged. In New Jersey, for example, the law has been stalled since 1997, in part because the governor did not think it was constitutional. In all but a few cases, in fact, the laws have been found to be unconstitutional. When on 28 June 2000 the Supreme Court overthrew the Nebraska law, it led to further rethinking among state lawyers. The lawyers in Nebraska planned to go back to the drawing board, and Laurence Tribe of Harvard Law School said that many states would follow suit. Missouri Governor Mel Carhanan commented that the Supreme Court decision 'makes it clear that a similar Missouri law is unconstitutional'. A commentator from New Mexico, however, said that he felt the Nebraska ruling would not effect the situation in New Mexico because the proposed state law was different in that, unlike the Nebraska law, it had a clearly define exemption to protect the woman's health. In Iowa, a commentator took a different approach, suggesting that the addition of a different judge could change the decision of the Supreme Court.

California and 26 other states had by June 2003 laws mandating punishment for harming a fetus during the course of a crime. Although the laws make an exception for voluntary acts such as abortion itself. On Christmas Eve 2002 Laci Peterson, who was eight months pregnant, disappeared and was found murdered. Her husband has been charged with two murders – that of the wife and of the child she was carrying. It is known that the woman planned to call her child Conner and it looks that a federal law on the issue now renamed the Laci and Conner Bill could be passed by the time this book is published.

So the anti-abortion groups have tried to persuade states to pass laws restricting abortion especially in areas where the Supreme Court was not specific. There appears to be a high level of activity and in the first five months of 2003 the right presented about 115 anti-abortion bills to state legislatures according to figures provided by the Centre for Reproductive Rights (Goldenberg 2003). Overall, therefore, the political system in the USA is such that there are great possibilities for the development of new laws and the controversy that develops with the potential changes.

In fact in some areas the states have also begun to attack contraception and in Missouri, where the right has recently gained control women under the age of eighteen have to receive their parents permission to obtain birth control pills (Goldenberg 2003).

6.4 Conclusion

I wrote an article for the British Journal *Political Quarterly* back in 1978 entitled: 'Abortion: why the issue had not disappeared'. In this article I considered the reasons why abortion was still a political issue in Britain whereas there had been no serious attempts to overturn other liberalizing measures such as homosexuality or the abolition of capital punishment. I proposed the reason for this to be that on top of the opposition of the right wing there was the added opposition of the Catholics. Dr Christopher Tietze, the leading US expert considered the position from an American perspective and told me that he was not surprised by the continuance of the controversy and that he expected abortion to be an issue well after his lifetime. He was right and abortion continues to be a major source of conflict in the USA in the way in which it is not in Britain.

There are a number of reasons for the greater controversy in the USA. First of all the doctrine of the separation of powers means that there is the potential for action to be taken within the judiciary, the Presidency, Congress and the individual states. This contrasts with the more unified situation in the United Kingdom. In addition, there is the fact that the Supreme Court decision left the USA with a very permissive law despite the fact that the society is very conservative. In addition the USA is much to the right politically compared to the UK and the rest of Western Europe. The fact that capital punishment has not yet been abolished also differentiates the USA from other developed countries and the maintenance of laws against homosexuality contrasts markedly to the political attitudes in Britain.

Chapter 7

The Politics of Legal Abortion in the UK since 1967

After the Abortion Act of 1967, many people felt that the issue was settled. There was a confidence about the changes. In the 1960s, suicide had ceased to be a criminal offence, the death penalty had been abolished, homosexuality had been legalized and birth control had become openly available to single people. It seemed that the legalization of abortion was just part of an overall change in attitude towards 'crimes without victims' (Schur 1965). However, in subsequent years there was a great deal of controversy and by the end of 1982 there had been ten Bills concerned with abortion, of which eight were intended to restrict the working of the Act. Since that time, however, things have been much quieter and we have seen that Britain has not had the degree of controversy over abortion that has occurred in the USA.

There does appear to have been further liberalization in behaviour. The changes in terms of greater freedom of sexual morality seem to have been consolidated. Living together before marriage is now generally seen as acceptable behaviour, and the continued movement towards sexual equality has enabled women to have greater control over their lives. Attitudes to abortion amongst the general public have also liberalized, and the medical profession now supports legal abortion. Since the passing of the 1967 abortion law, many of the activists believed that the issue had been decided and so moved on to other campaigns. For example, some prominent ALRA members wanted to spread birth control information in order to help to reduce the number of abortions. A passage from ALRA's Annual Report for 1969–70 read as follows:

> The executive committee believes that the abortion problem will assume a proper perspective in the eyes of many members of the public only when it is seen as part of an overall campaign to avoid unwanted pregnancies.

This suggested that the best course for ALRA, both from the point of view of reducing the need for abortion and of defending, and perhaps later extending, the Abortion Act, lay in a campaign for better facilities in the whole field. At the AGM in 1970, it was decided to vote over a large part of ALRA's reserves to the Birth Control Campaign. This move displayed a confidence that the Act could be maintained fairly easily and it was passed despite the opposition of a few key workers. Diane Munday, an activist particularly against the decision told me:

> I was out on a limb. You see I was the one that was going to these anti-abortion meetings and getting the feel of the audiences; seeing how unscrupulous they were in putting their case, and I've never underrated the Catholic Church and I think so many of our people do ... It is the oldest pressure group in the business. It is wealthy and powerful and one should never underrate its power.

In retrospect, it can be seen that many misjudged the opposition. However, it is in some degree understandable that the change which had been achieved after so long should be regarded as safe while its effects were being evaluated.

Meanwhile, the pressure against the Act came not from disquiet amongst the general population, nor from those performing the operations. Rather, there have been other factors involved. In fact the opposition can be divided into two.

7.1   Anti-Choice Forces

While the pressure from the supporters of the Act declined, pressure from the anti-abortionists increased. When abortion was illegal, those fighting the law had a number of advantages. The presence of an underground network providing abortions made a mockery of the provisions of the law, and those with access to the services of a Harley Street doctor often felt an obligation to others who were having to make do with unqualified and possibly unskilled operators. However, after legalization these advantages diminished, and the opponents of the law were able to capitalize on the changes. First of all abortion became visible for the first time, and statistics showed it to be relatively common. Furthermore, the number of recorded abortions kept rising in the years to 1973, and seemed to give credence to the theories about people becoming 'abortion-minded' and using abortion as a contraceptive. There were also problems arising from the fact that Britain was the first major Western European country to liberalize, so large numbers of foreign women began to come over, giving rise to comments about Britain being the 'abortion capital of the world'. Those arriving at the airports would not know where to go, so newspaper reports talked about 'taxi touts'. Attempts were made to create a moral panic and, while these were not totally successful, the fears aroused helped recruitment amongst those inclined towards an anti-abortion position.

7.1.1   LIFE

At the time of the 1967 Act SPUC was the only anti-abortion pressure group, but in August 1970 it was joined in battle by a second group, LIFE; this had its origins in the correspondence columns of the religious press, taking a position much closer to that held by the Catholic Church. When it was first formed, Norman St John Stevas, MP, spent half his weekly column in the *Catholic Herald* attacking it for 'dividing the forces of righteousness.' There was certainly the potential for conflict, for LIFE had the aim of outlawing all abortions. In a pamphlet entitled 'Fifteen Errors of the Abortionist' (n.d.) LIFE disagreed with abortion in rape cases, arguing that it 'won't undo the horrible fact of rape and will add a new horror'.

LIFE opposed the abortion of a disabled fetus, and arguing that 'to destroy a child because he or she is not perfect is elitist'. It also argues that while, after birth, the law gives the disabled person equal protection, before birth the person 'is officially worthless – to be hunted down by pre-natal diagnostic tests and aborted' (pre-birth screening). The differences in position were used to lead to disputes with SPUC. An article in *LIFE News* (Autumn 1978) declared:

> We have tried gradualism and found it does not work. We must be bold and go the whole 'hog'. We must fight on principles and openly tell the world that there can no more be a halfway house on this issue than there can on, say, piracy, blackmail, racism or torture. In the short run absolutism may seem absurd. In the long run it is the only thing that will succeed.

This was obviously a direct challenge to the gradualist stance taken by SPUC and this debate, of course, mirrors the earlier ones that occurred in the pro-choice movement in Britain. As in that case, it seems that the gradualists have kept the predominant position but even in its early days LIFE was hoping for a change:

> We must take courage from America. After a debate similar to ours, the absolutists are in charge there. The Right to Life movement has rejected gradualism, and makes no bones about going for total victory – an Amendment to the Constitution to override the fateful decision of the Supreme Court on 22 January 1973 which opened the floodgates of American abortion (*LIFE News*, Autumn 1978).

SPUC has moved closer to the absolutist position of LIFE in recent years. Consequentially, things have been more harmonious, and in September 2001, Professor Scarisbrick, the most prominent member of LIFE, was invited to speak at SPUC's national conference at Newcastle.

LIFE has many centres where it helps pregnant women and also engages in various political and research activities. One controversial piece of research it financed studied the relationship between abortion and breast cancer. On 5 December 2001, BBC News On Line carried a headline 'Anger over Abortion Cancer Study'. The claim was made by LIFE that abortion increases the risk of breast cancer by up to 50 per cent. However, the report quoted Professor Allan Templeman of the RCOG as saying 'No causal link between abortion and breast cancer has been proven'.

LIFE is opposed to the view that birth control can reduce unwanted pregnancies and in a press release (1 June 2001) Nuala Scarisbrick, a trustee, commented 'Since the safe sex message was introduced in earnest in the 1980s, there is no evidence that it has worked at all. On the contrary it has helped the spread of sexually transmitted diseases'. She went on to say (wrongly) that there were soaring teenage pregnancy rates and that the abortion rate increases year by year. Her proposed solution was that, as a matter of urgency, people should 'empower girls to say "no" and boys to respect this'. On 27 June 2002 LIFE published a press release headed 'No, No, No' which said it was outraged by a proposal that the Department of Health should supply free condoms and birth control pills to school children. Nuala Scarisbrick commented 'It will only cause more teenage pregnancy while doing nothing to stop the spread of STDs'. A LIFE leaflet entitled 'abstinence' suggested that a positive self-affirming choice would teach self control not birth control. Even those with sexual experience, it said, could start again and pledge to save sex until marriage. The leaflet included a space in which to sign the pledge.

7.1.2   *The Society for the Protection of Unborn Children*

After the Abortion Act came into force, SPUC needed to rethink its tactics. One rule it changed was the one which did not allow Catholics on to the executive. Phyllis Bowman, the SPUC Press Secretary, became converted to Catholicism and, in 1975, took over as director. In an interview with her, I suggested that SPUC had been more willing to compromise than LIFE (14 May 1979). She disagreed with me and set out her organization's position as follows:

With SPUC we have always stated categorically that we have people who accept abortion for general medical indications and those who take an absolute stand, and these have come together to fight against the Abortion Act 1967. That is not compromising; it is an agreed stand. The other thing is from my own point of view. I personally take an absolute stand on abortion. This is what I teach a child. On the other hand I have never fought for an absolute law. I do not think, in certain circumstances, if a woman were dying, you could force her to make a martyr of herself by law. I feel on this with the doctors who carry out abortions for genuine medical reasons. Aleck Bourne put this in a nutshell. He once said to me that had he been able to save the baby of the girl who had been raped and to save the mother from her trauma, he'd have saved both. But with the abortionist, it is a deliberate act of killing to make sure certain humans don't survive.

Thus she would like all abortions made illegal except to save the life of the woman.

It seems from these comments that SPUC is taking a more moderate line than LIFE or the American organizations. I questioned her further as to whether she felt that going for minor changes, such as a reduction of the time limits, could weaken the pressure for a stronger Bill later. I drew attention to some opposition to piecemeal changes in the United States on these grounds. She replied that she felt that LIFE might take that view but: 'It's rather like saying in Nazi Germany that you wouldn't save certain Jews because you couldn't save the lot. I find that argument arrogant.' However, as mentioned in the discussion of LIFE, SPUC has increasingly moved to a more absolutist position. This led to a major conflict in the late nineties which resulted in Phyllis Bowman leaving the organization she founded, in acrimonious circumstances.

In the current parliament (2003), the chances of an anti-abortion bill are slim and the chance of one being successful nonexistent. Consequently, SPUC has been working on a number of issues. It fought the plan of the government to sell the 'morning after' pill without a prescription and, in 2002, mounted a challenge to the that pill on the grounds that it was an abortifacient under the 1861 Offences Against the Person's Act. This was rejected by the courts; however. SPUC is actively involved in trying to prevent the 1967 Act from being extended to Northern Ireland. It also had some success in opposing the case of Diane Petty, a woman with motor neurone disease who wanted the right to assisted suicide. She lost in both the UK and the European Courts and eventually died of natural causes in 2002.

7.2   Pro-Choice Organizations

Several of these have been important. In the 1970s, an organization called The
Coordinating Committee in the Defence of the 1967 Act (Co-Ord) was formed,
and this was an umbrella group to which most of the major organizations
belonged. I was appointed adviser to the group on my return from the USA
in 1978. This organization did not aim at extending the Act. It was disbanded
after the Corrie Bill fell in 1980, in part because it was clear that the anti-choice
groups had shot their bolt, and also because the agenda was now to extend the
Act to give women the right of choice in this area that they had elsewhere.

7.2.1   Abortion Law Reform Association

This is by far the oldest of the groups advocating an extension of abortion
rights. In chapter eight, we shall see that it was behind the extension of the
law to include rape in 1938, and was also the primary group behind the 1967
Act. In the 1970s it moved to advocate a woman's right to choose, and when
the National abortion Campaign (NAC) was formed as the mass movement
it played a special role. For example, ALRA was invited to organize the mass
lobbies of parliament, while NAC provided the people to lobby. Its role also
included commissioning opinion polls, writing to MPs, carrying out research,
writing reports and developing educational materials for schools.

In 1975, ALRA changed its aims to promote a woman's right to choose
abortion up to 12 weeks of pregnancy, and in 1977 this right was extended to
viability. However, in 2002 at its AGM, ALRA took the view that it should
seek abortion on request up to 14 weeks, and that there should be no change
in the law from 14 weeks to viability.

Apart from activities mentioned elsewhere such as working with *Woman's
Own* on a poll at the time of the Corrie Bill, the organization has made various
contributions. For example, it became concerned that there were not enough
doctors being trained in abortion techniques; I cooperated in carrying out a
survey of the views of consultants, the evidence of which was publicized.
Another survey conducted by Jane Roe looked at the availability of abortion
according to area, publicizing those areas where women were more likely to
have to pay for their operations.

7.2.2   National Abortion Campaign

This organization was formed in 1975, and differed from ALRA in that it aimed to be a mass organization. On 21 June 1975, 20,000 people demonstrated against the James White anti-abortion Bill and in October the same year the group had its first national conference. It called for:

- free abortion on demand on the National Health Service;
- the incorporation of private clinics within the National Health Service;
- no forced sterilization with abortion;
- increased research and training;
- the removal of anti-abortion doctors from positions where they can obstruct women's choice.

In addition, it has always had a policy of not permitting men on to its management committee, although I was once invited to speak to it. For a time it was taken over by a group of supporters of Trotsky and took rather extreme positions calling, for example, for abortions to be legal throughout the whole pregnancy. At one Co-Ord meeting, Madeleine Simms proposed that NAC should be excluded because of its extreme views. She took the view that it could be helpful to the movement if there were these 'wild women of the left' next to whom the other organizations would appear moderate: 'We could say to MPs we are the reasonable ones.' The expulsion did not occur.

In 1999 there was a move by the Royal Bank of Scotland to enter into a business relationship with Pat Robertson, the ultra right-wing president of the Free Congress Association. NAC published a press release (26 May) which attacked the proposal and reprinted one of Robertson's statements which said: 'Feminism is about being anti-family and it encourages women to leave their husbands, kill their children, practice witchcraft, destroy capitalism and become lesbians.'

The NAC Newsletter in 2001 reported that, in the General Election of that year, the Pro Life Alliance did not have enough candidates to repeat its 1997 feat of fielding sufficient Parliamentary Candidates to receive free advertising space on national television services. Furthermore, it reported their share of the vote was 26 per cent lower than in 1997. In 2002, the NAC website contained words of support for Catholics for a Free Choice, with its campaign for the Catholic Church to participate in the UN like the other world religions as a non-governmental organization and not as a state.

7.2.3   *Pro Choice Alliance/Voice for Choice*

The Pro Choice Alliance was formed in 1988, its two main proponents being two ALRA members, Hilary Jackson and Fiona Simpson. At the end of 1988 Hilary rang Jane Roe to 'kick start the organization'. They were hoping for a Labour victory in 1992, which would open the way for a new bill to give women the right to choose. The further victory for the Conservatives meant that this strategy would have to go on the back burner.

One organization that did develop, however, was the All-Party Parliamentary group to promote abortion rights. Members of the government do not belong to the group, but in February 2003 there were 70 MPs in the group and 37 peers. With the victory of the Labour Government in 1997, optimism was renewed. Jane Roe (personal interview 19 November 2002) commented:

> We had a great deal of support. We felt 'our friends are now in parliament'. People like Patricia Hewitt and Harriet Harman were keen supporters of ours. Betty Lockwood was very supportive and she said that we should pursue abortion on request. She introduced us to Baroness Joyce Gould and the All-Parliamentary Group was set up with about 20 active members. In 1998 we changed to Voice for Choice, still under my leadership. However, there were two problems in introducing a bill. First we had to get a supporter high up in the ballot, and secondly the person would need the support of the government. Our chief supporter, Joyce Gould, was very close to the prime minister and her first loyalty was to the Labour Party. One of our most prominent supporters, a female Labour MP, was number eight in the ballot, and even she would not take a Bill. Increasingly, back benchers are taking what are in fact government Bills. In the long term this is probably much better for their careers. In fact, we heard that there had been an informal agreement not to introduce an abortion bill for ten years; our strategy was therefore to continue to argue for a woman's right to choose, but to do so in the realisation that this would not occur; meanwhile, we worked towards an improvement of services on the NHS.

7.2.4   *Family Planning Association (FPA)*

The FPA has an important role in working for improved education on issues related to contraception and abortion. In Autumn 2002 its Chief Executive, Ann Weyman, gave evidence to the Health Select Committee, urging that women should be provided with abortion on request to cut through the present over-bureaucratic procedure. Amongst her other recommendations were:

* nurses should have a greater role in performing abortions;
* abortions could take place out of hospital settings, in clinics and health centres;

- women should have greater control over the method of abortion offered to them. Only a third of services provided medical abortion;
- the second stage of medical abortion could be administered by the woman herself at home (FPA 2002b).

The FPA is without doubt the major educational force in the UK in the area of fertility control and is an organization well respected by both academics and politicians.

These, then, are the major organizations in the UK.

7.3   Early Attempts at Restriction

In July 1969, Norman St John Stevas tried to introduce an amending Bill into the House under the ten-minute rule. His measure claimed to be merely rectifying certain abuses with the support of the medical profession. A 'ten-minute rule' Bill does not stand a chance of becoming law but is, rather, a method of raising an issue for possible consideration later. He was defeated by 11 votes. In the following year, a similar Bill was introduced by Bryant Godman Irvine, but since this was also facing defeat, its supporters talked it out to prevent a vote being taken. These defeats led to the view that the Abortion Act was safe so long as a Labour government was in power. When the Tories won in 1970, Norman St John Stevas began to seek out support for a change in the law. However, as he explained in his column in the *Catholic Herald*: 'There is little chance of getting amending legislation without a preceding full scale enquiry ... I have worked for it for more than three years' (Hindell and Simms 1971, p. 221).

The Lane Committee, formed in June 1971, set out to investigate the way the Act was working, not its underlying principles. Evidence was received from 194 organizations and 529 individuals, and overall the Committee seems to have carried out its research thoroughly. The Report published in April 1974 largely supported the way that the Act was being operated:

> We have no doubt that the gains facilitated by the Act have much outweighed any disadvantages for which it has been criticised. The problems which we have identified in its working, and they are admittedly considerable, are problems for which solutions should be sought by administrative and professional action, and by better education of the public. They are not, we believe, indications that the grounds set out in the Act should be amended in a restrictive way. To

do so … would be to increase the sum of human suffering and ill health, and probably drive more women to seek the squalid and dangerous help of the back-street abortionist (Lane Report 1974, p. 184).

However, while it did propose a reduction of the time limit to 24 weeks, it was obviously a great blow to the anti-abortionists.

7.3.1 James White Bill

This had its Second Reading on 7 February 1975 and was passed by 203 votes to 88, and then went, by agreement, to a Select Committee. It set out to restrict the grounds for abortion – in particular, to exclude abortions performed on social grounds; although James White, the MP for Glasgow Pollock, and sponsor of the Bill, said that he did not take a 'hard line on abortion' and that abortion should be available for women with problems (Hansard, 7 February 1975). However, White argued that the Act was being interpreted too liberally, and that certain doctors would perform abortion on request for cash, which was against the wishes of the sponsors of the original Act. He stated that he and his supporters 'want to make the 1967 Act work as it was intended to work' (Hansard, 7 February 1975).

The Bill jolted the labour movement into action; and in 1975, the Trades Union Congress (TUC) Women's Advisory Council, the TUC and the Labour Conference all opposed the Bill and called for abortion on request. With these developments the abortion rights movement took a new turning and, for the first time, the advocates of free choice began to develop mass support of a kind that could match the opposition. There was, however, by no means total support for abortion on request. Many of those in the agencies felt that the existing position should simply be defended. The doctors' organizations that opposed restrictions reflected this divide. Doctors in defence of the 1967 Act took the view that it would work to keep the Act as it was, but a second group, 'Doctors for a Woman's Choice', aimed to give women the right to choose especially in the early months of pregnancy. In later years this group has increased in importance.

The Select Committee was seen by some in the anti-choice groups as a second delaying tactic to the Lane Committee, however, it aimed to examine Mr White's proposals in some detail. The Committee was viewed by pro-choice groups as simply a device for forcing restrictions. They believed that the talk of abuses of the Act was just a tactical ploy in order to cut back services, and there is no doubt that in this they were at least partially correct.

The Lane Committee had already sifted the evidence, so at best the Select Committee could only repeat the analysis of the same material. Faced with sitting through what they felt to be a charade, the six pro-choice members on the Select Committee resigned.

The level of debate in the Committee left something to be desired, for in the published evidence virtually all the old arguments against contraception were revised and used against abortion. Professor Scarisbrick of LIFE talked of abortion as 'national suicide', the Rev. John Stevenson of the Church of Scotland said abortion undermined the family unit (Select Committee 1976, p. 160), Margaret White of SPUC said it increased mental disturbance and LIFE quoted the suggestion of the Wynns (1973) that abortion in a high percentage of cases led to sterility (Select Committee 1976b, p. 22). However, the most bizarre point came when Leo Abse, an anti-abortionist but a supporter of birth control, used the argument that 'great men would not be born' against the Methodists, who were the most liberal of the religious groups giving evidence. John Wesley, the leader of the Methodists was the fifteenth child, and one of the favourite arguments against contraception was that if Susanna Wesley had used it there would have been no Methodist Church. It was strange that a champion of birth control should use this argument (Select Committee 1976b, p. 176).

The recommendations coming from the Committee were relatively mild. The main one was that there should be a reduction in the time limit to twenty weeks, with certain exceptions for fetal or maternal health. There was, however, no advocacy of a change of grounds. On this issue the report stated: 'Your committee … make no recommendation: a decision must be left to the individual consciences of Members' (Select Committee 1976a, p. 5). These proposals were so mild that the press officer of BPAS toyed with welcoming the report as a justification that the Act was working well. However, others suspected that the proposals were designed to obtain a large majority on a mild Bill which could then be stiffened at the committee stage: the proponents of later restrictive Bills would say that they were following the recommendations of the Select Committee.

After the Select Committee reported in July 1976, there were several minor Bills which attempted to legislate its recommendations or some variant of them. The first two, introduced by William Benyon, Conservative MP for Buckingham in 1977, and Sir Bernard Braine (Conservative MP for Essex South East) in 1978, both had little chance of success. One of the crucial arguments was that the time limit for abortion should be reduced from 28 weeks at least to 24 weeks as recommended by the Lane Committee, or to twenty weeks as suggested by the Select Committee. The argument for a reduction found support in parliament and from the general public. However, the anti-abortionists did not want just this change. Their aim was to gain as many restrictions as possible. One of the divisions was over whether to accept a mild change, which could then prevent others at a later date. The issue of compromise was also one for the pro-choice groups. For example, at the time of the Benyon Bill in 1977, secret approaches were made to those on the Parliamentary Select Committee for a very mildly restrictive Bill. There was support for this amongst some pressure group operators, who saw it as a way of getting the abortion issue out of the way without having any real affect on availability. However Jo Richardson, MP, told me that she and the other women on the Committee believed in fighting all along the line. The Benyon Bill therefore fell when it ran out of time at the end of the parliamentary session. Braine's Bill was a ten-minute rule Bill and so it did not progress.

7.3.2   John Corrie Bill

Once the Conservatives had won the election by a substantial majority in 1979, it became clear that an anti-abortion Bill was a distinct possibility and that it would have a good chance of becoming law. The Scottish Conservative MP John Corrie drew number one in the ballot, and announced his intention to introduce a Bill which would reduce the time limit of abortion to 16 weeks. It would also restrict the grounds of abortion by abolishing the rule that a woman could obtain an abortion if the risk to her health by continuing the pregnancy was greater than if the pregnancy were terminated.

The parliamentary conditions mirrored many of those present at the time of the passage of the original Act in 1967. First of all there was a government with a substantial majority. Next, the timing of the election meant that there would be a long parliamentary session and finally, there were people in positions of power who would favour the Bill. Norman St John Stevas, for example, was leader of the House and in charge of the parliamentary timetable. Margaret Thatcher was known, too, to be in favour of some change. The Bill was also aided by a well-orchestrated publicity campaign. In the run up to the General Election, there were three stories of abortions resulting in live births. Two of these were known earlier, but the stories were released at the time of maximum impact. The anti-abortionists were clearly attempting to strike at the most sensitive area – late abortions – just as, in the past, advocates of legalization had concentrated on cases of rape. The tactics worked in that a great many Members of Parliament felt that they should back Corrie's Bill to reduce the time limit. This contributed to the high support at the Second Reading on 13 June 1979 with seven out of ten (71 per cent) of those voting being in support (Marsh and Chambers 1981, p. 105). There was a great deal of confusion, but the official voting breakdown showed that the Conservative support was overwhelming, with 93 per cent voting in favour, compared to only 40 per cent of Labour. All the seven voting Irish MPs supported the Bill. The wide difference between Labour and Conservative members in voting patterns is a continuation of the situation since the 1960s, and also compares with experience in the United States. The voting patterns in 1979 also confirm my earlier finding (Francome 1978b) that members who supported abortion rights were also opposed to capital punishment: 101of the 102 members who voted against Corrie also opposed the death penalty, while supporters of Corrie voted for capital punishment by a majority of 128 to 97 (Francome 1984, p. 176). The likely effect of the changes was open to debate. Although Professor Scarisbrick had said that the number of abortions would be reduced by about two-thirds, Corrie denied this and, at a later date, said he wanted to reduce the number of abortions by 20 per cent (*Guardian*, 13 July 1979).

After success at the Second Reading, a bill passes to the Committee Stage. The role of the Parliamentary Committee is to consider the Bill in some detail and to report back to the House of Commons for a Third Reading. The composition of the Committee is in proportion to the vote at the Second Reading. Consequently, Corrie and his supporters had almost total control of what changes were to be introduced. However, supporters of the Bill were divided. A group which included Michael Ancram, Conservative MP for Edinburgh South, wanted the Bill to remain very restrictive, while Corrie and some allies were more willing to make concessions.

The tactics of the pro-choice MPs were clear. There was no opportunity to filibuster the Bill or get any changes at this stage. They therefore had to wait to introduce any substantial amendments on the floor of the House of Commons, where they felt that the Bill could be watered down. Parliament's procedure is that the Committee discusses the Bill and, at the Report Stage, the whole House can consider anything the Committee has missed. If any amendment has been considered in Committee, it cannot be discussed again at Report. The tactics of the opponents of restriction were, therefore, to change the Bill as far as possible by force of logic, but not to introduce any amendment they felt could pass at Third Reading.

In the weeks leading to the Report Stage of the Bill, which was due to start on 8 February 1980, it was clear that both sides would aim to organize as many events as possible to influence parliamentary opinion. The Bill's supporters arranged their Mass Lobby of the House of Commons on 30 January 1980, and the pro-choice groups organized theirs for the following Tuesday (5 February). Estimates suggested that at least 10,000 were present on each occasion, and the opponents of the Bill were pleased that they were able to match the anti-abortionists in organizing this kind of event.

It was also necessary to monitor public opinion, and three polls were published between 1 February and 6 February 1980. I contacted *Woman's Own*, and the magazine agreed to pay for a Gallup Poll (sample: 1,004) that would contain more questions than any previous poll. Gill Cox, the *Woman's Own* researcher, agreed the final wording of the questions with Gallup's Bob Wybrow. We were anxious that the questions should reflect the abortion decision as closely as it could be arranged. The final wording of the crucial question on the right to choose was therefore: 'Do you think that the choice as to whether or not to continue a pregnancy should or should not be left to the woman in consultation with her doctor?'

The result showed that more than four out of five women, and seven out of ten men, agreed with the right to choose. This result gained wide publicity and was carried in all the national newspapers. The opinion of the women in the survey was considered particularly important. The *Observer* editorial, for example, read:

MR. CORRIE'S BAD BILL

Mr. John Corrie's Abortion (Amendment) Bill, which goes back to the floor of the House of Commons this week, is a partisan measure. Its supporters are many and various, but the backbone of the 'restrictive' movement is Roman Catholic. The Church abhors the destruction of the foetus as a 'crime' against a 'person'; it is a matter of conscience. The Corrie Bill floats on a powerful tide. Fortunately, it is not too late for Parliament to recognise that the right to exercise one's own conscience is not the same as to ram that conscience down the throats of others. The right of a woman to take responsibility for what happens to her own body is also a crucial part of the debate.

Four out of five women, according to a survey conducted last week for 'Woman's Own', think the choice should be left to the woman concerned in consultation with her family doctor. A majority of all adults believe the law should be left as it is or made more liberal. Members of Parliament, who are pre-dominantly male and in that sense unrepresentative in an issue of this kind, should take serious note of the fact that this proposed reform is not wanted by the public at large, and most definitely not wanted by women (*Observer*, 3 February 1980).

These results were broadly confirmed by a survey in the *Sunday Times* (3 February 1980) which also showed that most people were in favour of a reduction in the time limit. However, another Gallup Poll sponsored by SPUC and published in the *Daily Mail* on 6 February 1980 asked people whether they agreed with 'abortion on demand' and the results seemed to show that most people were in favour of restrictions.

Apart from polls and lobbying, both sides used other techniques to demonstrate support. On 25 January, Willie Hamilton, MP put down an 'early day motion' which pointed out that the Bill intended to change the criteria for abortion (*Times*, 29 January 1980). The opposition put down an alternative motion showing support. The medical profession continued its opposition to the Bill, and Doctors for a Woman's Choice on Abortion organized its own lobby at the House. These ways of influencing the climate of opinion were obviously important, but it was clear that time was going to be a crucial factor. The future for the Bill looked very uncertain when the Speaker selected 28 groups of amendments for debate (Ferriman 1980). Labour MP Jo Richardson told a group of women gathered to protest at the Bill that, with that number of amendments, 'I could keep going every Friday until July' (8 February 1980). The Members voted for a number of changes, and raised the time limit from 20 to 24 weeks. There was also evidence that the members' support for the Bill was diminishing. On 14 March 1980 Corrie was given an extra day, but when a vote was taken to close the debate it was lost by seven votes. At this point it was clear that the Bill was dead, and the following week Corrie announced he was going to withdraw it. The opponents of the Bill were pleasantly surprised that they had succeeded in stopping it and many within the pro-choice groups felt they had blunted the opposition's attack. ALRA's newsletter stated (April 1980):

> After many months of hard fighting against the Corrie Abortion (Amendment) Bill, one can now feel for once that we have really defeated the anti-abortion lobby. The extent of opposition to this attack on the 1967 Act has been so great that in the end the Bill did not only run out of time in Parliament, it also clearly lacked the political and public will for it to succeed … Of course we are not so naive as to believe that this will be the last we'll hear of the anti-abortionists. But their serious failures will inevitably hinder any future plans they may have.

The confidence amongst pro-choice groups that they had temporarily defeated the anti-abortion lobby was strengthened when Timothy Sainsbury dropped the idea of introducing an anti-abortion Bill in 1981. It seems that he was advised not to stir up the issue again, and for the first time in a number of years pro-choice groups felt that they were winning the long-term battle.

Two events in 1982 seemed to confirm this fact. The first was the failure of the Pope's visit to galvanize the anti-abortion movement. Many within the pro-choice camp were concerned that the Pope's popularity would stimulate anti-abortion feeling. The day before he arrived, however, a poll was published which showed that the British support for the right to choose an abortion was at an all-time high of 80 per cent (Francome 1982). It also showed that Catholics in Britain did not agree with official Church doctrine, and the *Daily Mail* (27 May 1982) reported:

> The survey contains some bad news for the Pope who arrives in Britain tomorrow. Seven out of ten Roman Catholics support the woman's right to choose, in opposition to the official teachings of the Church.

With this kind of evidence receiving wide publicity, the Pope's statements on the abortion issue could be seen in a wider context. SPUC attacked the poll in its newspaper (*Human Concern*, Summer 1982) and Phyllis Bowman was quoted as saying: 'The pro-abortion Gallup Poll was published in the week prior to the visit of John Paul 11 to Britain, and was obviously intended to undermine anything which the Pope said on ethical issues.' The report continued by attacking Gallup, a little unfairly in my opinion, since the major questions had all been asked before, and the date of publication was my decision and not Gallup's. Next, in 1982, MPs at the top of the Ballot (including Corrie) refused to introduce an abortion Bill. On 6 December 1982, the anti-abortionists tried a back door method of introducing a restrictive Bill into the House of Lords. It was, however, defeated at its Second Reading, by 57 votes to 42. The vote is of interest in part because it shows the social composition of the active members of the UK's highest chamber. The earlier differences according to party were confirmed by the vote. A total of 33 Labour peers opposed the bill, a ratio of ten to one, while Conservative peers were in favour by a ratio of four to one. However, many Conservatives abstained. Five of the Church of England Bishops voted for the Bill and one against. Phyllis Bowman of SPUC pointed out that 70 Catholic peers had been written to five times, but only 15 had voted, and one of these had opposed the Bill (*Universe*, 17 December 1982).

7.4   Reduction in the Time Limit

At the time of the 1967 Act, the time limit for abortion in England and Wales was set by the 1929 Infant Life Preservation Act at 28 weeks, which was linked to viability. There was no legal time limit in Scotland. There was some debate about whether the time limit would be adjusted automatically, if viability increased. This is the argument of Simon Lee, Professor of Law at Queen's University Belfast, who criticized the anti-choice groups. He said that such groups were mistaken to campaign for a reduction in the time limits because 'given developments in technology, now that foetuses could be delivered at 24 weeks, the 1929 time limits self-adjusted' (1995, p. 22). However, there were many who wanted a formal change in the law, and an amendment to the Human Fertilization and Embryology Act 1990 provided the opportunity, introducing a 24-week limit. However, the Act also introduced a new ground for abortion: 'grave permanent injury to the physical and mental health of the pregnant women.' There is no time limit for this, nor is there for 'the substantial risk of serious handicap.' The pro-choice groups at the time were reasonably happy with the safeguards to women and felt, rightly, that this relatively minor change would defuse the issue of abortion for subsequent years.

There was an attempt at the report stage to extend the Abortion Act to Northern Ireland, but this was defeated by 276 votes to 131. Lee suggested that the UK would defend this decision on the basis of the presumed difference in moral climate. However, he drew attention to the fact that this was not accepted by the European Court of Human Rights in the case of homosexuality remaining illegal in Ireland.

7.5   Women's Perceptions of the law

In 1992 Marie Stopes International carried out a study of women's perceptions of abortion, and commented 'In Britain, in the new millennium, in many respects abortion is the last taboo'.

MSI set out to determine what women wanted from abortion services. It found that women did not realize the legal restrictiveness of the current law. For example, fewer than one in four (24 per cent) women realized that, for an abortion to proceed the signatures of two doctors are required. When asked who should make the decision, only 4 per cent supported the current legal framework. Almost nine out of ten (88 per cent) believed that the decision should be with the woman concerned.

In Britain, the fact that a local anaesthetic rather than a general anaesthetic has increasingly been used is not widely known. Consequently, almost six out of ten (59 per cent) women believe that a general anaesthetic is the only treatment available to women in Britain. Only one in eight respondents (13 per cent) were able to identify correctly the 24-week legal limit on abortion. In fact, almost one in three (32 per cent) believed the legal limit was just twelve weeks. However, this might not be so surprising since my earlier research, with Wendy Savage, showed that many doctors would not carry out abortions after the first trimester.

The respondents were clearly unaware of how common abortions were in Britain. Only one in eight (12 per cent) correctly identified one in three women as having an abortion. The majority thought abortion was much rarer with 53 per cent, thinking it was one in five or fewer. In fact, almost a quarter (23 per cent) thought it was only one in ten (Marie Stopes International 2003).

What is clear from this is that most women do not have problems obtaining abortions, and they also believe that it should be readily available. This may be one of the major reasons why there is not more pressure in the UK to liberalize the law to give women the right to choose.

7.6   The Situation in Northern Ireland

The 1967 Abortion Act does not apply to Northern Ireland. There, consequently, the law is governed by the 1861 Offences Against the Person's Act amended by the 1945 Criminal Justice (Northern Ireland) Act and the 1938 Bourne Decision (see Chapter 9).

The Chair of the Equal Opportunities Commission for Northern Ireland set out the conditions for Women from Northern Ireland: They have abortions, but they do not have them at home – they go to Britain. They must pay for their terminations, and in this sense they suffer from discrimination. This particularly affects those who are economically disadvantaged who must endure an unwanted pregnancy, incur great debt, or have an illegal abortion. The fact that abortion is largely illegal in Northern Ireland means that certain antenatal tests, commonly available in Britain, are not routinely offered to women in Northern Ireland. The situation is such that women in Northern Ireland are prey to isolation, fear and loneliness to a greater extent than are women elsewhere in the UK.

My study of gynaecologists in Northern Ireland showed that 95 per cent carried out some operations, although 5 per cent said they would only do so if the fetus would not survive. More than two-thirds supported a change in the law which would leave any abortion decision to the woman and her doctor. At face value, it could seem that they would want women given the right to choose; however, answers to further questions suggest that this is not the case. Fewer than half wanted the introduction of the British law, and there were different attitudes towards whether abortion should be legal in different conditions. For instance, 70 per cent thought there should be abortion for risk to the health of the woman, while only 8 per cent said there should not the others answered 'depends'. Seven out of ten (70 per cent) also said there should be abortion for rape, which just over one in ten (11 per cent) opposed. In the case of fetal handicap, just under three in five (59 per cent) said this should be legal and 3 per cent said it should not (Francome 1994a). My survey of GPs in Northern Ireland found that seven out of ten (70 per cent) said that the decision as to whether or not to continue a pregnancy should be left to the woman in consultation with her doctor. Fewer Catholic doctors were in favour, with only just over half (55 per cent) in agreement (Francome 1994b).

In June 1993, the Standing Advisory Commission on Human Rights issued a document on the issue written by Simon Lee. It observed:

> The law on abortion in Northern Ireland is so uncertain that it violates the standards of international human rights law. It could not withstand a challenge before the European Court of Human Rights at Strasbourg. The Government should bring forward proposals to clarify the law without waiting for such a defeat (1995, p. 16).

He went on to say that Northern Ireland should have the confidence to devise a better law than exists in Britain.

7.7   The Future

In October 2002 I spoke to Madeleine Simms, who gave me her views on what should be happening. She told me that when the Labour government took office in 1997 with a 100 women MPs, she had high hopes of obtaining abortion on request in the first three months of pregnancy. She wrote about such a change to Patricia Hewitt, the Minister for Women, whose husband was very active in the pro-choice movement. However, the minister said that she did not think the issue was primarily a women's issue, and referred Madeleine to the Minister of Health. At the ALRA AGM in October 2002, Mary Porter argued that public opinion favoured abortion on request; the UK had now fallen behind other countries, and that medical practice has changed, so a strong case could be made for a change in the law. She proposed a five-stage strategy to accomplish this change. First, the production of a good document which would bring out the anomalies of the current law and explain the necessity for change, followed by a working conference where the major organizations would give commitment to change. Next, the internet would be used to develop the campaign, leading to a second conference at which members of the public would be involved. This would, in turn, lead to the introduction of a private member's bill.

However, the government does not seem to want such a change. At the ALRA AGM in 2002, Barbara Chamberlain said the position seemed to be 'We love Tony Blair, we like being in power and so go away and be nice women'. In view of such comments, and the fact that the leaders of all the three main parties have links to the Catholic Church, it seems that a liberalization of the law is unlikely. Some people are not concerned about this, however. Tim Black, the director of MSI, takes the view that people should just get on with improving services. The view of Madeleine Simms is that, since the purchasing of abortion services on the NHS is controlled by local purchasers – the primary health care trusts – people can make things change by exerting local pressure.

Chapter 8

When Abortion was Illegal I

During the eighteenth and nineteenth centuries there was a great increase in world population, largely due to improvement in the death rates. The population more than doubled from 728 million in 1750 to 1,608 million in 1900. The population of Europe rose faster than that of the world as a whole, to 401 million in 1900. In Britain the population multiplied three and a half times between 1801, when the first census was taken, and 1900, and its share in the population of Europe rose from 5.7 per cent to 9 per cent. It would have been higher but for continued emigration (Royal Commission on Population 1949, p. 7). There was also large-scale migration leading to much greater increases in the population in North America, which rose from 1.3 million in 1750 to 81 million in 1900 (Royal Commission on Population 1949, p. 7).

France was the country best known for successfully carrying out preventive checks and this was largely due to the successful use of coitus interruptus. It seems that the aristocracy first began practising the method, for in the eighteenth century their average family size was less than half that of the peasantry and their fertility rates were remarkably low in the later childbearing years (Potts and Selman 1979, p. 167). By the nineteenth century the knowledge of this method had percolated through to the rest of society, to such an extent that a French bishop sought a papal ruling to address the fact that young married men did not want to have too many children and yet could not 'morally restrain themselves from the sex union'. He complained that if questioned about their practices too closely, they absented themselves from mass. On 8 June 1842, the Holy High Court of Doctrine ruled that the father confessor need not investigate the matter; so the control of family size by the French received the tacit acceptance of the Church (*New Generation*, August 1922).

8.1   Growth of Victorian Morality

In Britain before the nineteenth century, it was mainly the middle classes who had conservative sexual attitudes, often attacking the upper class for its behaviour. In 1755, or example, *The World* talked of the vices and immorality amongst the wealthy, and commented: 'What should banish a man from all society, recommends him to the rich' (Thomas 1969 p. 87). Amongst the peasant groups there was clear recognition that young people would want to express their sexual feelings, and the main problem was to enable courtship to continue without a premature pregnancy occurring. In the absence of contraceptives, various garments were devised. In Wales, for example, women in their teens would be given a 'courting stocking', a garment which completely covered them from the waist down with room for both legs. Young people were allowed to sleep together on condition that this was not removed, and the practice was called bundling (Baker 1974, p. 14). This was also practised in the United States, and became common in Pennsylvania and New England where it was stated that the couple kept their clothes on to save fuel. In Britain, the social pressure against intercourse diminished once a couple began to court seriously. Hair (1966, 1970) calculated that between a third and a half of brides were pregnant on their wedding day. The evidence therefore shows that chastity was not the dominant practice nor even the dominant ideology, and the growth in Victorian morality is linked to the social and economic developments occurring during the nineteenth century.

One factor is the movement of the peasantry from the land. They had been driven off, by the economic pressures linked to the enclosure movement, and pressed to work in factories where the conditions were far worse than those they had encountered in the rural areas. Many people were working such long hours that their homes became almost a dormitory, and in this way the factory system destroyed much of family life. There was a great amount of poverty, which did not encourage young people to act with forethought and restraint, and the movement from the rural setting further broke down the informal sanctions on sexual behaviour. Thus the rural norms were no longer applicable and were replaced by widespread anomie. Francis Place, not one of those inclined to bewail the lack of morality, nevertheless commented in 1832 about the working-class poor: 'Girls become unchaste at a very early age as a matter of course; the whole family live in one room; and … hearing what they hear and seeing what they see, they never arrive at any notion of self respect, and the consequences are certain' (1930, p. 326). This change affected the poorer classes, while non-marital sexuality was associated with poverty, filth, drunkenness and other features of life from which the middle classes wished to disassociate themselves. Many adopted the values expressed by the religious leaders and rose up the social hierarchy. For example John Wesley, the Methodist leader, had taught his followers to work hard and be frugal: 'We must exhort all Christians to gain all they can, and to save all they can; that is, in effect, to grow rich' (Weber 1968, p. 175). Though Wesley himself opposed wealth and gave much of his money to charity, his followers tended not to follow his example but used their wealth to help their rise in social status. Commentators in the USA made similar comments. Cowan (1880, p. 122) stressed the strong correlation between work and chastity. 'Everyday employment should be as much of a necessity to every man (and woman) as is eating. A man who is constitutionally lazy and careless about working is nearly always a licentious man. An idle life and a chaste and continent life cannot possibly be found in the same individual.' A combination of these status and ideological factors must count as a major reason for the strength of the belief in chastity amongst the middle classes.

Another factor was that urbanization increased the possible segregation of the sexes. In the rural areas there had been less of a distinction between work and leisure, and women often had their own tasks in the household. In the town, however, there were few acceptable jobs, so middle-class women spent their time in piano playing or in other 'accomplishments', to enhance their position in the marriage market. This sexual segregation had sometimes occurred in the eighteenth century, but the numbers involved grew and the divisions hardened. Women were, therefore, restricted in the ways in which they were able to develop their personalities, and consequently were not valued on any grounds approaching equality. They were placed on a pedestal and were supposed to embody the virtues of society but not soil their hands with the 'evils of the world'. This idealization led to their chastity being greatly valued. As Hannah Gavron (1966, p. 64) rightly pointed out: 'The more a society places women on a pedestal as in modern Brazil or Victorian England, removed from the realities of life, the greater will the virginity of brides be prized. However, the less the division between male and female, the less is virginity considered important.' The movement to the towns also made it more possible for the middle classes to ignore sexuality. In the countryside this is difficult for it is evident in the normal cycle of animal life.

In addition, in the nineteenth century, there was a fear of sex that was related to a number of myths. One was that men had better restrict their emissions or they would be drained of energy, hence the use of the term 'to spend' rather than 'to come' for orgasm. Benfield (1972) suggests that this meant that women were a potential threat and that 'women's latent boundlessness' posed a threat to male strength and, through this, to civilization. A woman was a 'sperm absorber'. So the general idea of 'saving', transferred to the sexual field, accentuated the sexual divisions. There were some people who argued that birth control was dangerous. Routh told the Obstetrical Section of the BMA, in 1878, that women who practised contraception risked acute and chronic inflammation of the uterus, galloping cancer, permanent sterility and mania leading to suicide; and that men also risked mania involving loss of memory and mental decay.

It seems that the middle classes in the United States had an even greater fear of sexuality than their British counterparts. In 1907, Robinson noted the great fear of ejaculation amongst his clients and complained: 'A patient who notices a drop or two of semen is sure he is on the way to the insane asylum' (Benfield 1972, p. 349). Such extreme views did not seem to exist in Britain; neither did the practice of removing the clitoris. Benfield discussed the fact that in the United States the belief existed that it was so abnormal for women to enjoy sex that clitorectomy was often performed. There is evidence of operations from 1867 to at least 1904. In contrast, the British gynaecologist who performed a clitorectomy in 1858 was expelled from the London Obstetrical Society.

McGregor (1957) suggested that 'Few aspects of the period are more astonishing than the successful imposition of middle class standards on the overt sexual behaviour of the aristocracy'. One factor may be that the British upper classes were very worried by the French Revolution, which some felt was connected to immorality. The 1878 edition of the Annual Register said: 'The French revolution illustrated the connection between good morals and the order and peace of society' (Thomas 1969). It went on to argue that licentiousness could lead to the breakdown of the society. However, probably a more important factor in the middle-class domination of the sexual norms in the United Kingdom and the USA was the growth of the school system. In 1811, the Anglicans founded the 'National Society for Promoting the Education of the Poor in the Principles of the Established Church' which took over many of the schools. Armytage (1964, p. 91) comments: 'Its aim was heroic; nothing less than shouldering the whole burden of the national education.' By 1814 it had 230 schools and 40,484 pupils. In 1833 the government agreed to give money towards church building costs, so the first steps towards a national system of education were taken, a system which was strongly influenced by conservative attitudes and where religious instruction was prominent. In this way, the restrictive ideas of the middle classes, which in early times had been minority beliefs, increasingly came to be considered as the 'proper' behaviour which should be accepted as a matter of course.

In the USA, the fact that settlers came from widely differing backgrounds raised problems in understanding between different groups. Many nuances of social behaviour could be misinterpreted, so people had to develop a directness in communication. The rules had to be spelled out; consequently, the United States has had a much greater tendency to constrain behaviour by legal means and by carefully drafted codes of behaviour. Furthermore many immigrants came from countries where there were rigid sex divisions, so a double standard of sexual behaviour was imported to the United States. A final point is that when the immigrants entered US society, they had low status and were expected to become socialized into the American way of life. When the American middle classes saw deviant behaviour in immigrant groups, they regarded it as a result of lack of knowledge. Moral entrepreneurs drew attention to the high proportion of recent immigrants engaged in deviant activity. For example, the 1874 Annual Report of the Society for the Suppression of Vice (p. 6) gave the nationality of those arrested under the pornography laws: 46 were Irish, 24 were English, 20 were other nationalities and only 34 were American. So only just over one-quarter were native-born Americans, and the Society aimed to educate the 'unsocialized' deviants.

A second difference between the societies was the lack of an upper class in the United States to restrain some of the excesses of the middle classes. This is evident from the fact that when the British Obscene Publications Act was passed in 1857, it was only working-class literature which was to be suppressed: the upper class managed to insert a clause excluding works of 'literary merit' from the statute. A third difference was that there were no laws prohibiting alcohol or pre-marital sex of the kind that existed in the United States. The effects of these major differences on the debate will be considered.

8.2   Abortion Laws

During the nineteenth century most countries of Europe tightened up their provision of abortion. A law was introduced in Belgium, as in France, in 1810; the German law, based on the Prussian Penal Code of 1851, was adopted by the German Reich in 1871 (Kommers 1977); Portugal also made abortion illegal in 1854 and Holland in 1886 (amended in 1911). One slight legal movement in the other direction was in Sweden where, in the seventeenth century, abortion had been made punishable by death, but an 1864 law reduced the sentence to imprisonment for six years (Linner 1968). At the beginning of the nineteenth century, all countries under British common law allowed abortion at least until quickening – the time when movement could be felt in the womb (about 15 weeks gestation). Quickening was an important legal concept and no woman could be executed if she had passed the quickening stage, so a special jury of women was formed to feel a condemned pregnant woman's stomach and determine whether there was movement. If there was, the woman could not be executed. Parry translated a commentary published in about 1290 on the law in force at the time: 'The woman commits homicide who by potions and drugs of that sort, shall have destroyed her animate child in her womb' (1932, p. 95). British law was changed in 1803, and abortion was made illegal throughout pregnancy. In large part this was because abortion was regarded as being dangerous to women. The law also changed the law on infanticide which it said was too punitive. Hitherto, women who had concealed their pregnancy and whose child died would often be convicted of murder simply on this evidence; now, the law said that other evidence was needed (*The Times*, 29 March 1803).

The *Lancet* pointed out that for a woman quick with child the administration of a 'noxious or destructive substance' was made a capital felony. However, there was no proscription on carrying out abortions on a woman quick with child by using instruments. The *Lancet* argued that this loophole allowed abortion to save a woman's life, and vainly tried to prevent its closure (11 April 1829). However, later in the year the law was changed. The maximum penalty for aborting a woman quick with child was to be death. For a woman in an earlier part of pregnancy, the penalty was to be transportation (to Australia) for up to 14 years, or three years imprisonment with the possibility of a public whipping (Parry 1932). The death penalty was removed in 1837 and the law was changed with the Offences Against the Person Act, Sections 58 and 59 in 1861. The abortion provisions were:

> Section 58:
> Every woman being with child, who with intent to procure her own miscarriage shall unlawfully administer to herself any poison or other noxious thing … and whosoever, with intent to procure the miscarriage of any woman whether she be or be not with child shall unlawfully administer to her or cause to be taken by her any poison or other noxious thing … with the like intent shall be guilty of felony, and being convicted thereof shall be liable … to be kept in penal servitude for life.

> Section 59:
> Whosoever shall unlawfully supply or procure any poison or other noxious thing … knowing that the same is intended to be unlawfully used or employed with intent to procure the miscarriage of any woman, whether she be or be not with child, shall be guilty of a misdemeanour, and being convicted thereof shall be liable to be kept in penal servitude for the term of three years.

The law therefore made attempts at abortion illegal even if the woman was not pregnant. The specification that abortion was illegal only if the action were taken 'unlawfully' implies that legal abortion could take place in certain circumstances, a point which was to become relevant to UK, New Zealand and Australian law in later years. The 1861 Act passed through without controversy, which is not surprising, for the establishment views during the large part of the nineteenth century were that even birth control was suspect, if not illegal. The British 1861 Act was subsequently introduced into the laws of the Empire.

At the beginning of the nineteenth century English common law applied in the United States, which meant that abortion could be carried out until quickening. There was no equivalent to the British 1803 Act. Consequently, when a man named Bangs was charged with using drugs to cause an abortion, he was freed by the Massachusetts Supreme Court on the grounds that the indictment did not specify that the woman was quick with child. This case was used as a precedent in other trials including one in 1880 (Mohr 1978, pp. 5, 265). Connecticut became the first state to pass a law in 1821; it prohibited abortion on a woman 'quick with child' but left it legal for the early part of the pregnancy. In 1828, New York became the first state to pass a law without specifying that the woman should be quick with child. Means said the primary reason for the law was a desire to protect maternal health, and argued that in the early part of the nineteenth century abortion was a dangerous operation. He gave figures to suggest that the death rate from sepsis after surgery for abortion, even when performed in hospital, was over 30 per cent in 1828, when New York's first abortion law was passed (Means 1971, p. 385). Further, he argued, this was much higher than the maternal mortality rate of less than 3 per cent, so the danger of the operation was the key factor behind legal restrictions. This New York law does not seem to have led others to follow suit. In fact by 1840, only five of the 26 states banned abortion throughout pregnancy and a further five had a law banning abortion after quickening (Francome 1986, p. 30). This was to change in the latter half of the century when Mohr alleged that doctors were the primary force calling for abortion to be illegal and that the main propelling reason behind the pressure was a desire to professionalize medicine. He said that the 'anti-abortion crusade was nearly perfect' as a method of establishing the position of the regular physician. By raising its dangers and abuses, doctors could encourage the state to employ sanctions against their competitors (Mohr 1978, p. 164).

8.3   The Practice of Abortion in the USA

In the early nineteenth century, one source of demand for abortion came from single women. In a series of public lectures in 1839 Professor Hodge, the well known anti-abortionist, said that the majority of abortions were 'to destroy the fruit of illicit pleasure, under the vain hope of preserving reputation' (Hodge 1854). It seems that the number of abortions increased in the 1840s and continued at a high level. Mohr commented:

> As a reasonable guess, abortion rates in the United States may have risen from an order of magnitude approximating one abortion for every twenty-five or thirty live births during the first three decades of the nineteenth century to an order of magnitude possibly as high as one abortion for every five or six live births by the 1850s and 1860s (1978, p. 50).

Hale (1860) published an estimate that one in five pregnancies ended in abortion and that nine out of ten married women had attempted one. He said that in his home town of Chicago, he had met women with both ten children and ten abortions (Francome 1986, p. 31). Thus, there was a rise in the number of abortions, and a change in that it became largely married women who sought them. In 1800, the average American woman bore seven children. Family size reduced between 1840 and 1850, and by the end of the century it was halved to 3.6 per woman. In the mid-nineteenth century, the best known abortionist was called Madame Restell. She tried pills first, but used other methods if necessary. Her advertisements were relatively disguised, but other people were quite overt in their claims. For example on 4 January 1845, the *Boston Daily Times* advertised Dr Peter's French Renovating Pills claiming 'although very mild and prompt in their operation, pregnant females should not use them, as they invariably produce a miscarriage' (Mohr 1978, p. 53).

In 1854 Professor Hodge published *Criminal Abortion* in which he commented on the prevalence:

> We blush while we record the fact, that in this country ... educated, refined and fashionable women – yea in many respects women whose moral character is, in other respects, without reproach; mothers who are devoted, with an ardent and self-denying affection, to the children who already constitute their family, are perfectly indifferent respecting the foetus in utero. They do not seem to realise that the being within them is indeed animate (pp. 17, 18).

This latter comment is a reference to quickening. In 1859, a committee of the

Suffolk County Medical Association reported three reasons why abortion was common throughout society. One was that the belief in quickening meant that mothers did not believe the fetus was alive until movement was felt in the womb – at perhaps 15–18 weeks. Next, doctors did not concern themselves with fetal life and the third reason was 'defects in our laws, both common and statute, as regards the independent and actual existence of the child before birth as a living being'. The high number of abortions led to regular physicians, under the leadership of Horatio Robinson Storer, attacking the practice. He argued that they were dangerous for the woman's health and, like many others in the nineteenth and early twentieth century, quoted the work of Tardieu which stated that 34 abortions carried out by non-physicians led to 22 deaths (1866, p. 15). The campaign led to at least 40 anti-abortion statutes being passed from 1860–80.

In the 1860s, the British medical press began to comment on the high US abortion rate. In May 1863, the *BMJ* carried an article in which it quoted comments in the *American Medical Times* that the number of advertisements in newspapers testified to the 'wide and almost universal prevalence' of abortion (Francome 1986, p. 34).

We shall see below that in 1868 the British medical establishment became aware of abortion as part of 'baby farming'. This was the practice of parents abandoning their children. Women would often pay a sum of around five pounds to have their children taken by baby farms. One estimate in the 1860s was that each year more than 30,000 children were placed in the hands of baby farmers (Acton 1878, p. 281). Many of these would have died of mistreatment. On 3 November 1870, the *New York Times* introduced an editorial: 'Margaret Waters, the baby farmer, was executed on Tuesday. London paper.' It went on to congratulate the British authorities and argued that there were similar practices in New York:

> From a 'palatial mansion' in fifth Avenue down to wretched chambers in the slums of Chatham Street, there is accommodation for the perpetuation of infant murder suited to every rank and condition of life … In the rural districts of this State there are quiet unpretending cottages, which seem, amid embowering foliage, the chosen abode of innocence and peace, but from these places wasted baby forms are carried into nameless graves (Francome 1986, p. 35).

The article argued that respectable citizens had ceased to express indignation because they felt powerless, but that now was the time for people to rouse themselves. With this article, the paper began a year-long anti-abortion campaign. It followed up advertisements, and expressed satisfaction when a Dr Wolf received seven years imprisonment for carrying out illegal terminations. However, the numbers did not seem to reduce, and on the 23 August 1871 it called abortion 'The Evil of the Age' as the operations continued. The *New York Times* campaign did get abortifacient advertisements to disappear, for a time but by 30 January 1872 it had to admit that they had returned. In fact, it was not the *New York Times* but the puritan, Anthony Comstock, who had the greatest effect on the provision of abortion. In 1873, he persuaded Congress to pass an act which made it an offence to provide any article or medicine for causing an abortion except by a physician of good standing. It also banned the advertisement and sale of birth control appliances. He used the law to pursue abortions energetically. The Second Report of the Society for the Suppression of Vice (1876) said that 49 abortionists had been arrested, of whom 39 had been convicted and sentenced. In 1878 he succeeded in buying abortifacients from Madame Restell who committed suicide the day before her trial. Comstock also had an effect on advertisements for abortion. However, in 1888 Pomeroy said that the law on abortion was a 'dead letter' and that the operation flourished in the highest places, while the medical profession not engaged in it was silent (p. 56).

In January 1907, the journal *Critic and Guide* published an article directed towards new medical graduates which pointed out that they would be asked to carry out abortions very early in their careers. The author, Robinson, commented: 'An abortionist who is aseptic and not too clumsy, can enjoy a lucrative practice, with very few deaths, and the man who refuses to perform abortions will make enemies of many influential persons' (Francome 1986, p. 39). There were various estimates of the number of abortions in the USA in the early twentieth century. One piece of research was based on correspondence with nearly 100 doctors. A Dr Hunter estimated that there were over 100,000 abortions resulting in 6,000 deaths each year (*Medical Age*, March 1906). A major work on abortion was that of Taussig in 1910. He analysed the data of 348 women who had been pregnant: 58 per cent of them had had either induced or spontaneous abortions. One in ten admitted to having had an instrumental abortion, although Taussig commented that it was difficult to get a confession to this criminal act. Overall, he estimated 80,000 criminal abortions in New York and 6,000 to 10,000 in Chicago (p. 5). William Robinson estimated that between one in ten and one in four doctors carried out abortions regularly, and that over a million abortions were performed in the USA each year (*Critic and Guide* 1911, p. 209). In 1917, Robinson revised his estimate to say that three-quarters of doctors carried out abortions at some time (*Critic and Guide*

1917, p. 47). Robinson was also the first known consistent activist for legal abortion, and from 1913 called for it to be legalized in the early months of pregnancy (Francome 1986, p. 41).

8.3   Abortion in Britain

In Britain in the early nineteenth century, a common drug for the use of abortion was savin oil of juniper. In fact the first prosecution under the 1803 Act was in 1811 when a man was accused of giving his girlfriend a concoction made by pouring boiling water over a shrub called savin. However, he argued successfully that her feelings of shame were so great that she had threatened to commit suicide and that he had only given her the drug for amusement (Potts, Diggory and Peel 1977).

At this time, also, the medical profession sometimes carried out an abortion to protect the woman's health or life. The earliest reference I have found to this was in 1828, and it tells us something about the medical practice of the time. A woman was in shock and the doctor said that the pregnancy needed to end:

> I stated my opinion that nothing could be done but to bring on premature labour. The doctor (consulting) assented and I then suggested the use of ergot of rye; and if that failed, the necessity of puncturing the membranes. This was agreed to, and on the same day (Saturday) I proceeded to bring on labour. For this purpose I administered about half past eleven o'clock a wine glassful of infusion of ergot of rye made by infusing ergot of rye in half pint of boiling water.

The woman was five and a half months pregnant when the house next door had caught fire (*Lancet*, 20 September 1828). He continued to say that he had to perforate the membranes to complete the abortion and stressed the value of ergot of rye in such cases.

There was some dispute about the frequency of abortion. In a lecture in 1837, a Professor Thomson said that medicines taken to produce abortion sometimes worked; however, he felt the incidence was rare and occurred mainly amongst the poorer groups: 'Should pregnancy in the unmarried female of rank take place, the disgrace can more easily be concealed; but in the middling and the lower ranks it occasionally happens that drastic purgatives are taken to procure abortion' (*Lancet*, 28 January 1837) In 1844, a doctor wrote to the *Provincial Medical and Surgical Journal* (8 May) saying that he had attended three unmarried females who had used 'herbs' to abort, and commented: 'These are not solitary cases, but I believe, they are constantly occurring and rather on the increase than otherwise.' By the middle of the century, it seems that abortionists had become established. An editorial in the *Lancet* (30 July 1853, p. 101) reported that abortion was common and that 'handbills addressed to female domestics are dropped down the kitchen areas, conveying in ambiguous but unmistakable terms, the information that pregnancy may be cut short'. In 1861, the *Lancet* published another editorial stating that illegal abortion had become a money-making activity carried out by both sexes (23 March).

In 1868 the *British Medical Journal* (*BMJ*) organized a vigorous campaign against 'baby farming' which targeted infanticide and adoption as well as abortion. The campaign ran from 8 February to 4 March. A female abortionist told the investigating officer that if the lady were too far gone the baby could be adopted and sent into the country with payment of a good sum. If the lady was earlier in her pregnancy, she could have an abortion for a larger sum. She commented that it was 'hard that people could not have a little enjoyment without being put to such inconvenience afterwards' (*BMJ*, 8 Feb). The *BMJ* series stressed that their investigators had only visited the better class of establishment. Another woman used a doctor who charged 50 guineas in addition to the 20 guineas for her own services. In an editorial (29 February 1868), the *BMJ* drew out the implications of its findings and complained that the middle-class women were setting a bad example: 'Shall we ever be able to teach our kitchen maids that the murder of a fetus is a crime, while they know that their young mistresses can be directed by their milliners to places of agreeable retirement, with pianos, muslin blinds and jocular attendants where such a transaction is a twenty six-year old tradition' (p. 197).

The *BMJ* campaign had no effect in reducing abortion. At some point the fact was realized that lead was an effective abortifacient. However, it had side effects: it could cause blindness, and a woman died of lead poisoning in 1893 (Parry 1932, p. 36). There were letters on the prevalence of abortion in the *BMJ* (17 September and 1 October 1898) and later in the year the *Lancet* mounted a major campaign against abortificient pills which lasted from 10 December 1898 to 1 April 1899. It pointed to an important blackmail case that was in progress. Three brothers, aptly called Chrimes, had been advertising abortifacient pills, and in the space of two years received replies from 12,000 women. The brothers wrote to them, in the guise of a public official, saying there was evidence that the woman had committed the awful crime of preventing the birth of a child and that arrest would follow unless two guineas costs were received. The blackmail was discovered, and the prosecution drew attention to the fact that the police intercepted £800 in a few days (*Lancet*, 31 December 1898, pp. 1, 807). The brothers were sentenced to long periods of imprisonment. The *Lancet* felt the case would have stopped the trade, but on 25 February 1899 it reported that it had over 100 newspapers before it 'in which occur the advertisements of persons of whose pretensions to procure abortion there can be no doubt'. It began an aggressive campaign of naming the offending newspapers, and on 11 March 101 were reported; subsequent issues listed nearly 100 more.

A third campaign was against lead pills (diachylon); this issue was brought to prominence by Professor Arthur Hall in the *BMJ* (18 March 1905) and in an article with Ransom the following year (24 February 1906). The pills produced abortion, but could also cause blindness and death. Women of childbearing age in some areas were routinely examined to discover if they had the blue line on their gums which was symptomatic of lead poisoning. An editorial in the *BMJ* (24 February 1906) called for legislation on the pills, but this did not occur.

Although the medical profession in the late nineteenth century UK was still firm in its opposition to abortion, it often took a more sympathetic view to the plight of the woman than might have been expected. For example, in 1896 (8 August), the *Lancet* said that while illegal abortion was wrong, it was unfair that women should have to shoulder the blame:

> We believe we are right in saying that the procuring of abortion otherwise than for reasons which can be medically justified is banned by the civil and ecclesiastical law of every civilised country, and as constructive murder it is right it should be so. But the whole question teems with difficulty. It certainly appears unjust, and very possibly is actually so, that a woman who driven and harassed by shame and fear resorts to the questionable remedy of abortion should be liable to severe punishment, while the man who is equally responsible for the child goes free.

The profession was also against giving evidence to the police about abortions. In 1896 Lord Brampton told a grand jury: 'I doubt very much whether a doctor called in to assist a woman, not in procuring an abortion, for that in itself is a crime, but for the purpose of attending her and giving her medical advice, could be justified in reporting the facts to the Public Prosecutor, such action would be a monstrous cruelty' (*Lancet*, 5 February 1916). The issue was raised again in 1914 when Mr Justice Avory had to deal with a situation where three successive doctors had attended a woman who had received an illegal operation, but had not given information to the police: there were, therefore, no grounds for conviction (*Lancet*, 5 February 1916). Following this, on 27 January 1915, the Council of the BMA passed a resolution: 'That the Council is of the opinion that a medical practitioner should not in any circumstances disclose voluntarily, without the patient's consent, information which he has obtained from that patient in the exercise of his professional duties' (*Lancet*, 5 February 1916). So the doctors sometimes took a much less vindictive view on abortion than might have been the case. In fact, in some ways there seems to have been a degree of empathy with the woman who often found herself in difficult circumstances.

Perhaps the best information on abortion practice before the First World War was the book *Report on the English Birthrate* (Elderton 1914). The research was completed in 1911 and the report published in 1914. Her evidence was largely obtained by writing to various medical correspondents under the auspices of the Eugenics Society. She opined that the reduction in the birth rate might lead to the death knell of the British Empire, and that the effective legalization of contraception with the 1877 Bradlaugh/Besant trial was a crucial factor. However her report did not show much evidence of contraception – rather, it was abortion that women were using to control their fertility. In Bradford, for example, the birthrate fell from 25 per 100 married women aged 15–55 in 1851, to 14 in 1901. Her correspondent commented: 'There is a good deal of abortion practice in this district, and for every case that comes to notice there are hundreds that do not.' Her fullest analysis, however, was for the City of York where she had three informants. Women sometimes asked their doctor for a drug to cure a slight irregularity and then took a large dose. Others used the many pills available in the town – Widow Welsch's female pills, steel pills and a common remedy of gin and gunpowder. In addition to the medical correspondents, evidence was obtained from several wives. One woman's husband earned 24 shillings a week but was often ill. She observed:

> Six out of ten working women take something, if it is only paltry stuff ... one tells another. There's no hawking here; its all done in secrecy ... sometimes they can take a druggist's shop and it does no good, the child comes out just the same; but it's puny, it's half starved. I knew a child which was nine months old but only weighed about four pounds; they kept it alive a twelve month then it died. The mother died too. She had been taking all sorts and went into rapid consumption. Our folk go on taking what weakens them, and they can't make it up like the rich. One woman said to me 'I'd rather swallow the druggist shop and the man in it than have another kid' (Elderton 1914, p. 136).

Two other women 'of most respectable type' said that abortion was all but universal with at least seven but probably eight out of ten working women taking abortifacient drugs. One of them said

> They'll rise money for that, if they rise it for nothing else. The working class are equally bad, bad as the rich. I think nearly all of them have a try and there's many that half poison themselves. You'll hear them talking 'Oh I ain't going to have any more I knows summat' (Elderton 1914, p. 137).

Elderton stated that while her best evidence was from York, she had no doubt it was representative of a wide range of towns. In Birkenhead, for example, she reported:

> Women of all classes will ask doctors frankly as to the best methods of prevention and whether they are injurious to health, and also of the best and safest method of abortion … Women will frankly state how they avoid pregnancy and recount how they have tried everything to bring an undesired pregnancy to a premature end. Bitter apple, lead plaster, nutmegs, etc. have been taken in many cases with acute symptoms; a few cases have been reported of attempts to introduce knitting needles into the uterus in order to produce abortion. Advertised pills are very much tried (p. 80).

Elderton reported that the only place births had not declined was Liverpool, and this should be put down to the Irish connection. Her book was given wide publicity in the *BMJ* (26 December 1914) and also in *The Malthusian* (January 1915) – the main journal supporting birth control at the time. Indeed, her research may have been the basis of an estimate in *The Malthusian* (14 May 1914) that 100,000 working women took abortifacient pills each year.

In addition to indigenous abortions, it seems that at the beginning of the twentieth century many British women went to France for abortions. A Dr Blondel talked of 'sundry English women, both married and unmarried, who had crossed the channel simply to have an abortion brought on' (*Lancet*, 14 May 1907, p. 1257). A Mrs Burgwin visited France around 1913 and told the Birthrate Commission (1917, p. 220) that, over and over again, doctors had told her that rich English women went to Paris for abortions. One said: 'We have got 50,000 criminal abortions taking place in Paris in a year and we find that numerous English women resort to that city to be relieved of their pregnancy.' This trade continued into the 1930s (Ellis 1933).

**8.4   Why Abortion was Common in the Nineteenth and Early
Twentieth Century in the USA and UK**

The first factor was the failure to spread contraception. The campaign for
contraception began similarly in the UK and the United States, but diverged
towards the end of the nineteenth century. In 1822, Francis Place published his
Principles of Population in which he proposed that society should introduce
contraception (Place 1930). He argued that opposition to contraception from
those such as Thomas Malthus on the grounds that it would lead to unchastity
was not very relevant to the working class, for they had little chastity either
before or after marriage. He proposed that the most effective method of
diminishing 'promiscuous intercourse' was young marriages. In the summer
of 1823 Place began his public propaganda. He published three pamphlets on
contraception, and had them distributed to the working classes through radical
sources. It seems that it was Place who persuaded John Stuart Mill to write
and distribute literature in favour of contraception – for which he spent a few
days in prison. Place wrote of his success: 'I have received a multitude of
thanks from persons who have been saved from poverty and misery or whose
circumstances have been improved by the practice recommended' (Place 1930,
p. 311). Place was also influential in the early agitation for contraception
in the United States. He convinced the editor of the Republican, Carlile, to
support it. Carlile advocated contraception in his journal, and also published
a pamphlet 'Every Woman's Book'. Owen also published a tract entitled
'Moral Physiology' which was the first booklet on contraception printed
in the United States, and which, in its first five years, had a circulation of
20,000–25,000 copies. Owen was also important because he encouraged Dr
Charles Knowlton who, in 1832, published – at first anonymously – a pamphlet
called the 'Fruits of Philosophy'. This was republished in England a year or
two later, and was pivotal in the legalization of contraception in the United
Kingdom. A Bristol bookseller had been sentenced to two years' hard labour
for issuing the 'Fruits of Philosophy' interleaved, it was alleged, with obscene
pictures. Charles Bradlaugh and Annie Besant decided to challenge the law, and
republished Knowlton's pamphlet in order to precipitate a test case. They were
duly charged and the trial began on 18 June 1876 (Banks 1954). The Solicitor
General argued that the real aim of the book was 'to suggest to people that
they might enjoy the pleasures of sexual intercourse with or without marriage
and yet avoid offspring' (*The Times*, 19 June 1876). Later in the trial, he set
out the criteria on which to judge the book: 'The proper test of it is this – that
it is a book which no decent man would dare to place into the hands of a

decent woman.' The main thrust of Bradlaugh and Besant's defence was that the population was being restrained by the enormous mortality amongst the poor. They pointed to the fact that many of the children were unwanted, and Annie Besant stressed the high level of infanticide. However, the Lord Chief Justice in his summing up clearly stated his concern that contraception would lead to a breakdown in the social order:

> Though these means are recommended to those who are married, they may equally be used by those who are unmarried, and that if at present unlawful intercourse is restrained by the apprehension of its natural result – in the birth of offspring – the removal of that restraint may remove one of the restraints on vice and one of the safeguards on morality.

One of the witnesses whom Annie Besant questioned about abortion was Dr Drysdale. He stated that it was common among both rich and poor women, and then agreed with her comment that it was better for health if people used contraception. The defendants were found guilty, although the foreman of the jury absolved them of any corrupt motives in publishing the book. They were initially sentenced to six months' imprisonment and fined £200, but won on appeal. The trial was a watershed in birth control history in the UK. The publicity surrounding the trial and the subsequent appeal brought contraception to the forefront of public discussion. Sales of Knowlton's pamphlet grew from about 1,000 a year before the trial to 125,000 copies between March and June 1877 (*The Malthusian*, February 1914). Pro-contraceptive organizations were set up in many towns and *The Malthusian* newspaper was formed, its main slogan being 'A crusade against poverty'. One problem was that contraception was marketed as part of an overall doctrine that poverty could be eliminated by the poor restricting the number of their children, rather than on the grounds of free choice. This led to such groups as the socialists in Britain opposing contraception at least until the First World War and so it did not spread as rapidly as it might have done. Therefore many unwanted pregnancies ended in abortion.

Although the Malthusians were radical on contraception, in the period up to 1915 they were totally opposed to abortion. There were several reasons for this, the most important being the belief that abortion was dangerous. In this respect, the major piece of research quoted during the period was that of Tardieu. In May 1881 *The Malthusian* carried an article on 'an excellent pamphlet on the great danger to human life of criminal abortion'. It commented that the pamphlet pointed out that 'Dr. Tardieu, of Paris, had shown that 60 poor women had lost their lives out of 116 cases when criminal abortion had been made use of, either from loss of blood or from inflammation'. This research was widely quoted, even after the First World War and despite the fact that on 19 April 1902 the *Lancet* criticized it. Brouardel (1901) reported a series of 72 abortions without a death, and later observers such as Parry (1932, p. 88), talked of Tardieu having had an exceptional series. However, in the intervening period it was often believed that abortion was very dangerous, so it was opposed for this reason.

Secondly, the Malthusians maintained that abortion resulted in the removal of potential life. When arguing this point of view a Mr Carpenter, lecturing to men only, contrasted contraception with abortion, for there 'the only life destroyed was that of the spermatozoa themselves and these were constantly being destroyed anyway' (*The Malthusian*, March 1887).

The third reason for opposing abortion was a political one. *The Malthusian* tried to distinguish between abortion and contraception in order to facilitate the wider acceptance of their arguments. In *The Law of Population*, Annie Besant pointed out that Dr Fleetwood Churchill had legally given many methods of inducing premature labour and inducing abortion. She continued, 'surely the prevention of conception is far better than the procuring of abortion' (Besant 1877, p. 36). This kind of argument, that contraception was a substitute for abortion, was one that was continuously used in the following years and is still relevant.

The leaders of the medical profession were largely opposed to birth control in the second half of nineteenth century UK. For example, in 1871 the *Lancet* called contraception 'a form of bestiality' (30 September). However, in the 1890s the opposition of the medical profession began to weaken somewhat, and its members began to use it in their private lives. As late as 1905, however, the *Lancet* (21 October) quoted with approval a Professor Simpson who had spoken against the decline of the birthrate and had praised the Jews for fulfilling the commandment 'Be fruitful, multiply and replenish the earth'. In 1910, the *BMJ* attacked the view that there was some connection between mental disturbance and contraception, stating that if that was the case 'the proof has yet to be furnished'. The movement towards liberalization continued through the early part of the twentieth century so that, by February 1914, *The Malthusian* could claim that medical opposition to contraception had collapsed, and that the increase in the number of its medical vice-presidents was evidence that definite support had begun.

While the thrust of the British change in the period 1870–1910 was towards greater liberation in terms of contraception use, in the USA there was a popular movement against sexuality led by Anthony Comstock. His personality dominated the debate from the 1870s to 1915. When he began it, the social conditions were ripe for his purity campaign. The growth in the number of abortions had led to a great deal of concern. In 1872, with financial help from Young Men's Christian Association (YMCA) members, he began to attack virtually all aspects of sexuality, not distinguishing between pornography, abortion and birth control. One tactic he used was copied from *New York Times* reporters, and their method of gaining information about abortion by pretending to seek one for a friend. In 1872, in an important case, he arranged for a police captain to knock on the door of an abortionist and to say that a previous patient was dangerously ill. They raided the premises to find 'a young girl in a semi-nude condition lying on a sofa'. She told the police she was six weeks pregnant and had gone there for an abortion, and Comstock prosecuted the doctor involved (*New York Times*, 31 August 1872). Comstock was concerned that the law was not strong enough and he agitated for a federal statute. This was introduced in Congress by C.L. Merrian on 1 March 1873 in a speech which praised Comstock. He described how, in a relatively short time, Comstock had seized and destroyed 182,000 obscene pictures, more than five tons of obscene books and over 30,000 obscene rubber articles (condoms). He also announced that he had arrested more than 50 dealers, and six more were dead. Comstock, flushed from these successes, became America's primary moral entrepreneur, and a law was passed making the spread of birth control and abortion knowledge through the post illegal. This was a Federal statute and so applied in all the states. It gave Comstock the legal backing he needed to repress literature and prevent the publication of advertisements for contraception and abortion. He therefore set about preparing for a great campaign. At the first Annual Meeting of the Society for the Suppression of Vice (1874), Comstock announced 'The Society which has for some months past been in contemplation, is now organized and ready for aggressive action'. It had the backing of many businessmen, and Comstock was the major driving force.

It was not until Comstock changed the focus of his attack from pornography to contraception that he met any real opposition. Many in the middle classes had used contraception for some years. The *Medical and Surgical Reporter* in 1888 carried a whole series of articles, in one of which D.E. Matteson described four procedures: the syringe with astringent, withdrawal, condoms and, finally, a silk sponge 11″ in diameter with a thread attached, which was recommended. Comstock did not take any action, despite the fact that this discussion was illegal. However, as the amount of overt pornography declined, he began to take a much greater interest in repressing contraception, which brought him into conflict with totally different groups. Now, he was effectively attacking a segment of the middle class – and they were more willing to fight back. The major early pioneer of contraception in the United States was William Robinson. He began his campaign in 1903, and in 1907 made his opposition to Comstock's activities quite clear in an article in the journal he edited: 'Unfortunately the man who is at the head of the vice crusaders is a stupid ignoramus utterly devoid of sense and judgement.' If Comstock had just attacked obscene pictures, he continued, there would be no reason for opposition; but 'He has started to prosecute retail druggists and supply houses who sell, and manufacturers who produce, a certain kind of rubber or fishskin article' (Medico-Pharmaceutical *Critic and Guide*, February 1907, p. 2). This comment could have warned Comstock of the problems he would meet. He was facing a new opposition. Naturally he did not like the *Critic and Guide*, but he could do nothing about it, especially as Robinson was careful not to print information about contraceptive methods.

On the question of abortion, Robinson took a pragmatic approach. In a paper he read before the Eastern Medical Society, in 1911, he said that it was much better to teach contraception, but that as long as illegitimacy was viewed as being such a matter for shame, there would be a great demand for abortion (1933, p. 26). Furthermore, he stated that if the operation were not performed by a professional it would be carried out by a non-medical person and so in certain circumstances it was justifiable. But although he took this view, he publicly claimed he had never carried out an abortion and that he did not regard it as the pressing issue. One of his major criticisms was that the law treated abortion and contraception as if they were the same thing. In 1916, he called for contraception to be separated from both abortion and pornography in the statute (he felt it was not politically possible to legalize it) and in his writings he continually attacked those who treated the different issues together (*Critic and Guide* 1916, p. 125), so Robinson was responsible for one of the major strands of the contraceptive movement. However, there was an alternative source of pressure which, in contrast to Britain, came from the socialist movement and was rooted in the subculture largely located around Greenwich Village. It was the socialists and anarchists who questioned the traditional attitudes. Emma Goldman, one of the most prominent members, had been introduced to contraception when she was taken to a meeting of the French Malthusians in 1900. She became one of the major early proponents, and was also in contact with Margaret Sanger who became the largest single influence in the United States

Thus, in the period up to the First World War, the birth control movements in both countries were hampered. In the UK it was because it was limited to conservative Malthusian doctrines and in the USA because it faced a puritan backlash. People knew that birth could be controlled but had limited means of artificial prevention.

A second reason for the high number of unwanted pregnancies in the USA and the UK was that in both countries the safe period was mistimed. Virtually everyone believed that conception was most likely around the time of the menstrual period. The view seems to have been based on the work of the German scientist, Theodor Bischoff, who in 1853 published his discovery about eggs in the genital tract of dogs on heat. He found that the eggs were released at the time of menstruation, and wrongly assumed that women's periods must be similar to being on heat and that women were most likely to get pregnant at this time.

The birth control pioneer Annie Besant (1877) popularized this view in her work and Elderton (1914) commented primly 'Most women in the country districts know that a human is more likely to be impregnated around the time of menstruation, and a great many avoid this time when sober'. After the First World War, Marie Stopes published the wrong safe period in her best selling book *Married Love*. This information was particularly important to Catholics, who had received permission to use the safe period in 1853 and whose priests regularly quoted the incorrect information (Francome 1984b).

The chief rabbi cast doubts on the view of the safe period in 1917, since observant Jews had no intercourse until 12 days after the start of the menstrual period but did not have smaller families than non-observant Jews (Francome 1986, p. 22). However, the first time people had really strong information was in 1925 when a study by Siegal was reported in Britain. He studied 320 German soldiers and their wives after the men had been home on leave for periods of two to eight days. He found that there were no conceptions after 21 days of the cycle, and that his sample was most prolific six days from the start of the menstrual cycle. This latter figure is eight days earlier than we might now expect; however, it led to a re-evaluation in the UK. The *New Generation*, the journal of the neo-Malthusian, commented that Siegal's work 'proves beyond question that there is some truth in the doctrine of the safe period, and it also proves that this period comes later in the cycle than is commonly supposed' (January 1925, p. 10). In the USA, books giving the wrong dates were still being published in 1928, and it was not until the early 1930s that the menstrual cycle was understood.

There were several other factors. For many women, the extent of their poverty meant that they were often struggling to make ends meet. Extra children would have meant that they were unable to care adequately for those that were already born. Elderton reported that in some cases the men were not too willing to cooperate in terms of birth control, so the women would be faced with an unwanted pregnancy and would decide to seek a termination. Overall, it is likely that the number of abortions in both the UK and the USA were very high and above that occurring in the 1920s.

8.5   Conclusion

The evidence of this period, to the beginning of the First World War, shows that abortion was common in the USA and the UK despite being illegal. In fact, it may well be the case that in the 20 years or so before the war began there were proportionately more abortions per woman than at any time before or since.

Chapter 9

When Abortion was Illegal II

After the First World War, commentators on both sides of the Atlantic noted the change in sexual morality. One focal point was the behaviour of young people, with the growth of youth culture and a distinctive style of dress. In the United States, young women had become 'flappers', a term coined in England and used to describe young women who were assertive and independent, who had casual courtships and who possibly granted 'permissive favours' to young men. In Britain, too, there was a good deal of discussion about the new freedom of the young. The *New Leader* drew attention to the fact that young people under the age of 25 could earn three to four times more than they could before the war. This had led to the growth in the numbers of cinemas, motorcycles, cars, cafes and dancing places which catered for those even with little to spend. It also mentioned the cure for venereal disease and the growth of birth control (23 November 1928).

The extent to which liberalization occurred in the USA is a matter for discussion, and there is some evidence that matters were changing before the First World War. For example, women in the USA reaching their teens after 1910 had twice as much premarital sex as those reaching puberty in the immediately preceding years (Gordon 1977, p. 193). This suggests that liberalization may have occurred earlier in the United States and without the effect of the war. Another piece of evidence is provided in the decline of chaperonage, which had been common in the late nineteenth century. Mrs J. Borden Harriman, describing her first visit to a ball in 1888 stated 'No girls ever went anywhere except with a chaperon or a maid' (1923, p. 36). However, Scott Fitzgerald commented 'As far back as 1915 the unchaperoned young people of the smaller cities had discovered the mobile privacy of the automobile' (McGovern 1968, p. 318). In contrast, the end of chaperonage in the UK does not seem to have come until the conditions of war made it difficult to enforce. Vera Brittain tells us that at first she was closely observed, but that 'the free and easy movements of girl war workers had begun to modify convention' so that after the war there was no attempt to reintroduce the same restrictions. 'How different was the peaceful independence of a post war courtship'.

In the United States, the role of the war in this regard seems more uncertain. In some respects it had a conservative effect on the dominant ideology. In the

USA, Germany was demonized and, in contrast, Americans were idealized as paragons of virtue; and changes were introduced to try to ensure that their soldiers did not engage in sexual behaviour or get drunk. Later, the idea grew that the whole population should receive a spiritual renewal. During this period, alcohol was prohibited (1917), prostitutes were harassed, and young women were encouraged to keep the soldiers on the straight and narrow path with such slogans as 'Do your bit to keep him fit'. The anti-vice societies also grew in size as conservative values received support. However, despite all the official puritanism, the reality of behaviour was somewhat different. The problems of venereal disease and unwanted pregnancy meant that in 1917 the decision was taken to give condoms to the troops. This was one factor leading to sexual behaviour becoming freer, and thus the gap between official attitudes and actual behaviour becoming wider. Schmalhausen even talked of the 'sexual revolution', and stressed the strong effect of the First World War in 'remoulding the conventional direction of sexual anarchism' (Calverton and Schmalhausen 1929). Judge Ben Lindsey also stressed the role of the war in liberalizing sexual behaviour, suggesting that many young men became 'inoculated with continental standards'. He said that before the war he had talked to a hundred boys, half of whom admitted that they had been with prostitutes in the red light district. With the changed conditions, however, boys were turning to girls in their own class (1925, p. 54). So it seems that despite the differing ideologies between the two countries, the liberalization of behaviour occurred in both.

A crucial factor in the period between the wars was the growth in the availability of contraception. It is not clear what effect it had on the abortion rate. In fact the effects of liberalizing contraception on the number of abortions may vary. If the abortion rate is low and women expect to have large families, then the introduction of birth control may lead to rising expectations of controlling fertility; and if contraception fails, abortion may increase as an alternative. However, where the abortion rates are higher, the improved availability of preventative measures is likely to lead to the abortion rates falling. One can see that the high rates present in Russia in the 1990s could easily be reduced by a coherent family planning policy.

The post-war liberalization of attitudes facilitated the spread of contraceptive knowledge in both the UK and the USA. In 1918 Marie Stopes published her book *Married Love*, and in 1921 she opened the first birth control clinic in Britain. Stopes had been a member of the Malthusian League in the war years, but gradually began to reject its overall theories of society. She let her membership lapse and, after the war, began fighting for birth control as a single-issue campaign.

In the 1920s some medical opposition continued, as did that in the Church of England. However, changes were afoot. At the 1921 Church Congress, Lord Dawson, the King's physician, caused a tremendous stir in a speech which attacked restrictive attitudes towards sexuality. In a passage widely quoted on both sides of the Atlantic he stated:

> To tell you the truth, I am not sure that too much prudent self restraint suits love and its purport. Romance and deliberate self control do not, to my mind, rhyme very well together. A touch of madness to begin with does no harm. Heaven knows, life sobers it soon enough. If you don't start life with a head of steam you won't get far (*The Malthusian*, November 1921).

Lord Dawson went on to call for the Church to support birth control, and this speech did much to break down the resistance of the middle classes. Most of the press comments were favourable, but the *Sunday Express* (16 October 1921) printed a hostile editorial entitled 'Lord Dawson Must Go'. However, it also drew attention to the fact that, for the first time in the national life of Britain, birth control had been given such prominent support. Later Lord Dawson helped towards the acceptance of birth control, at the Lambeth Conference of 1930, by 193 votes to 67. The statement declared that 'where there is a morally sound reason for avoiding complete abstinence, the Conference agrees that other methods may be used' (*The Times*, 15 August 1930). By 1930, therefore, organized Church opposition to contraception within marriage was over except for Catholics. The Malthusians had become eminently respectable, and their Ball of 1933 was patronized by a princess and presided over by a High Court judge. The major opposition came from the Catholic Church which provided a basis from which opponents of change could work.

The situation in the United States was different. *Medical World* of December 1932 called contraception premature abortion and commented primly about intercourse: 'Nature originated the sexual act for procreation only, and not as a diversion, amusement or business.' It changed its mind three years later, but on 6 January 1935 the *Brooklyn Eagle* reported that nine books and magazines, largely dealing with birth control, were banned from entry to the United States. Similarly, on 2 January, the *Buffalo Times* (New York) reported that the Post Office Department was asking for increased power to prosecute people who sent birth control propaganda and devices through the post. Also in 1935, the President of the Medical Society of New York attacked the advocates of contraception 'who wished to destroy life ... It must be a sign of moral insanity that birth control in its widest and vilest application should be so extensively practised'. The medical profession did not support contraception until 1937; when it decided that its members could provide information to their patients (Francome 1986, p. 43).

The failure of the medical profession to provide birth control information in much of the inter-war period led to a great amount of desperation amongst women, especially if they did not know of an abortionist. The following letter was published in Margaret Sanger's *Birth Control Review* in January 1918:

> I am a poor married woman in great trouble and I'm writing to you for help. I was married in June 1915 and I have two children a little boy 21 months & a girl 4 months and I will be only 17 years old this month and I'm in the family way again. I'm nearly crazy for when my husband finds out that I'm going to have another baby he will beat the life out of me. My husband isn't very strong; he had two operations since we were married and can't do no hard work and doesn't earn much and then there is always trouble, when we haven't enough money he goes out and drinks for all that he gets hold of. ... I'm sure I'm in the family way though my family doctor won't tell me for he doesn't want to tell me.

9.1 The Catholic Church, Birth Control and Abortion

Noonan (1967, p. 502) explains that the opposition of the Church to fertility control only became important after the First World War. Before that time, it had not campaigned actively to persuade non-Catholics to adopt its viewpoint. In part, its reaction may have been a backlash against the more aggressive methods of the birth control proponents, and an attempt to arrest some of the social changes that were beginning to take place. One practical reason for the Catholic Church to oppose fertility control was that a high average family size was necessary in order to keep up numbers. Sometimes Catholics argued that their views against artificial contraception would lead to a faster increase in numbers than that of non-Catholics. For example, a doctor speaking to the Southend Branch of the National Council of Women in 1923 asserted 'Our people will never adopt these practices, and we shall breed out the Protestants and England will become Catholic again' (*Birth Control News*, December 1923).

The best known of the opponents to contraception in Britain was Dr Halliday Sutherland, a Catholic convert, who in his book *Birth Control* (1922, p. 3) warned that 'The path of the Malthusian League, although at first glance an easy way out of many human difficulties, is in reality the broad road along which a man or a nation travels to destruction'. Sutherland became famous when defeating Marie Stopes in the House of Lords in 1923. He had alleged that her method of birth control was dangerous and she sued him for libel. After the trial, he stated: 'This propaganda of birth control had spread through the country with little to stop it until it reached the invisible and invincible frontiers of the Catholic Church, but there the battle had been joined' (*BCN*, February 1924). At first the opposition was unorganized, but in 1926 Sutherland was behind the formation of the League of National Life which aimed to be 'undenominational and non-political' with a membership open to anyone, but did not disguise the fact that it was largely supported by Catholics (*The Universe*, 23 July 1926). The general climate of opinion, however, was against this group. The percentage of Catholics in the population was relatively low, and the teaching of the rhythm method undermined many of their arguments. This was also realized by Sutherland, and when, in 1947, he reflected on the problems he and his allies had faced, he commented:

> Knowing that it was useless to quote religious sanctions in neo pagan Britain, we sought to defeat the contraceptionists by proving their propaganda to be contrary to the laws of biological, economic and ethical science. We failed. We witnessed the medical profession betray its trust; we saw the white flag hoisted over Lambeth Palace; we were in Whitehall in 1931 when the Ministry of Health first permitted advice on contraceptives to be given in antenatal clinics (Simms 1975).

Sutherland's movement was the forerunner of modern anti-abortion movements, and it is instructive to consider how the arguments of opponents of artificial contraception are still used by anti-abortionists today.

*   *Birth control is murder.* In 1914 the *Daily Mirror* carried an article supportive of birth control. In reply the Catholic newspaper *The Universe* argued that the regulation of the birth-rate meant the killing of the unborn child and the suppression by intention of the potential child in conception: 'It is open and unashamed war upon babies … What care we for the future of family or fatherland? Confront the natural law of life with the hedonists' law of death. Kill, Kill, Kill, and "let us eat drink and be merry for tomorrow we die"' (*The Malthusian*, April 1915, p. 30).
*   *Birth control leads to sterility.* Sutherland stated in the *BMJ* that birth control practices were harmful to men and women and that 'sterility is less common in countries such as Ireland and Spain where birth control is not practised'

(30 July 1921, p. 169). Other people would go even further: Dr F.J. McCann, a surgeon at the Samaritan Hospital, argued during the Stopes/Sutherland libel suit that contraception was always prejudicial to a woman's health, and is sometimes dangerous to her life (*BCN*, March 1923).

- *Birth control will destroy the family.* In 1929 a leaflet *Birth Prevention* issued by the British League of National Life, argued that birth control 'leads to a disintegration of the family upon which nation and Empire are founded' (*New Generation*, August 1929, p. 90). It is difficult to see why small families should be seen as destruction. However, there was an extension to the argument; this was that the fall in numbers meant that 'ends of families' were not being reached and that for this reason many great men would not be born. This argument was used by the Catholic Archbishop of New York in justification of instructions from his office to close one of Margaret Sanger's meetings. He argued (wrongly) that John Wesley was the eighteenth child and that 'one of the reasons for the lack of genius in our day is that we are not getting the ends of families' (Sanger 1932, p. 211). Against this argument, the birth controllers stressed the fact that many 'great men' were born high in the birth order – for example Jesus and John the Baptist. Another argument they used was that it would have been better if some men had not been born. William Robinson wrote later, in his *Critic and Guide*, of the misery society would have escaped if the mothers of Dillinger, Hitler, Al Capone, Goering and Oswald Mosley had used birth control (Francome 1984, p. 59).

- *Race suicide.* In August 1921, the *Malthusian* asserted that the 'only objection to birth control which has any appearance of reason is its supposed effect on the defensive power of the nation' (p. 62). The political movement to the right in Germany and Italy had led to birth control clinics being closed. In 1926, an Italian law made it an offence to distribute Malthusian teaching or any other 'means of prevention of conception, or any regulation of female fertility' (*BCN*, December 1926). This argument was also important in France and on 7 May 1918, as the war drew to a close, French bishops used the military argument against birth control: 'Let the lesson not be lost. It is necessary to fill the spaces made by death, if we want France to belong to Frenchmen and to be strong enough to defend herself and prosper.' Two years later France banned birth control, and this was seen as a victory by the Catholic Church.

The *Catholic Times* commented that the French government had realized it was 'now unable to provide sufficient troops' (28 October 1922). The League of National Life was sympathetic. Sutherland called the work of Hitler and Mussolini in this area 'heroic efforts', and commended the Nazi penal code of November 1936 which made 'the public ridicule of marriage or of maternity, and all propaganda in favour of birth control and abortion, into criminal offences' (Simms 1975, p .713).

The failure of the League of National Life was to be expected, although its pressure did have some effect on the British Labour Party for a time. In 1927, the Labour Women's Conference voted by 581 votes to 74 for contraceptive information to be given to the poor, but the full Labour Party rejected the motion. The three main opposing speakers were Irish Catholics, and Stella Browne accused the Labour leadership of surrendering to Roman Catholic threats (*Malthusian*, November 1927). One of the arguments was that many Catholics would leave the Labour Party if it endorsed contraception. Marie Stopes attacked this view in a letter to the New Leader, arguing that the Catholic Church, through its approval of the safe period was now in favour of birth control (28 December 1928). In drawing attention to this fact, she was pointing to a problem for those defending the Church's position: once the rhythm method was widely known to be acceptable, many of its traditional arguments against birth control had much less plausibility.

In the USA, too, it was the Catholic Church which was most opposed to birth control. When the first American Birth Control Conference was held in New York on 11–13 November 1921, it began with the formation of the American Birth Control League, with Margaret Sanger as its president. On the final day, there was a mass meeting to discuss whether or not birth control was moral. A hundred police officers appeared, intent on preventing the meeting. The next day it became clear that the raid was made after an order from the Archbishop. His secretary commented 'Decent and clean living people would not discuss a subject such as birth control in public' (Kennedy 1970, p. 96). The differences between the denominations became clear in 1935 when a Cardinal condemned birth control as a violation of divine law. However, a coalition of 13 liberal Protestant and Jewish clergymen argued that birth control was a scientific development which was sanctioned by the Deity (Kennedy 1970, p. 144).

In recent years the Catholic Church's attitude to abortion and childbirth has been presented as one of being 'pro-life'. However, if we look back into the first half of the nineteenth century we see that its position is much more due to its application of religious rules – even if these led to the death of women. One of the problems of the doctrine according to the Catholic Church was the belief, stated clearly in the British Catholic newspaper *The Universe* (22 May 1936), that 'It is now, and always has been, the mind of the Church that unbaptised infants go to hell'. So in order for the fetus to avoid this fate, it was considered that the mother's life should in certain circumstances be sacrificed. A book published largely for Catholic nurses was entitled *Moral Problems in Hospital Practice*, and was in its fifth edition in 1935; the book commented that in certain circumstances, such as war, it was sometimes a man's duty to die. Similarly:

> A parallel case is the situation of a woman in a difficult labour, when her life and that of her unborn child are in extreme danger. In this situation, it is the mother's duty to die rather than consent to the killing of her child. The first fact in the world is that justice, law, order, should be observed no matter what the cost; better that ten thousand mothers should die than one foetus be unjustly killed.

This book was obviously well read and it was even reviewed in the *BMJ*, which was critical of the disregard for the woman's life. However, the book was reflective of the views of other theologians. For example A.J. Shulte, a professor of Liturgy stated that if ever a pregnant woman's life were in danger 'a physician has no right to destroy the child's life. I say now with all seriousness that it is better that one million mothers die than to have one innocent little creature killed' (Francome and Baird 1988). There is evidence that the failure to permit abortion to women in danger did lead to deaths, and the *BMJ* reported a doctor who had seen eight Catholic women patients die over a 25 year period because they had either refused or been refused termination of pregnancy (*BMJ*, 11 December 1937). Similarly, in the USA, Taussig told of the medical problems he faced in the treatment of Catholic women. However, in an incredibly practical way, he explained that sterilized water might help save the lives of Catholic women who at the time were being condemned because of the application of the Church's teaching:

> The sterilisation of holy water and its use in various operative procedures on the pregnant woman are now being resorted to increasingly. Although, it seems possible that the Church may in time consent to the sacrifice of the foetus in certain cases, provided that the cardinal principle of baptism be adhered to by the introduction of sterilised holy water through a catheter in the uterus, thus saving mothers with serious diseases, as of heart or kidney, whose lives are now sacrificed (Taussig 1936, p. 399).

One of the reasons for the death of some women was the attitude to pregnancies which occurred in the fallopian tubes instead of the uterus (ectopic pregnancies).

There is no way that such a pregnancy can go to term, so the life-saving removal of the tube would appear to be logical; indeed, this is the current position of the Church. However, as the Catholic Encyclopaedia explains, it was decided on 20 March 1902 that an abortion in this case is not lawful (1913, pp. 46–50). This position was maintained, it seems, until after the Second World War. However, by 1963, the leading British Catholic layman, Norman St. John Stevas, argued quite incorrectly that abortion for an ectopic pregnancy had always been allowed by the Church (St John Stevas 1963, p. 40).

Another practice which caused the death of many women was intrauterine baptism. Finney explains why it should be carried out if there is doubt that the child would be born alive:

> You as Catholic are convinced, you believe, as Mother church teaches, that without baptism the child is deprived of the vision of God for eternity; do not then be deterred by difficulties or doubts, but give the child at least the chance of eternal happiness.

> METHOD:– use a syringe which has been rendered aseptic and fill it with boiled water. If the membranes have not broken, they must be ruptured and the amniotic fluid discharged. The syringe is then carefully inserted into the vagina, and the water directed against the child's head, while at the same time you say the form of baptism … As there is always doubt with regard to the validity of intrauterine baptism, in practice you should baptise again conditionally after it is born, pouring water on the child's head and saying: 'If thou art not baptised, I baptise thee in the name of the father and of the son and of the holy spirit.'

Although an aseptic solution was supposed to be used, in many cases the women received infections from which they died – and again, it is welcome that such a practice has died out.

9.1.1   Birth Control or Abortion

Marie Stopes genuinely opposed abortion, and was also concerned that the issue might harm her fight for birth control. At the time many people confused the two methods, and typical were the comments she made at a meeting in May 1923 when she insisted that her members should differentiate between birth control and abortion, and let the world know that her organization 'would have nothing to do with abortions, in spite of the numerous and often pathetic appeals' (*BCN*, June 1923). In contrast, research reveals that Margaret Sanger only opposed abortion for tactical reasons. In her pamphlet *Family Limitation*, first published in 1915, she approved abortion: 'No one can doubt that there are times where an abortion is justifiable but these will become unnecessary when care is taken to prevent conception.' In *Birth Control Review* (May 1919) she pointed out that abortion could be a safe operation: 'We know that abortion, when performed by skilled hands, under right conditions, brings almost no danger to the life of the patient and we also know that particular diseases can be more easily combated after such an abortion than during a pregnancy allowed to come to full term.' A year later, she again took a less than censorious attitude: 'The woman who goes to the abortionist's table is not a criminal but a martyr; a martyr to the bitter, unthinkable conditions brought about by the blindness of society at large' (Sanger 1969). She went on to argue the case for contraception as its substitute. British birth controllers were critical of her stance on this matter, and in February 1915 *The Malthusian*, when reviewing *Family Limitation*, criticized its passage on abortion:

> It is unfortunate that in Mrs. Sanger's otherwise excellent pamphlet she tells women that if they intend to have an abortion they should do so without delay … Mrs. Sanger has informed us that she has not advocated abortion, but that the practice is so common in America, and so generally spoken of, that she felt it desirable to warn women against the use of drugs, and against delay if abortion had been determined upon (p. 11).

When Sanger returned to the United States to face trial for breaking the Comstock law with *Family Limitation*, Marie Stopes organized a group of nine English birth control supporters, including the author H.G. Wells, to write to President Wilson saying that the United States was the only 'civilized' country in the world where the spreading of birth control information was a criminal offence, and asking for presidential action (*The Malthusian*, November 1915). The President was particularly impressed that Wells had signed it. From the early 1920s Sanger did not argue the case for abortion, but simply stated that with contraceptive usage it would become unnecessary. However, this does not mean that she changed her fundamental position on the subject – in fact, at least from 1933 she began to help patients get abortions (Reed 1978, p. 118). In one documented case, a woman was given a pregnancy test and referred to a sympathetic physician. Given the risks involved it is surprising that evidence of even one case was available, and it suggests there may have been a system of referrals. There would, for example, be very little risk in referring regular patients who had suffered contraceptive failure.

9.2   Abortion in the Inter-war Period

The liberalization of attitudes and the spread of contraception were clearly factors influencing the number of abortions. The legalization of abortion in the Soviet Union in 1920 was another factor. It was the first country in which this had occurred in modern times, and this affected the debate in both Britain and the United States. As early as 1914, the most eminent society of physicians had called for all laws to be removed (*The Malthusian*, September 1926). The law had two main effects on the debate elsewhere. First, it showed that change was possible, and radical groups were able to point to it as an example of what could be accomplished. Secondly, and this was probably more important, it revised the estimates of the safety of the operation. Until that time it had been widely believed that abortion was an unsafe operation. The Soviet authorities drew comparisons with Germany where, in 1924, 4 per cent of abortions were estimated to have resulted in death: in Moscow, it was fewer than one-tenth of 1 per cent (*New Generation*, September 1926). The Soviets publicized their results and, in 1929, sent a delegate to the First Congress of the World League for Sexual Reform in London. The figures suggested that abortion mortality and morbidity had decreased 'almost to vanishing point', and British medical men took an interest and, on a number of occasions, visited the country to watch the procedures. One such observer, L. Haden Guest, reported in the *Lancet* (5 December 1931) that, in a Russian series of 40,000 cases, there were only two deaths. A few months later the journal commented that if the evidence of the Russian experience of abortion were accurate: 'It will from the strictly medical point of view, deserve serious consideration by those planning new legislation appropriate to the outlook and habits of our time' (*Lancet*, 19 March 1932, p. 627). The US-based doctor Taussig paid a visit to the Soviet Union in 1930 and devoted a whole chapter on its approach to legal abortion in his influential book (1936).

9.3   Abortion Debate and Practice in the USA

The first modern activist for birth control in the USA, William Robinson, also became the first systematic proponent of the legalization of abortion. This mirrors Britain where the Malthusians were the first agitators on both issues. William Robinson seems to have taken a consistent position on abortion which, from his published works, can be summarized as follows:

- abortions occur in great numbers and the operations are usually carried out by doctors;
- this is a situation which should be deprecated and it is much better to substitute contraception;
- although contraception is much better, abortion is a relatively simple and safe operation and cannot be regarded as murder, for only a few cells are destroyed;
- the law on abortion should be repealed, to allow it in the early months of pregnancy.

Robinson's estimation of the number of abortions rose from 1 million a year in the 1910s to 2 million in the 1930s. He said he had little respect for the professional abortionist but that he was morally superior to the judges and hypocrites who condemned him: 'He has saved many a family from shame and humility, and many an unfortunate young girl from a suicide's grave' (*Critic and Guide* 1925, p. 136). He also pointed out that 'an altruistic physician does it, when necessary, for a nominal fee, and often altogether gratis' (Robinson 1933, p. 25). He believed that the law on abortion was illogical, so when, in 1908, the *New Orleans and Surgical Journal* reported a symposium on illegal abortion, he criticized it as being 'one physician vying with the other in his expression of execration of the crime of abortion, the same talk that the fetus is a living human being from the moment of conception' (*Critic and Guide* 1908, p. 380). But despite this opinion, he did not at this stage call for legalization. His views did not become known until 1913, when he criticized the radical statements of the German Professor Kocks who called for abortion throughout pregnancy. Robinson said that he did not agree that all restrictions should be abolished irrespective of gestation; he preferred to seek legalization of abortion in the early stages of pregnancy, asserting that: 'Abortion is a nasty business ethically, aesthetically and physically, although not infrequently it is fully justifiable as the lesser of two evils' (*Critic and Guide* 1913). He maintained this position when an American commentator, Herman Dekker (1920), began calling for legal abortion, and gave him space to write a series of articles in the *Critic and Guide*. Dekker's basic argument was that legalization of birth control had gone through two stages. First, although illegal it became widely used; and secondly, it became accepted legally. Abortion, he suggested, was now in the first position: 'in the process of becoming ethically approved, the first stage of wide-spread practice has already been completed' (*Critic and Guide* 1920, p. 336). One of the arguments underlying Dekker's proposals for abortion was that the 'lower classes' did not use contraceptives, so those of poorer quality were reproducing themselves to a greater degree. He claimed that if both contraception and abortion were practised, it would eliminate the effects of what many saw as 'reverse Darwinism'. Robinson opposed Dekker's standpoint as being too radical and not giving enough weight to the possible problems of abortion. He said that it should only be used in exceptional cases where contraception had failed (*Critic and Guide* 1921, p. 24). This view of Robinson's, that abortion should only be used sparingly, led him to be very critical of some young people who took a much more relaxed attitude. One day in 1929, a young woman came to his office and requested an abortion. As she had already had three, Robinson was angry: 'I do dislike a certain type of modern young woman who indulges promiscuously and uses contraceptives rather reluctantly, preferring repeat abortions, which she regards as lightly as tossing down a cocktail or a glass of whiskey' (*Critic and Guide* 1929, p. 428). It is likely that there was an increase in the number of abortions in the USA after the First World War. A survey of doctors known to have performed abortions led to an estimate of 550,000 terminations a year, taking into account different patterns in rural districts. One doctor confessed to having performed 18,000 abortions at $50 each. It was stated that the citizens supported this abortion practice. By way of illustration, the anonymous author commented that one of his respondents referred to one doctor as the 'leading abortionist in town' in a matter of fact way just as one might say 'There is the Brooklyn Bridge' (Francome 1986, p. 42).

In 1924 another commentator, Ettie Arout, stated that educated married women volunteer quite frankly that they have two or more abortions regularly every year and that they experienced no difficulty in securing economic and efficient service (Francome 1986, p. 42). Margaret Sanger stated in her autobiography that ideas of what to do with an unwanted pregnancy were passed from mouth to mouth. To bring on the abortion women tried a variety of techniques including herb teas, turpentine, rolling downstairs, inserting slippery elm and knitting needles. However, many women used the community operator: 'On Saturday nights I have seen groups of from fifty to one hundred with their shawls over their heads waiting outside the office of the five-dollar abortionist' (Sanger 1938, p. 89).

From the 1920s, Robinson took the view that the birth control issue was won, so he felt able to permit himself to devote some energy to the subject of abortion. In his book *Sex, Love and Morality* (1928) he made a forthright call for legalization: 'Abortion up to the end of the third month should be made perfectly legal, when performed by a physician and at the request of the woman.' Five years later he devoted a whole book to abortion in which he reiterated his earlier views.

By the early 1930s, other doctors like Rongy (1933) were supporting Robinson's call. There was also some pressure for the reform of the laws from a women's group who formed the Association for Reformation of the Abortion Law in 1932 (Taussig 1936, p. 426). This aimed to broaden the grounds to include cases of rape, seduction, infirmity, likely handicap, destitution and divorce. However, the group does not seem to have been very strong, and could have had little hope of success in a society which had not even legalized the spread of contraceptive information. There was never anything in the United States of comparable influence to ALRA, for reasons which are partly historical and partly due to the social conditions. In Britain, the neo-Malthusian movement had by the 1920s lost its role as the major organization pushing for contraception, and was looking for a new issue. It was therefore able to alter its policy on abortion and provide an immediate structure within which pro-choice agitation could operate. In the United States, no similar organization existed. William Robinson and subscribers to the *Critic and Guide* played a social role similar to that of the Malthusians, but Robinson was a lone organizer and when he died in 1936 his magazine closed.

Perhaps a more important factor was the failure of the birth control movement to break down the Comstock Laws until 1936, and the fact that the American Medical Association did not accept contraception until 1937. If this breakthrough had come at a time when Margaret Sanger was younger, she may well have been the person to launch off in a new direction. As it was, she went into semi-retirement. Planned Parenthood's leadership saw its major task to be the spreading of contraceptive knowledge: adoption of abortion as an issue would frustrate the main aim – a view it shared with Marie Stopes and the Family Planning Association in Britain. For this reason, the United States was lacking the effect of an active pressure group for abortion. However, although abortion was a statutory offence in every state, there were wide variations in penalties, and provisions were not uniform. In six states there were no legal exemptions; in thirty-nine states abortion was allowed to save the life of the woman; and a further three states and the District of Columbia also allowed abortion if there was a threat to the health of the woman. In Mississippi, alone, the operation was legal at the discretion of the medical practitioner (Birkett 1939, p. 165; Taussig 1936).

9.4   Abortion Debate and Practice in the UK

The first known call for a change in the UK abortion laws was from Stella

Browne in *The Malthusian* in March 1915. She put forward a number of reasons for liberalization. First, she said that a reliable contraceptive had not been discovered, so pregnancy might occur even when the greatest care had been taken and there were overwhelming reasons why a child should not be born to the people concerned. Secondly, the education of young people in sexual matters was only just beginning, and she argued that it was grossly unfair to penalize ignorance. Thirdly, she stated that the laws left people open to blackmail because of the need for secrecy and the fact that the operation had mainly fallen into the hands of the criminal class. She also pointed out that those performing the operation were often unskilled and produced permanent injury although, despite these factors, those with 'any knowledge of the lives of working class women will prove that the professional abortionist is sometimes the truest friend and benefactor' (p. 22).

Stella Browne also argued that prejudice against abortion was not due to medical science, but was based on Christian canon law which stated that from the time of conception there was a right of baptism. She said that thinking people would wonder why embryonic life alone should be considered sacred. She then referred to the war and suggested that the world should be made fit for children to be raised. Just after this article was published, reports began to arrive of the problems of French women who were pregnant because they had been raped by German soldiers. The *BMJ* noted the claims that such women should have a right to abortion, and also that there was some support for a change in the law (20 March 1915). *The Malthusian*'s view was that it was pleased to see the question raised, but that 'we have a better remedy, and it would be folly for us to waste our energy and resources in championing an imperfect one'. It claimed that when the knowledge of preventive methods became universal, abortion would only become necessary in rare cases where birth control had not been employed or had failed, and where there were serious medical or eugenic reasons against the birth. In the meantime, *The Malthusian* said that it would confine itself to advocating contraception, and that the real advocates of abortion were its opponents on the birth control issue.

Although the Malthusians were not prepared to endorse abortion, they were receptive to the writings of Stella Browne and others on the subject. Throughout the 1920s, statements favouring the legalization of abortion were treated sympathetically in its journal the *New Generation*, although the Malthusian League did not make it part of its official policy. In the early 1930s the *New Generation* began to consider seriously the need for an organization to fight the abortion laws. An article in 1931 commented: 'Instead of a new society being formed, it would be better if the Malthusian League were to take the matter up. It would be fitting that the first society in the world which advocated birth control should also be the first to advocate legalized abortion by a qualified surgeon' (December 1931, p. 134). Although the Malthusian League did not take up the suggestion, throughout the 1920s and early 1930s it was the only organization carrying abortion information on a regular basis. Furthermore, it was members of the Malthusian League who set up the Abortion Law Reform Association in 1936.

During the 1930s, as many European countries moved to the right, the movement for free abortions in Britain might have expected to receive serious setbacks. However, a number of factors prevented this, amongst them the actions of Mr Justice McCardie. He had grown convinced that the 1861 Abortion Act was out of touch with the realities of life, so on 30 November 1931 he publicly attacked the law. Two women had come before him and pleaded guilty to aborting themselves. He could have sent them to prison for life, but instead he just bound them over. In his summing up, he said, 'I express the view clearly that in my opinion the law in regard to illegal operations should be substantially amended. It is out of keeping with the conditions that prevail in the world around us'. Addressing Mrs Elsie Golding, he continued:

> Your case illustrates well what I have just said. You are a woman of most excellent character. You have been brave in the midst of sorrow to bear the burden of providing for your family. You had seven young children born in poverty and almost doomed to poverty for all their lives. You had no money. Your husband is lazy and you feared that another burden was to fall upon you. I can well believe you, because judges know more of human life than many people think. I shall not send you to prison but will bind you over for two years.

Then the Judge, turning to the jury with raised hand, said: 'A mother of seven children, gentlemen' (*New Generation*, December 1931). Two weeks later, on 11 December 1931, McCardie went even further and refused to sentence a woman who had committed an abortion on another. He pointed out that she was charged with a law passed 70 years earlier, and maintained that, since then, the national point of view had greatly changed. He went on to say that he thought abortion cases would continue so long as the knowledge of birth control was withheld, and he called for the law on abortion to be amended (*New Generation*, January 1932). The comments were influential in liberalizing attitudes and in response, six months later, the BMA set up a committee to consider a change in the law on abortion. L.A. Parry, the leading UK authority, told the BMA that McCardie's remarks had led to his becoming more open minded on the issue himself (*New Generation* August 1932, p. 89).

We saw earlier that it was women's groups, especially in the Labour Party, that were the most forthright in the matter of birth control. Radical women were also prime movers of the pressure group for the reform of the abortion law. A notable victory for the pro-choice groups in the early 1930s was to obtain the support of the Co-operative Women in 1934. There were 1,360 delegates to the Annual Meeting, and the following resolution was passed with only 20 dissidents:

> In view of the persistently high maternal death rate and the evils arising from the illegal practice of abortion, this Congress calls upon the Government to revise the abortion laws of 1861 by bringing them into harmony with modern conditions and ideas, thereby making of abortion a legal operation that can be carried out under the same conditions as any other surgical operation. It further asks that women now suffering from imprisonment for breaking these antiquated laws, be given amnesty (*New Generation*, July 1934, p. 78).

Two years later, on 17 February 1936, ALRA was set up. Its leaders had been working for change for many years, and the new association was an extension of previous activities. It was chaired by Janet Chance and to a large extent financed by her husband, Clinton, who was very active in the birth control movement during the First World War. He had also provided the money for Margaret Sanger to set up her birth control clinic in 1922. Stella Browne was the most militant of the three principal organizers; the Secretary, Alice Jenkins, noted: 'Stella never wavered from her uncompromising belief in the woman's right to abortion up to the viability of her child. Janet and I shared her opinion but, mistakenly or not, believed that we could further our views better by a less forthright declaration' (Jenkins 1960, p. 59). This division of opinion about reducing demands for political reasons was one that became important in both Britain and the United States. By 1938 ALRA had 274 members, hardly a mass movement but a reasonable size for the kind of organization that it was. Its greatest victory in the 1930s was the trial of Aleck Bourne which, as we shall see extended the law to cover rape.

Legal abortions were available to rich women after the First World War, as was made clear in a speech by Thomas Eden, Consultant Physician at the Charing Cross Hospital, at the Obstetrics session of the Annual Meeting of the BMA in 1926. He stated that it was impossible to lay down rigid criteria for abortion: 'It is an ethical question of great interest to what extent we, as doctors, have the right to insist that a woman shall pass through an ordeal which she is unwilling to face' (*BMJ*, 7 August 1926, p. 237). He gave the example of a barrister's wife who had two children very quickly and then became pregnant again. Both she and her husband took the view that, since the prospective baby was theirs, they should decide whether or not she should have an abortion. Eden confessed to being shaken by their view, but when he consulted a senior colleague, the doctor agreed with the patient and her husband, so the abortion was carried out. Furthermore, at a later stage the woman had another abortion.

Thus, many doctors took a very liberal line on abortion. However, others were concerned that the law did not specifically allow for abortion, even to save the woman's life, and that it was worthwhile for pro-choice groups to try to extend the law more formally. A Committee, set up by the BMA, reported in 1936 that the law was in need of clarification. Bourne, a member of ALRA's Medico-Legal Council, decided to try to find a suitable subject for a test case. The opportunity came in 1938 when a girl aged 14 years and 9 months was raped and became pregnant. Joan Malleson, who was a member of ALRA's Medico-Legal Council, saw her, and wrote to Bourne on 21 May 1938 to say that she had been consulted by the organizer of the Schools Care Committee about a girl of 14 [who] was assaulted in Whitehall by some soldiers.

> The facts were that she was with two girl friends, who ran off and left her, and she was held down by five men and twice assaulted. She went on to say the girl was pregnant and asked whether someone of his standing was prepared to risk a *cause celebre* and undertake the operation in hospital. 'Many people hold the view that the best way of correcting the present abortion laws is to let the medical profession gradually extend the grounds for therapeutic abortion in suitable cases, until the laws become obsolete, so far as practice goes. I should imagine that public opinion would be immensely in favour of termination of pregnancy in a case of this sort.'

Bourne replied to say that he was interested in this case of rape, and would be delighted to have the girl admitted to St Mary's hospital in Paddington and curette her. In his book *A Doctor's Creed* he said that he had carried out an abortion for rape before and would have no hesitation in doing it again. He also said that he had decided, the next time he did it, to write to the Attorney General and invite him to take action. On the morning he performed, the abortion the police arrived and he told them he wanted them to take action against him. It was not clear who, had in fact, contacted the police in the first place; it seems clear that Bourne did not do so, since he had promised the girl's father that he would keep the matter as secret as possible in order to save the girl's mother from worry (*BMJ*, 23 July 1938). In his summing up at Bourne's trial, Mr Justice MacNaghton stated that the traditional view was that abortion was justified only if it were done to preserve the life of the woman. However, he said that too narrow a view must not be taken of the meaning of these words. Any serious impairment of health might reach a stage where there was a danger to life, and anything which threatened health might justify the operation. In fact he went further, and asserted that it might be the duty of the doctor to perform the operation and religious scruples would be no excuse for not doing so. 'If the life of that woman can be saved by an operation and a doctor did not perform it because of his religious views, he would be in great peril of being brought before this court on a charge of manslaughter for negligence.' Bourne was acquitted, and the decision passed into English case law.

During the inter-war period, there was great concern over the number of deaths from illegal abortion in England – between 400 and 500 deaths every year, in the period from 1926 to 1935 (Birkett 1939, p. 6). The BMA Committee set up to consider the problem in 1934 published a report which suggested that perhaps 16–20 per cent of pregnancies ended in either spontaneous or induced abortion (British Medical Association 1936). The Birkett Committee (1939, p. iii) was set up in 1937: 'to enquire into the prevalence of abortion, and the law thereto, and to consider what steps can be taken to secure the reduction of maternal mortality.' The report opposed a suggestion from ALRA that there should be a general legalization of abortion, partly because it would lead 'promiscuous sexual intercourse to be more common' (Birkett 1939, p. 85). It recommended that the Bourne decision should be formalized in law, and also attempted to estimate the total number of abortions each year. It applied the BMA estimate to the total number of annual births of 600,000 and reached a figure of between 110,000 and 150,000 spontaneous and induced abortions each year (p. 9). The British Medical Association (1936) had suggested that spontaneous abortions were a relatively small proportion of the whole. However, Birkett took the view that 'perhaps 40 per cent of the abortions in this country are due to illegal interference' (1939, p. 11).

A year later David Glass, an ALRA member, suggested that the 60-40 proportion should be reversed and that probably 60 per cent of all abortions were illegal. He argued that, taking into account under-reporting, it is 'not at all impossible that there are about 100,000 illegal abortions annually in England and Wales' (Glass, 1940). This figure was given great publicity in 1947 in an ALRA pamphlet 'Back Street Surgery' (Chance et al. 1947). On the front cover, the pamphlet declared itself to be 'A study of the illegal operation, which is performed probably about 100,000 times a year in England and Wales'. Inside it gave Glass as the source, and this became the most widely quoted figure in the period leading to the 1967 Act.

Although there may be doubt as to the exact number of abortions in the 1930s, there is no doubt that it was widely used and that in Britain the illegal abortionist was often a valued member of the community. It is not difficult to see why. In 1926, Lord Buckmaster gave the House of Lords the following case history: 'A woman who was married at the age of seventeen had, by the age of thirty four, had eighteen pregnancies and eleven live children' (*Birth Control News*, May 1926). Buckmaster asserted that this case was not unusual. The illegal abortionist was usually only discovered if there was a death. Even then, it seems that the local community often continued its support. In 1930 a woman, Mrs Lee, who charged from 2s 6d to 10s for an abortion, was sentenced to five years' penal servitude; as a result:

> A big demonstration began when Mrs. Lee was taken away from the Shire Hall. The crowd, which consisted mainly of women, cheered when Mrs. Lee, in charge of a wardress, came out of a rear door of the Shire Hall, and many crowded round the car. A sobbing woman, apparently a relative of Mrs. Lee, insisted on kissing her before she was helped into the motor which was waiting. Another woman pushed her way towards Mrs. Lee saying, 'Let me kiss her; I must kiss her'. From the car Mrs. Lee waved kisses to her friends and as the car left the precincts of the Shire Hall the cheering was renewed. There was great anger against the witnesses who caused Mrs. Lee's conviction. The cheering was changed to 'booing' when witnesses in the case were seen at the windows of the building, and shouts such as 'Come out of it!' and 'Come down, you dogs!' were heard (*Gloucester Journal*, 14 June 1930).

The view that abortion was accepted by the mass of people gets other support. Birkett, for example, stated that 'the law relating to abortion is freely disregarded among women of all types and classes' (1939, p. 118). Evidence of the method of abortion is provided by Parish who studied women in Camberwell treated for abortion from 1930–34. Of 1,000 cases, 485 women admitted illegal interference, and in 426 cases the method was known. Two in five of the abortions were produced by both a syringe and drugs in combination, a quarter used just a syringe and just over a quarter used only drugs. The other 9 per cent used a variety of methods including knitting needles, a catheter and (in one in 25) slippery elm bark.

In 1938, a 'moral panic' about slippery elm was reported in the medical literature, and the *British Medical Journal* (14 May) printed a picture of the bark as removed from a woman's bladder. The bark was derived from a tree found in Central and North America. It was prepared by being separated from the trunk, having the outer corky portion removed and then being dried. It was sold in flat pieces several inches long, a few inches wide and a few millimetres in thickness, and contained material which approximately doubled in size when the bark was soaked in water. Small pieces were placed into the cervical canal, by the woman herself or by another, and the abortion was procured partly on account of the presence of a foreign body and partly because of dilation of the cervix following swelling of the bark.

At the outbreak of the Second World War there was no country in the world where women had the right to choose an abortion even in the early months of pregnancy. However, a number of countries did allow abortion on some grounds.

Chapter 10

Future Developments

An article at the beginning of 2003 stated that a woman's right to choose in the USA was now under greater threat than at any time for a century. The Republicans control the White House, the Senate and the House of Representatives at least until 2004 (Campbell 2003). In the eyes of the author, Duncan Campbell, this gives the opponent of abortion the opportunity to make a number of challenges. He drew particular attention to three likely developments. The first was a renewed attack on partial birth abortions which has occurred, the second a change in the law to allow hospitals to refuse to carry out abortions without losing federal funding and the third was the creation of a new crime, that of the taking a minor across state borders for an abortion. These changes are in addition to possible changes in the composition of the Supreme Court which could lead to earlier rulings being reversed.

These comments were echoed by a June 2003 article which stated that today's young women belong to the 'post aids generation' who are far more cautious about sex than those who came of age in the 1970s. They are less likely to suffer from unwanted pregnancies than previous cohorts (Goldenberg 2003). Public opinion also seems to be moving against abortion rights. An opinion poll published in June 2003 found that 47 per cent of Americans considered themselves as pro-choice and 48 per cent as pro-life. There seems to have been a decline in support for abortion rights amongst first year students from 67 per cent to 54 per cent during the past decade (Goldenberg 2003).

The crucial question is, of course, the possibility that *Roe v. Wade* could be overturned. If it was, and individual states were allowed to make decisions as they were before 1973, it would lead to a great amount of debate and the production of many bills. It would inevitably mean that the 'right to choose' would be abrogated in many states, and that women, consequently, would once again have to travel great distances for their abortions. However, in 2003 an article published the day after the anniversary of the Supreme Court decision argued that a reversal of *Roe v. Wade* was not likely. The authors commented:

> If Bush, who opposes abortion, nominates an overtly anti-abortion justice to the Supreme Court, he would risk angering a public majority with little hope of

achieving his goal. He would need to replace two current justices who uphold abortion rights, with two who would strike them down. And confirmation would be difficult in a Senate where the Republican Majority is only 58–48 – including at least three republicans who support abortion rights (Enda and Henderson 2003).

A similar comment was made by Anne Storer, the national chair of Republicans for Choice. She said that the administration was doing a lot of 'back dooring, fine tuning around the edges to keep the base happy'. However, on the crucial question of overturning *Roe v. Wade* she said 'They know they can't do it. They know there'd be revolution in the streets'.

Commentators noted that one of the problems for Bush was that he needed to gain more support among suburban women to help with his re-election. This may be a reason that when, in 2003, he addressed the annual March for Life rally in Washington DC, he did so by telephone rather than in person. R. Baker commented that this enabled the President to help to rally the troops without wading in too far (Enda and Henderson 2003).

If these assessments are correct it will mean that the action is going to be around the periphery, and a number of proposals have already been made. There will be a ban on later abortions (partial birth abortions). It may become a federal crime to circumvent parental consent laws by taking a minor across state lines for an abortion; hospitals and other health care providers may be able to refuse to do abortions without losing federal money and it may become a crime to kill or injure a fetus during an attack on a pregnant woman. These changes may cause some difficulties for women with problem pregnancies, but will not challenge the fundamental freedom obtained for most in *Roe v. Wade* (Enda and Henderson 2003).

One question is whether women under eighteen should be allowed to have an abortion without parental consent or court approval. However, having said this, many of those who are opposed to choice will welcome the introduction of some restrictions. Consequently, there are likely to be numerous debates within the states.

There is also the long-term consideration of the safety of clients and staff in the context of abortion violence. There are several contributory reasons for the greater violence in the USA than elsewhere. First, the law was made by a Court decision, and is consequently out of step with attitudes in many of the Conservative areas. We have seen that such states as Utah condemned the decision. Secondly there is much greater access to weapons in the USA, and all those murdered (in this context) have been shot. The strict gun laws in

Britain make access difficult. Another of the differences from Britain is that abortion facilities are far more visible in the USA. In Britain they have been carried out to a much greater degree in hospitals, where they would only be a small part of wide-ranging services.

There have been some welcome developments in that the extreme violence seems to have subsided somewhat. Data show that in the year 2000 over half (56 per cent) of providers faced harassment against abortion. However, apart from picketing, the kinds of harassment have declined since 1996 (Henshaw and Finer 2003). Furthermore, the mainstream abortion organizations such as National Right to Life and March for Life have been advocating a non-violent approach. For example, at the annual march in Washington DC on the anniversary of the Supreme Court decision (22 January) in 2002, the director of the organization March For Life, Nellie Gray, sent out a news release which had some soothing words. 'Abortion is an issue which bitterly divides our country and we need to treat those in disagreement with respect and civility.' However, much of the language used by the organization is such that it might inflame some people. Furthermore, in addition to the mainstream organizations, there are others such as Operation Rescue which are far more militant. In Britain there have been isolated incidents, but by no means such a degree of violence and harassment.

The major British organizations have been outspoken against violence. For example, when there was a report that some US groups were publishing photographs of women seeking abortions on a website, the UK group LIFE published a press release (10 June 02) which was unequivocally headed 'LIFE condemns American anti-abortion scare tactics'. LIFE said that women seeking an abortion deserved sympathy. In most cases, they did not want an abortion but felt they had no choice.

We have seen that abortion has not been such a controversial issue in the UK in recent times. At first, in Britain, after the act was passed, there was a great deal of pressure for it to be overturned. However, as we have seen, the failure of the Corrie Bill in 1980 was a great setback for the anti-abortionists. Its defeat in the face of all its advantages led to their being in a worse position than if no attempt had been made. The degree of opposition evident around the country has made Members of Parliament much more hesitant about becoming involved in the issue. It also showed pro-choice groups how to hold up any action in parliament, which means that no Bill is likely to succeed except in the unlikely event that the government gives it time.

At the time of the Corrie Bill, one of its main advantages was that the time limits for abortion clearly needed some harmonization. In Scotland, for example, there was no time limit at all. In England and Wales the upper time was set at 28 weeks by the 1929 Infant Life Preservation Act. But this was changed by the Human Fertilization and Embryology Act of 1990, which reduced the time limit to 24 weeks in most cases. We have seen that there were exceptions to this time limit if there were serious problems, and the pro-choice groups were reasonably happy with the new restriction, especially as it was felt to remove the issue from the political arena. In retrospect, this assessment was realistic and abortion has not been a divisive issue. In this respect, there has been a great difference between the UK and the USA.

10.1   The Case for the Right to Choose

There are several reasons for the right to choose an abortion, the first of which is that forcing or attempting to force a woman to have a baby against her wishes could lead to very poor child care. A number of US laws restrict the rights of anyone under 18 to have an abortion without parental or court consent. Parents who would force their child to have an unwanted baby are likely to have other problems.

An important point is that the vast majority of teenagers faced with an unwanted pregnancy will one day wish to have children when the social conditions are right. Forcing a woman to have a baby at a young age may militate against the family. These women could have an abortion at an early age, but later be able to have a family in improved social conditions where the involvement of the father is likely to be much greater. Each year, one million American teenagers become pregnant and more than eight out of ten of these pregnancies are unintended. Chastity is very rare. Four out of five American women begin intercourse before the age of 20 and by the age of 20, about 40 per cent of women have been pregnant at least once. Teenagers who have a baby are more likely to drop out of school, to develop extra health problems, to need public assistance, to have children who are more likely to suffer deprivation; and they are more likely to divorce (Dudley 1996). If many of these women were forced to have a baby against their will, it would cause immense social problems.

The evidence from chapters 8 and 9 shows that abortion was common even when it was illegal. We have also seen that women will travel for their operations. The Polish situation is a case in point. In 2003, a report in the *Guardian* was headed 'Abortion issue threatens Polish admission to the EU Economic Community'. It pointed out that the Catholic Church is demanding a special clause in an EU membership recognizing the 'separateness' of Poland's position on abortion. This demand for change came only days before the treaty was presented to the European Parliament. The decision for Poland to enter the Community will have to be ratified by a referendum. The Polish government, which very much wants entry, is concerned that the potency of the abortion issue could lead to Poland rejecting membership:

> The government caved in to pressure from the church by sending a note to Brussels this week seeking assurances that 'no EU treaties or annexes to those treaties would hamper the Polish government in regulating moral issues or those concerning the protection of human life' (Traynor 2003).

During the Cold War era abortion was legal in Poland, but in 1993 a new law was enacted banning the practice. In 1997 the law was liberalized to allow abortion in cases where the woman's life was in danger or in cases of rape or incest. This abortion ban has led to illegal abortions flourishing, and also to women travelling to the Czech Republic where abortion is legal. This development shows a turn round from the situation in the 1970s, when Swedish women used to go to Poland for their abortions. It also shows that abortion cannot be legislated out of existence. What is needed, therefore, is to give women the freedom to choose and to provide the education that enables them to make informed decisions.

Bibliography

Abma, J.C. and Sonenstein, F.L. (2001), 'Sexual Activity and Contraception Practices Among Teenagers in the United States 1988 and 1995', *Vital and Health Statistics*, Series 23, No. 21.

Abortion Law Reform Association (1997), *Report on NHS Abortion Services*, ALRA, London.

Abortion Law Reform Association (2000), *Improving Access to Abortion: A Guide* ALRA.

Acton, W. (1878), *Prostitution*, 2nd edn, Frank Cass.

Arkes, H. (2002), 'George Bush Can Gently Help a Pro Life Culture', Internet.

Armytage, W.H.G. (1964), *Four Hundred Years of English Education*, Cambridge University Press.

Associated Press (1996), 'Clinton Vetoed Partial Birth Abortion', *Minnesota Daily*, 4 April.

Associated Press (2000), report from AP, 2 January, Internet.

Baker, M. (1974), *The Folklore and Customs of Love and Marriage*, Shire Publications.

Banks, J.A. (1954), *Prosperity and Parenthood*, Routledge.

Barnett, W.E. (1973), *Sexual Freedom and the Constitution*, University of New Mexico Press.

Benfield, B.B. (1972), 'The Spermatic Economy: A Nineteenth Century View of Sexuality', *Feminist Studies*, Vol. 1, No. 1 (Summer), p. 341.

Besant, A. (1877), *Law of Population*, Freethought Publishing.

Birkett, W.N. (1939), *Report of the Inter-departmental Committee on Abortion*, HMSO.

British Pregnancy Advisory Service (2002), *Early Medical Abortion*, BPAS, Solihull.

British Pregnancy Advisory Service (2002a), *What You Need to Know Abortion Care*, BPAS, Solihull.

Brouardel, P. (1901), *Avortement*, J.B. Bailliere et Fils.

Buck, P.S. (1968), *The Terrible Choice*, Bantam.

Bunker, J.P. (1970), 'Surgical Manpower', *New England Journal of Medicine*, Vol. 282, No. 3, pp. 135–44.

Burkeman, O. (2002), 'Bush has Many Enemies. But he did not Expect them to Include Nancy Reagan', *Guardian*, 30 September, p. 3, col. 1.

Calverton, V.F. and Schmalhausen, S.D. (1929), *Sex in Civilisation*, Macaulay.

Campbell, D. (2003), 'Anti Abortionists Plan New Offensive', *Guardian International*, 3 January.

Carmen, A. and Moody, H. (1973), *Abortion Counselling and Social Change*, Judson Press.

Carstairs, G. (1962), *This Island Now*, Hogarth Press.

Cartwright, A. (1970), *Parents and Family Planning*, Routledge.

Chance, J., Edge, M. and Ryan, M. (1947), *Back Street Surgery*, ALRA.

Churchill, W.S. (1972), *My Early Life*, Fontana, 1st edn 1930.

Cisler, L. (1970), *Abortion Law Repeal Sort of*, New Yorkers for Abortion Repeal.

Coffey, P. (1976), 'When Is the Killing of the Unborn a Homicidal Action?', *Linacre Quarterly*, Vol. 43, No. 2, pp. 85–93.

Coleman, J. (1966), *Equality of Educational Opportunity*, Department of Health, Education and Welfare, US Government.

Cowan, J. (1880), *The Science of a New Life*, Cowan and Co.

D'Agostino (2001), Internet at Abortion/Crime under the Heading Human Events, 2 July.

Dekker, H. (1920), 'The Ethical Grounds of Abortion', *The Medical Critic and Guide*, Vol. 23, pp. 336–40.

Donovan, P. (1981), 'Half a Loaf: A New Anti Abortion Strategy', *Family Planning Perspectives*, Vol. 13 (December), pp. 262–68.

Doyle, A. (1977), *Do You Need Permission to Save an Unborn Baby?*, Committee to Defend Pro Life Groups.

Drinan, R.F. (1967), 'The Inviolability of the Right to Be Born', in D. Smith (ed.), *Abortion and the Law*, Western Reserve University Press.

Dudley, S. (1996), 'Teenage Women, Abortion and the Law', NAF home page.

Eccles, M.E. (1978), 'Abortion: How Members Voted in 1977', *Congressional Quarterly*, Vol. 36, No. 5 (4 February), pp. 258–67.

Ehrlich, P.R. (1976), *Population Bomb*, Ballantine.

Ehrlich, P.R. and Ehrlich, A.H (1970), *Population Resources and Environment*, W.H. Freeman.

Elderton, E.M. (1914), *Report on the English Birthrate*, Eugenics Society.

Ellis, H.H. (1928), *Studies in the Psychology of Sex*, vol. VI, F.A. Davies Co.

Ellis, H.H. (1933), *Psychology of Sex*, Heinemann.

Enda, J. (2002), 'Now Says President's Nominee "Inappropriate" for US Attorney', *Miami Herald*, 1 February.

Enda, J. and Henderson, S. (2003), 'Reversal of "Roe" Not Likely', *Philadelphia Enquirer*, 23 January.

Eppel, E.M. and Eppel, M. (1966), *Adolescents and Morality*, Routledge.

Feminist Campus (2003), 'A Brief History of Anti Abortion Violence Patterns', Internet.

Ferriman, A. (1980), 'Women Clash with Police at Commons', *The Times*, 9 February.

Finer, L.B. and Henshaw, S.K. (2003), 'Abortion Incidence and Services in the United States in 2000', *Family Planning Perspectives*.

FPA (2002a), *Sexual Health Agenda*, Vol. 5, Issue 3, Summer.

FPA (2002b), *Sexual Health Agenda*, Vol. 5, Issue 4, Autumn.

Francome, C. (1976a), *Youth and Society*, unpublished MA thesis, University of Kent, Canterbury.

Francome, C. (1978b), 'Abortion: Why the Issue has not Disappeared', *Political Quarterly*, Vol. 49, No. 2, pp. 217–22.

Francome, C. (1978c), 'Catholics – Sex, Contraception and Abortion', *Breaking Chains*, No. 10 (November).

Francome, C. (1980a), 'Birth Control: A Way Forward', pamphlet to Celebrate Centenary of Marie Stopes Birth, Marie Stopes House.

Francome, C. (1980b), *Public Opinion on Abortion*, ALRA.

Francome, C. (I 980c), *Social Forces and the Abortion Law*, PhD thesis, Council for National Academic Awards (CNAA).

Francome, C. (1980d), 'Abortion Policy in Britain and the United States', *Social Work*, Vol. 25, No. 1, pp. 5–9.

Francome, C. (1980e), 'Abortion Politics in the United States', *Political Studies*, Vol. 28, No. 4, pp. 613–21.

Francome, C. (1982), *Gallup on Abortion: 1982*, ALRA and Doctors for a Woman's Choice on Abortion.

Francome, C. (1984), *Abortion Freedom*, Allen and Unwin, London and Boston.

Francome, C. (1986), *Abortion Practice in Britain and the USA*, Unwin Hyman, London and Boston.

Francome, C. (1992), *If you Ever Go Across the Sea to England*, Middlesex University. London.

Francome, C. (1994a), 'Gynaecologists and Abortion in Northern Ireland', *Journal of Biosocial Science*, Vol. 26, pp. 389–94.

Francome, C. (1997), 'Attitudes of General Practitioners in Northern Ireland towards Abortion and Family Planning', *Family Planning Perspectives*, September, pp. 234–6.

Francome, C. and Freeman, E. (2000), 'British General Practitioner's Attitudes toward Abortion', *Family Planning Perspectives*, Vol. 32, No. 4, July, pp. 189–91.

Friedan, B. (1963), *The Feminine Mystique*, W.W. Norton.

Furedi (1995), 'The Abortion Law in Northern Ireland', Family Planning Association, Northern Ireland, Belfast.

Gavron, H. (1966), *The Captive Wife*, Penguin.

Gillie, O., Wallace, M., Ashdown-Sharp, P. and Zimmerman, L. (1975), 'Abortion Tales Revealed as Fantasies', *Sunday Times*, 30 March, p. 1.

Glass, D.V. (1940), *Population Policies and Movements in Europe*, Frank Cass.

Goldenberg, S. (2003), 'When Does Life Really Begin', *Guardian*, 6 June, Section G2, p. 6. col. 1.

Goldstein, A. (2001), 'Medical Coverage of RU 486', 31 March, p. A9.

Goode, E. (1970), *The Marijuana Smokers*, Basic Books.

Goodhart, C.B. (1973), 'On the Incidence of Illegal Abortion', *Population Studies*, Vol. 27, pp. 207–34.

Gordon, L. (1977), *Woman's Body, Woman's Right*, Penguin.

Goreau, A. (1981), 'Book Burners: The Threat to Literature', *New Statesman*, 25 September.

Guttmacher, A. (1967), *The Case for Legalised Abortion Now*, Diablo Press.

Hair, P.H.E. (1966), 'Bridal Pregnancy in Rural England', *Population Studies*, Vol. 20, pp. 233–44.

Hair, P.H.E. (1970), 'Bridal Pregnancy in Rural England Further Examined', *Population Studies*, Vol. 24, pp. 59–70.

Henshaw, S.K. and Feivelson, D.J. (1996), 'Teenage Abortion and Pregnancy Statistics by State', *Family Planning Perspectives*, Vol. 32, No. 6, pp. 272–80.

Henshaw, S.K. and Finer, L.B. (2003), 'The Accessibility of Abortion Facilities in the United States, 2001'.

Heron, A. (ed.) (1963), *Towards a Quaker View of Sex*, Society of Friends.

Himes, N.E. (1930), 'Robert Dale Owen, the Pioneer of American Neo-Malthusianism', *American Journal of Sociology*, Vol. 35, pp. 529–47.

Hindell, K. and Simms, M. (1971), *Abortion Law Reformed*, Peter Owen.

Holland, M. (1981), 'Ireland's Bishops Decide', *New Statesman*, 3 April.

Hunter, A. (1981), 'In the Wings', *Revolutionary Socialism* (Summer).

Illman, J. (1976), 'Abortion Distortion', *General Practitioner*, 6 February.

IPPF (1974), *Survey of World Needs in Family Planning*, International Planned Parenthood Federation.

Isaaaon, W. (1981), 'The Battle Over Abortion', *Time*, 6 April.

Jafl'e, F.S., Lindheim, B.L. and Lee, P.R. (1981), *Abortion Politics*, McGraw Hill.

Jenkins, A. (1964), *Law for the Rich*, Charles Skilton.

Jenness, L. (1976), *Socialism and the Fight for Women's Rights*, Pathfinder Press.

Joyce, T. and Kaestner, R. (2000), 'Impact of Mississippi's Mandatory Delay on the Timing of Abortion', *Family Planning Perspectives*, Vol. 32, No. 1, pp. 4–13.

Kaiser (2001), update, *Abortion Policy and Politics*, Internet at abortion/state.

Kendall, M. (1979), *The World Fertility Survey*, Johns Hopkins University.

Kennedy, D.M. (1970), *Birth Control in America*, Yale University Press.

Ketting, E. and Schnabel, P. (1980), 'Induced Abortion in the Netherlands: A Decade of Experience 1970–80', *Studies in Family Planning*, Vol. 11, No. 12, pp. 385–94.

King, L.R. and Moser, C. (1979), *The Impact of Robbins*, Penguin.

Kommers, D.P. (1977), 'Abortion and the Constitution: United States and West Germany', *American Journal of Comparative Law*, Vol. 25, No. 2, pp. 225–85.

Lader, L. (1966), *Abortion*, Beacon Press.

Lader, L. (1973), *Abortion II – Making the Revolution*, Beacon Press.

Lane Report (1974). *Report of the Committee on the Working of the Abortion Act*, Cmnd 5579, HMSO.

Lauter, P. and Howe, F. (1970), *The Conspiracy of the Young*, World Publishing Co.

Lee, E. (1998), *Abortion Law and Politics Today*, Macmillan Press Ltd, London and St Martin's Press, New York.

Lee, S. (1995), 'The Abortion Law in Northern Ireland: The Twilight Zone', in Furedi (1995).

Lee, S. (1995a), 'An a to K to Z of Abortion Law in Northern Ireland: Abortion on Remand', in Furedi (1995).

Lindsey, B. (1925), *The Revolt of Modern Youth*, Boni and Liveright.

Linner, B. (1968), *Sex and Society in Sweden*, Cape.

Macfarlane, A. and Mugford, M. (1984), *Birth Counts*, HMSO, London.

Marie Stopes International (2002), *Women's Perceptions of Abortion Law and Practice*, MSI, London.

Marsh, D. and Chambers, J. (1981), *Abortion Politics*, Junction Books.

Martin, D. (1967), *The Sociology of English Religion*, Heinemann.

McGovern, J. (1968), 'The American Woman's Pre-World War I Freedom in Manners and Morals', *Journal of American History*, Vol. 55 (September), pp. 315–48.

McGregor, O.R. (1957), *Divorce in England*, Heinemann.

Means, C. (1968), 'The Law of New York Concerning Abortion and the Status of the Fetus 1664–1968: a Case of Cessation of Constitutionality', *New York Law Forum*, Vol. 14, pp. 411–515.

Means, C. (1971), 'The Phoenix of Abortion Freedom', *New York Law Forum*, Vol. 17, pp. 335–410.

Mohr, J.C. (1978), *Abortion in America*, Oxford University Press.

Murray, D. (2003), Internet at abortion/crime.

Myrdal, A. and Klein, V. (1968), *Woman's Two Roles*, Routledge.

NARAL (1972), *Newsletter*, Vol. 2, No. 2 (March).

NARAL (1978), *Newsletter*, Vol. 10, No. 3 (May).

NARAL (n.d.), *Abortion Questions and Answers*, undated leaflet, National Abortion Rights Action League.

Noonan, J. (1967), *Contraception*, Mentor-Omega Edition.

Office of National Statistics (2001), *Abortion Statistics* 20, Series AB, London.

Office of National Statistics (2002), *Abortion Statistics*, The Stationery Office, London.

Parry, L.A. (1932), *Criminal Abortion*, Bale; Carswell.

Pierce, R. (1963), 'Marriage in the Fifties', *Sociological Review*, Vol. 11, No. 2, pp. 215–40.

Place, F. (1930), *Illustration and Proofs of the Principles of Population: Including an Examination of the Proposed Remedies of Mr. Malthus and a Reply to the Objections of Mr. Godwin and Others*, Allen & Unwin.

Planned Parenthood (1945), 'Planned Parenthood's Campaign for 1945', pamphlet.

Planned Parenthood (1963), 'Plan Your Children for Health and Happiness', anonymous pamphlet.

Potts, M., Diggory, P. and Peel, J. (1977), *Abortion*, Cambridge University Press.

Potts, M. and Selman, P. (1979), *Society and Fertility*, Macdonald & Evans.

Reaves, J. (2002), 'Roe v. Wade v. Bush', *Time.com*, 29 January.

Reed, J. (1978), *From Private Vice to Public Virtue*, Basic Books.

Robinson, J. (1963), *Honest to God*, SCM Press.

Robinson, W.J. (1928), *Sex, Love and Morality*, Eugenics Publishing Co.

Robinson, W.J. (1933), *The Law against Abortion*, Eugenics Publishing Co.

Rongy, A.J. (1933), *Abortion: Legal or Illegal*, Vanguard Press.

Rosenblatt, R.A. (1995), 'Abortion in Rural Idaho', *American Journal of Public Health*, Vol. 85, pp. 1423–25.

Rostow, W.W. (1971), *The Stages of Economic Growth*, 2nd edn, Cambridge University Press.

Rowntree, B.S. and Lavers, G.R. (1951), *English Life and Leisure*, Longmans Green.

Sanger, M. (1932), *My Fight for Birth Control*, Faber & Faber.

Sanger, M. (1969), *Woman and the New Race*, 1st edn 1920, Maxwell Reprint Co.

Schur, E.M. (1965), *Crimes Without Victims*, Prentice-Hall.

Select Committee (1976a), *First Report of the Select Committee on Abortion*, Vol. 1, HC 573–1, HMSO.

Select Committee (1976b), *First Report of the Select Committee on Abortion*, Vol. 2, HC 573–11, HMSO.

Shareef, R. *Abortion and Crime: We Still Do Not Know the Truth*, Internet at roanoke.com, 4 October.

Simms, M. (1975), 'The Compulsory Pregnancy Lobby, Then and Now', *Journal of the Royal College of Medical Practitioners*, Vol. 25, p. 716.

Society for the Suppression of Vice (1874), *Annual Report*, New York.

Steinhof, P.G. and Diamond, M. (1977), *Abortion Politics*, Hawaii University Press.

Stopes, M.C.C. (1918), *Married Love*, The Critic and Guide Company.

Storer, H.R. (1866), *Why Not? A Book for Every Woman*, Lee and Shepard.

Sutherland, H.G. (1922), *Birth Control*, Harding and More.

Taussig, F.J. (1910), *The Prevention and Treatment of Abortion*, George Keemer.

Taussig, F.J. (1936), *Abortion – Spontaneous and Induced*, C.V. Mosby.

Thomas, D. (1969), *A Long Time Burning*, Routledge.

Titmuss, R.M. (1963), *Essays on the Welfare State*, Unwin University Books.

Traynor, I. (2003), 'Abortion Issue Threatens Polish Admission to EU', *Guardian*, Section 1, p. 17, col. 1.

Viguerie, R. (1981), *The New Right*, Caroline House.

Walbert, D. and Butler, J.D. (1973), *Abortion Society and the Law*, Case University Press.

Weber, M. (1968), *The Protestant Ethic and the Spirit of Capitalism*, Allen & Unwin.

Westfall, J.M, Kallail, K.J. and Walling, A.D (1991), 'Abortion Attitudes and Practices of Family and General Practice Physicians', *Journal of Family Practice*, Vol. 33, No. 1, pp. 47–51.

Willey, D. (1975), 'Reform Italian Style', *People*, Vol. 2, No. 3, p. 26.

Willke, B. and Willke, J. (1975), *Handbook on Abortion*, Hiltz.

Willke, J. (2000), Internet at Right to Life.

Wright, J.W. (2002), *The New York Times Almanac*, Penguin Reference, New York.

Wynn, M. and Wynn, A. (1973), *Some Consequences of Induced Abortion to Children Born Subsequently*, Foundation for Education and Research in Childbearing.

Index